FORTRAN 77
for
SCIENTISTS and
ENGINEERS

Second Edition

BERTRAND

W9-BKL-941

FORTRAN 77
for
SCIENTISTS and
ENGINEERS

Second Edition

J.N.P. Hume

R.C. Holt

Department of Computer Science
University of Toronto

RESTON PUBLISHING COMPANY, INC., Reston, Virginia
A Prentice-Hall Company

ISBN 0-8359-2065-8

©1985 by Reston Publishing Company, Inc.
A Prentice-Hall Company
Reston, Virginia 22090

All rights reserved. No part of this book
may be reproduced, in any way or by any means,
without permission in writing from the publisher.

10   9   8   7   6   5   4   3   2   1

Printed in the United States of America

CONTENTS

PREFACE

This book is intended to introduce computers to science and engineering students. No serious study of computers is viable without a solid underpinning in programming, in algorithms, and in basic data structures. It is our aim to provide this underpinning and while doing so to give interesting examples in the field of science and engineering, as well as from everyday life.

Although the computer is an absolutely essential tool to scientists and engineers in their professional life, it is, as well, an integral part of present-day society. We must all be computer literate. So our goal is a double one: to acquaint students with the ideas and technical terminology connected with computers and to provide a sufficiently detailed presentation of programming so that the computer can be used as a professional tool.

Programming in this text is taught using the Fortran 77 programming language. Fortran is the earliest of the common high-level languages, dating from 1956. It has had many improvements incorporated in it since then: by the American National Standards Institute in 1966 as Fortran 66, and in 1977 as Fortran 77. During this time important changes have occurred in programming, due to the efforts of computer scientists and engineers. It is no longer enough to know the details of a particular programming language in order to create programs; you must also know a great deal about what constitutes good programming **style**. Bad style leads to programs that may never work or, if they do, develop flaws as time goes on — flaws that no one can fix because the program is not understandable.

In the early days of computing, people used to say they were writing **code** for the machines; that is because machines understood code. Then high-level languages came along and we wrote programs for machines. Programs are for people; code is for machines. In fact the programs must be translated into code (by the machine) before they operate. We want to teach programming according to our best ideals of style so the programs you create are as understandable as possible to other people, and yourself. After all, this is just good scientific or engineering practice. We call the kind of programming that we are presenting **structured programming**.

Fortran 77 contains a number of language features that are **not** compatible with good style. These we have ruthlessly omitted. One of the basic elements of style is to streamline the programming language to what is really essential. On the other hand, Fortran 77, although much improved over Fortran 66, still does not contain some language features that are crucial to structured programming. Perhaps the most notable omission is the language construct for the **conditional loop**. This can be simulated using other Fortran language features but there are several problems: It is awkward, and there is no generally accepted way to do it. We have chosen one way and stuck to it, but there are others. Each person (that includes us) views their method as the best. Because rules of style are not universally prescribed in some manual, disagreements can occur.

Here are some of the things that are different about this book:

☐ Although Fortran 77 is not our ideal as a programming language, the use of Fortran seems to be entrenched in the world of scientific and engineering computation. So we have attempted to make the best of the situation and marry the elements of structured programming to Fortran 77 as reasonably as we can.

☐ Fortran grew up in the days of punched cards with batch processing of jobs but we will show it as a language to be used interactively at keyboard-screen terminals and with file storage on disks rather than as card images on tape.

☐ Most programming languages employ lower case letters as well as upper case to make programs more readable; Fortran is by tradition shown in upper case only. We take the plunge to lower case and believe that the resulting programs are much easier on the eye.

☐ Flow charts have all but vanished from good practice in software houses. Why should they persist in textbooks? We show only two examples.

☐ Fortran is not an ideal language for processing character strings; even the improvements of Fortran 77 do not bring it up to speed. We show examples of character string handling in Fortran 77 partly to permit its use, where essential in scientific or engineering applications. But we show more uses, such as in text processing, to illustrate how computers can handle words. No doubt an off-the-shelf piece of applications software (not written in Fortran) will ultimately provide the word processing needed for most scientific or engineering reports.

☐ No pseudo code is introduced: the statement in English of what is to be done by a program is transformed step-by-step into the Fortran program for doing it. At intermediate stages of the process the algorithm being developed is in a mixture of English and Fortran. A special intermediate language is quite unnecessary.

□ Programs are introduced as algorithms; the design of programs is presented systematically starting with small programs and building to larger programs. Through the use of subprograms, all programs can be constructed of small manageable components.

□ The interfaces between program components is carefully presented; details of argument - parameter correspondences and variables in common indicate what is most appropriate.

□ A study of structured programming in Fortran 77 will prepare a student to adapt quickly to other programming languages. We have tried to make sure that what is learned about a particular language has some generality. The syntax changes but the concepts remain.

□ Programming in a high-level language can seem mysterious unless some reference is made to how the computer actually performs the act of translation to its own language and the execution of machine code. It is part of being a reasonably well-informed programmer. Both these are briefly discussed.

□ A language like Fortran deals mainly with single variables or arrays. More complex data structures are extremely useful for many applications. For students of science and engineering an introduction to data structures and the selection of appropriate structures cannot be postponed. They are fundamental to good programming style.

□ Technical terms in this book are always defined by using them in context. Bold face type alerts the reader to the first appearance of such terms. Concepts are illustrated first by programmed examples; generalities follow particular examples. A systematic summary of new terms and concepts is given at the end of every chapter, for quick reference or for review.

□ New programming ideas are illustrated first by relatively simple examples involving little mathematics; more scientific examples follow. The exercises at the end of the chapter provide a good range of difficulty. In all there are over 250 programmed examples and problems. Science and engineering applications range widely over the various fields; a list is given in Appendix 7.

□ Common programming errors are noted and various means of debugging programs discussed.

□ The specifications of Fortran 77 as presented in this book are detailed in Appendix 1 and its syntax summarized in Appendix 2. A brief overview of the operating systems needed for interactive program development is given in Appendix 4. Appendix 5 presents an introduction to the Unix Operating System and Appendix 6 does the same for the VAX/VMS operating system.

A catalog of built-in Fortran functions is given in Appendix 3.

☐ The material in this book provides an excellent basis for a one semester introductory course at the University freshman level. Calculus is not essential although a few references are made to it. The introductory chapters can be covered quite quickly possibly as reading assignments. Local details regarding the operating system the student will be using must be provided by the time Chapter 4 is reached. The fundamentals of programming are complete by Chapter 11. Chapter 12 and 13 are very specific to numerical methods used in science and engineering applications. The applications chapters following on text processing, searching, and sorting could be omitted if desired. The materials on files and records, and on data structures provide a good way to finish. Some of these chapters could be omitted. It is intended that freedom of choice be left to the individual instructor. It is merely a matter of rationing the time spent on the different topics. The book provides everything needed to present a solid first course on computers.

The preparation of a text requires a large effort on the part of authors now that the final typesetting process is under their supervision. It could not have been done so expeditiously without the exceptional assistance of Inge Weber who did all the text editing on the computer. Testing of the programs directly from the text was capably handled by Harriet Hume who also prepared the index. The authors want also to thank their colleagues Professors T.E. Hull and Philip Sharp for their advice.

J.N.P. Hume
R.C. Holt

University of Toronto

FORTRAN 77
for
SCIENTISTS and
ENGINEERS

Second Edition

Chapter 1

INTRODUCTION

WHAT ARE COMPUTERS?

Computers are devices consisting of electric circuits with electronic elements that act as **switches** and **gates** in the circuits. When computers were first built starting about 1945 the electronic elements were vacuum tubes. About 1959, tubes were discarded in favor of transistors. Then it was found that the electronic elements could be integrated into the circuits and produced by special "printing" techniques. By the 1980s the integrated circuits had been miniaturized to such an extent that major components of the computer could be "printed" on a chip of silicon smaller than a fingernail. Today we can obtain desk top computers for personal use that are as powerful as ones that sold for over a million dollars in the early 1960s.

As the cost of computers has dropped in the last 25 years, the uses that have been found for them have skyrocketed. There is scarcely any part of our lives that has not been changed in some way due to computers. There has been what many refer to as a **revolution** in the way things are done. With the invention of the steam engine in the nineteenth century, machines were devised to handle physical materials: to transport them and shape them into useful objects. We had what was known as the **industrial revolution**. Computers are machines that handle information and process it so that it is useful to us. We have now what is called an **information revolution**, or a **computer revolution**. The revolution has been accelerated by the concurrent advances in the technology of **telecommunications**, which includes the use of satellites for long distance communication and the transmission of digital signals.

The machines of the industrial revolution did physical work for us. The machines of the information revolution do mental work for us. That is why the early computers were referred to as **electronic brains**.

The way that a computer operates is to take in information, transform it, and then put the transformed information out. If the computer transforms information in a fixed way, we would say it is a **special purpose machine**. Computers usually are **general purpose machines**. To operate, a computer must have in it a list of instructions which specifies how the information is to be transformed. This list of instructions is called a **computer program**. The information that is to be transformed is called **data**. A computer program can itself be read into a computer and this means that you can have various programs in the machine. This is why we say that our computers are general purpose; they can run, in sequence or in parallel, a variety of programs. Any computer that you intend to use must have some programs already stored in it so that you may read in your programs and have them operate. We call programs **software**; the computer itself is the **hardware**. The software stored in the computer that allows users to enter programs and run them is called the **operating system**. Programs that transform data for you are called **applications software**.

There is a great deal of applications software available for most computer systems. This means that you may not have to write programs for yourself. You only need to know how to run the application program. Usually an attempt is made to make it as easy as possible for the user to use an applications software package. The software is designed to make the system **user friendly**. An important part of software design is to make the interface between the machine and the user as simple as possible. After all, the purpose of computers is to do as much of our work as they can for us.

WHAT IS COMPUTER SCIENCE?

Computer science is concerned with the acquisition and organization of knowledge about computers and their use. As a science it is systematic in this activity; it is concerned with generalizations, structures, abstractions, models, fundamentals, and theories. Since computer science is an emerging science we must form new concepts. Some of these are adopted from more mature sciences. As with other sciences, mathematics is the language in which ideas and facts can be most precisely expressed. But we have in computer science another kind of language which did not exist before computers existed, the language of **programming**. In mathematics the concept of a set of instructions which specifies a procedure by which certain ends can be accomplished in a finite number of steps pre-existed computers. It was called an **algorithm**. Before computers there was not much interest in devising languages to express algorithms. A computer program is an algorithm.

Perhaps one way to look at computer science is to ask what is its premise. No doubt there are as many answers to this question as there are computer scientists. One answer worth consideration is that a computer scientist is concerned not just with a tool (or machine) such as lathe, or an automobile, or a pocket calculator with limited capabilities but with a machine that is capable of almost everything that can be done mentally by a person. Many jobs presently done by people can ultimately be done equally well by machines. This does not mean that we know yet how to get the machines to do everything and perhaps this will take a very long time. Nor does it mean that we would replace people by machines that do their work.

WHAT IS PROGRAMMING?

Programming is writing instructions for a computer in a language that it can understand so that it can do something for you. We will be writing programs in one particular **programming language** called **Fortran**. When these instructions are entered into a computer directly by means of a keyboard input terminal they go into the part of the computer called its **memory** and are recorded there for as long as they are needed. The instructions could then be **executed** if they were in the language the computer understands directly, the language called **machine language**. If they are in another language such as Fortran they must first be **translated**, and a program in machine language, called the **object program**, **compiled** from the original or **source program**. After compilation the program can be executed.

Computers can really only do a very small number of different basic things. The repertoire of instructions that any computer understands usually includes the ability to move numbers from one place to another in its memory, to add, subtract, multiply, and divide. They can, in short, do all kinds of **arithmetic calculations** and they can do these operations at rates that exceed a million a second. Computers are extremely fast calculating machines. But they can do more; they can also handle alphabetic information, both moving it around in their memory and comparing different pieces of information to see if they are the same. To include both numbers and alphabetic information we say that computers are **data processors** or more generally **information processors**.

When we write programs we write a sequence of instructions that we want executed one after another. But you can see that the computer could execute our programs very rapidly if each instruction were executed only once. A program of a thousand instructions might take only a thousandth of a second. One of the instructions we can include in our programs is an instruction which causes the use of other instructions to be repeated over and over. In this way the computer is capable of repetitious work; it tirelessly executes the same set of instructions again and again. Naturally the data that it is operating on must change with each repetition or it would accomplish nothing.

Perhaps you have heard also that computers can make **decisions**. In a sense they can. These so-called decisions are fairly simple. The instructions read something like this:

> if John is over 16 then place him on the hockey team
> else place him on the soccer team

Depending on the **condition** of John's age, the computer could place his name on one or other of two different sports teams. It can **decide** which one if you tell it the decision criterion, for example, over sixteen or not.

Perhaps these first few hints will give you a clue to what programming is about. The kind of programming we will present is called structured programming.

WHAT IS STRUCTURED PROGRAMMING?

The term structured programming is used to describe both a number of techniques for writing programs as well as a more general methodology. Just as programs provide a list of instructions to the computer to achieve some well-defined goal, the methodology of structured programming provides a list of instructions to persons who write programs to achieve some well-defined goals. The goals of structured programming are, first, to get the job done. This deals with **how** to get the job done and how to get it done **correctly**. The second goal is concerned with having it done so that other people can see how it is done, both for their education and in case these other people later have to make changes in the original programs.

Computer programs can be very simple and straightforward but many applications require that very large programs be written. The very size of these programs makes them complicated and difficult to understand. But if they are well-structured, then the complexity can be controlled. Controlling complexity can be accomplished in many different ways and all of these are of interest in the cause of structured programming. The philosophy of structured programming encourages us to keep track of everything that will help us to be better programmers. We will be cataloguing many of the elements of structured programming as we go along, but first we must look at the particular programming language we will be using.

WHAT IS FORTRAN?

Fortran is a language that has been developed to be independent of the particular computer on which it is run and oriented to the problems that persons might want done. We say that Fortran is a **high-level language** because it was designed to be relatively easy to learn. As a problem-oriented language it is concerned with problems of numerical calculations such as occur in scientific and engineering applications as well as with alphabetic information handling required by business and humanities applications. It is a **procedure oriented language** which means that it was designed to express algorithms.

A high-level language lasts much longer than machine languages, which change every five years or so. This is because once an investment has been made in programs for a range of applications, you do not want to have to reprogram when a new computer is acquired. What is needed is a new compiler for the high-level language and all the old programs can be reused.

Because of the long life-span of programs in high-level languages it becomes more and more important that they can be adapted to changes in the application rather than completely reconstructed.

A high-level language has the advantage that well-constructed and well-documented programs in the language can be readily modified. Our aim is to teach you how to write such programs. To start we will present a few features of the Fortran language at a time. What we will have presented at any time is a subset of Fortran. At each stage, as new concepts are introduced, new features of Fortran are presented and examples are worked out to illustrate the new concepts. We will not be burdened with any more details of the programming language than we actually need to provide concrete illustrations of the concepts that we are attempting to understand.

There is no substitute for a hands-on experience in learning a new subject; submit your knowledge to the test by creating your own programs and running them on your computer.

CORRECTNESS OF PROGRAMS

One of the maddening things about computers is that they do exactly what you tell them to do rather than what you want them to do. To get correct results your program has to be correct. When an answer is displayed by a computer you must know whether or not it is correct. You cannot assume, as people often do, that because it was given by a computer it must be right. It is the right answer for the particular program and data you provided because computers now are really very reliable and rarely make mistakes. But is your program correct? Are your input data correct?

One way of checking whether any particular answer is correct is to get the answer by some other means and compare it with the displayed answer. This means that you must work out the answer by hand, perhaps using a hand calculator to help you. When you do work by hand you probably do not concentrate on exactly how you are getting the answer but you know you are correct (assuming you do not make foolish errors). But this seems rather pointless. You wanted the computer to do some work for you to save you the effort and now you must do the work anyway to test whether your computer program is correct. Where is the benefit of all this? The labor saving comes when you get the computer to use your program to work out a similar problem for you. For example, a program to compute telephone bills can be checked for correctness by comparing the results with hand computation for a number of representative customers and then it can be used on millions of others without detailed checking. What we are checking is the method of the calculation.

We must be sure that our representative sample of test cases includes all the various exceptional circumstances that can occur in practice, and this is a great difficulty. Suppose that there were five different things that could be exceptional about a telephone customer. A single customer might have any number of exceptional features simultaneously. So the number of different types of customers might be 32, ranging from those with no exceptional features to those with all five. To test all these combinations takes a lot of time, so usually, we test only a few of the combinations and hope all is well.

Because exhaustive testing of all possible cases to be handled by a program is too large a job, many programs are not thoroughly tested and ultimately give incorrect results when an unusual combination of circumstances is encountered in practice. You must try to test your programs as well as possible and at the same time realize that with large programs the job becomes very difficult. This has led many computer scientists to advocate the need to **prove** programs correct by various techniques other than exhaustive testing. These techniques rely partly on reading and studying the program to make sure it directs the computer to do the right calculation. Certainly the well-structured program will be easier to prove correct.

THE OPERATING SYSTEM

In order that a computer can accept programs in Fortran and run them it must already have programs inside it. These are called **systems programs**. One of these systems programs is a Fortran compiler. Another is called its **operating system**. The operating system permits you to enter your program through the keyboard, make any alterations in it that are necessary (**edit** it), store it away in the secondary memory of the computer (**file** it), initiate compilation and execution (**run** programs), initiate printed output (prepare **hardcopy**), and so on. In the Appendix we will describe two particular operating systems, the Unix^{tm} operating system devised by Bell Laboratories and the VAX/VMS operating system of the Digital Equipment Corporation. These are two of the most commonly used operating systems. You will only have to learn about the particular operating system that you will be using.

In order to get the operating system to accept, edit, file, compile, or execute your Fortran program you must give it instructions through the keyboard. These are called **system commands**. So, in addition to learning the Fortran language for writing Fortran programs, you must also learn the **command language** of your own particular operating system.

CHAPTER 1 SUMMARY

The purpose of this book is to introduce computer programming. This is essential for those who intend to become computer scientists and for those in other sciences or engineering it will provide a sound basis for the use of computers. We have begun in this chapter by presenting the following terminology.

Computer — a device or machine consisting of electric circuits containing electronic elements and accompanied by devices by which it can communicate with its users.

Vacuum tube — an electronic element which could act in a circuit so as to produce the effect of a switch, to reroute electric signals, or a gate to selectively block signals. Tubes were used in the original computers built between 1945 and 1956.

Transistor — an electronic element which could replace vacuum tubes. It was called a solid state device and was much more reliable than a tube. Transistors started to be used about 1959.

Integrated circuit — a circuit in which the connecting wires and transistors were integrated and often produced by a form of reproduction like printing.

Silicon chip — the medium upon which the integrated circuits are now deposited. The circuits are miniaturized by photographic techniques and "printed" on the chip.

Large Scale Integration (LSI) — circuits in which thousands of electronic elements are contained on a single silicon chip often smaller than a fingernail. As more and more circuits have been placed on single chips, the term VLSI (Very Large Scale Integration) has come into use.

Personal computer — a microcomputer which can be placed on a desk and used by a single user at a time.

Information revolution — the change in society due to the advent of computers and modern telecommunications.

Special purpose machine — a machine (computer) programmed to carry out one specific task such as running a heating system.

General purpose machine — a machine (computer) into which many different programs can be read and which is thus capable of many different tasks.

Data — the information which is to be transformed by the program executing on the computer.

Software — computer programs.

Hardware — the computer itself, that is, the electronic curcuits and the input-output devices.

Applications software — programs that are written to perform specific tasks and which can be used by anyone who learns how.

User interface — what must be learned and understood by a user before use can be made of a computer system.

Computer science — the science concerned with the acquisition and organization of knowledge about computers and their use.

Algorithm — the mathematical term for a list of instructions by which some specific result can be obtained by a person or device in a finite number of steps. Programs are algorithms.

Program (or computer program) — a list of instructions for a computer to follow. We say the computer executes instructions.

Programming — writing instructions telling a computer to perform certain data manipulations.

Programming language — a language used to write programs that direct the computer to do work for us.

Fortran — a high-level programming language. Pascal, PL/1, Turing, Cobol, and APL are other high-level programming languages.

High-level language — a programming language that is designed to be convenient for writing programs. Fortran is a high-level language.

Procedure oriented language — a programming language suitable for expressing algorithms.

Compiler — a systems program that translates a program written in a high-level language, such as Fortran, into a language that can be executed on a computer.

Structured programming — a method of programming that helps us write correct programs that can be understood by others. The Fortran language has been designed to encourage structured programming.

Correctness of programs — demonstrating that a program will necessarily accomplish its stated purpose (its specification).

Operating system — a program that is kept in the computer and which permits users to operate the computer. It lets them submit programs, edit them, file them, compile them, and execute them.

Unix^{tm} — an operating system devised by the Bell Laboratories and used on a great variety of computer systems.

VAX/VMS — an operating system devised by the Digital Equipment Corporation for use on its VAX computers.

Command language — a set of commands that cause the operating system to perform certain functions for you. These are used to submit, edit, file, compile, and execute programs.

Chapter 2

THE STRUCTURE
OF COMPUTERS

A computer is a complex object composed of wires, silicon chips with electronic circuits on them, and so on, but we will not be trying to follow circuit diagrams and worrying about how to build a computer. What we will be interested in is the various main parts of a computer and what the function of each is. In this way your programming will be more intelligent; you will have a better idea of what is going on inside the computer.

FUNCTIONAL UNITS

We have already mentioned a number of things about computers. They have a **memory** where programs, numbers, and alphabetic information can be recorded. They can add, subtract, multiply, and divide. This means they have a part called the **arithmetic unit**. They can read information from a keyboard input and output results on a screen. They may also have a printer. The printer may output a whole line at a time or just one character at a time, like a typewriter. We say they have an **input** (for example, keyboard) and an **output** (a screen). Computers execute instructions in sequence. The part of the machine that does this is called the **control unit**. The arithmetic unit and the control unit are usually grouped together in a computer and called the **central processing unit** or **CPU**. So then the computer is thought of as having three parts, memory, input-output, and CPU.

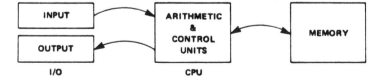

MAIN PARTS OF A COMPUTER

We will look at these different parts in turn but first we must see how numbers and alphabetic information can be represented in a computer.

CODED INFORMATION

You are probably familiar with the way that information used to travel over telegraph wires in the form of Morse Code. Perhaps you know that each letter or number is coded as a pattern of dots and dashes. For example, the letter A is a dot followed by a dash, E is one dot, V is three dots and a dash. The letters are separated from each other by a pause with no dots or dashes. The famous signal SOS is

$$\cdot\,\cdot\,\cdot \quad \_\,\_\,\_ \quad \cdot\,\cdot\,\cdot$$

This is an easy one to remember in emergencies. The Morse Code was designed so that the signal could activate some noise-making device and the listener could then translate the coded message back into letters. Modern teletype machines can send messages much faster because the machines themselves can be used to decode the messages. For these, a character is represented by a pattern of pulses, each pattern being of the same length. Instead of dots and dashes, which are two different lengths of electric pulses, they use one basic time interval and in that time interval have either a pulse or a pause. Each character requires 5 basic time intervals and is represented by a sequence of pulses and pauses. We often write down a pulse as a 1 and a pause as 0, and then the pattern for *b* is 10011, *i* is 01100, *l* is 01001. The word *bill* would be transmitted as

$$10011011000100101001$$

Strings of ones and zeros like this can be associated with numbers in the **binary system**. In the decimal system the number 342 means

$$3 \times 10^2 + 4 \times 10^1 + 2 \times 10^0$$

where 10^2 stands for 10 squared, 10^1 for 10 to the first power, that is 10, and 10^0 for 10 to the power zero, which has a value 1. In the binary system of numbers 1101 means

$$1 \times 2^3 + 1 \times 2^2 + 0 \times 2^1 + 1 \times 2^0$$

In the **decimal system** this binary number has a value $8+4+0+1 = 13$. We say that this number in the decimal system requires 2 **decimal digits** to represent it. In the binary system it requires 4 **binary digits**. We call a binary digit a **bit**. So the binary number representing the word *bill* has 20 bits, each letter requiring 5 bits. Sometimes we take the number of bits required to represent a character as a group and call it a **byte**. Then the word representing *bill* has four bytes. In a computer we must have a way of recording these bits, and usually the memory is arranged into **words**, each capable of holding a whole number of bytes.

In most computers a single letter is represented by a byte of eight bits. Typical microcomputers have a word length of two bytes. There are many different combinations of byte length and word length in different computers. This is something the machine designer must decide.

Because information is represented as a string of bits or binary digits, we say the computers are **digital** computers. Another quite different kind of computer called an **analog computer** represents numbers as electric voltages, the bigger the voltage the bigger the number. Analog computers are rarely used today although, in the early days of digital computers, analog computers provided a highly competitive way of doing certain scientific calculations.

PULSES, CLOCKS, AND GATES

Computers are often represented by diagrams giving their logical structure. The basic speed of a computer is determined by the time of one pulse. This pulse rate is controlled by a **clock**. The clock issues pulses at a uniform rate. The clock pulse signals are used to control the sequence of activity in the computer. Changes of **state** of the machine take place only at discrete times controlled by the clock. The clocks in typical computers tick at rates of tens of megahertz (millions of ticks per second).

The **logical diagram** of a computer is built up largely of **gates** which are devices made of transistors that control combinations of signals. An **and** gate is one in which a pulse must enter simultaneously on each of its incoming lines for a pulse to appear on its output line. We represent the **and** gate by a diagram

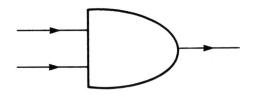

DIAGRAM OF *AND* GATE

An **or** gate is one in which a pulse appears on the output line if there a pulse on either or both of the input lines.

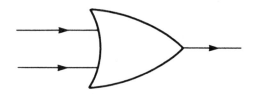

DIAGRAM OF *OR* GATE

A **not** gate is one in which there is only one incoming line and a pulse appears on the output line if in the clock interval a pulse does not appear on the input line and vice versa.

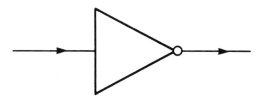

DIAGRAM OF *NOT* GATE

Groups of these basic gates can be interconnected to make a variety of other units or components which form the computer. One type of such component can act as a device for storing a binary digit. It is called a **flip-flop**. This is done by feeding the output of one **or** gate back through a **not** gate in as one input for another and vice versa. The other input to the pair of **or** gates comes from two **and** gates one of whose inputs is a pulse from the control unit, the other being a pulse that we want to store in the flip-flop.

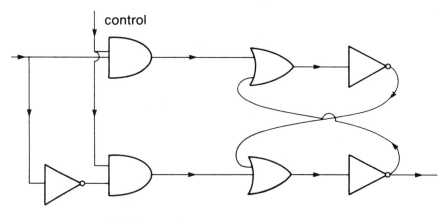

LOGICAL DIAGRAM OF FLIP-FLOP

When a pulse is given by the control, a pulse on the other incoming line to the flip-flop is passed to the output line. Because of the feedback between the **or** gates the pulse continues to be available on the output line. We say the pulse is stored. If, when the control pulse is given, there is no pulse on the incoming line then there will be no pulse on the output line and this condition too will persist. The result is a device capable of storing one bit of information. This type of storage device is volatile; the information would disappear if the power were turned off.

Flip-flops are very high-speed storage devices; they can be set and reset in a few nanoseconds (10^{-9} second). They are used in the high-speed storage registers of the computer. The main memory of the computer is more likely to be a metal oxide semiconductor (MOS) storage device.

MEMORY

Most machines record letters and numbers in the binary form because it is possible to have recording devices that can record, read, and hold such information. Most long term recording devices involve a non-volatile recording something like that on the tape of a magnetic tape recorder. There is a big difference, though, in the recording. On audio tape we have a magnetic recording that varies in intensity with the volume of the sound recorded. The frequency of the variations gives the pitch of the sound. For a computer, the recordings vary between two levels of intensity which you might think of as *on* and *off*. If in a particular region there is an *on* recording it could indicate the binary digit one and if *off* the digit zero. So on a strip of magnetic tape there would be designated areas that are to hold each bit of information.

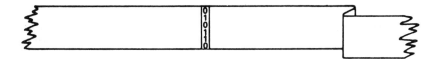

BITS RECORDED ON MAGNETIC TAPE

Binary digits can thus be recorded on reels of magnetic tape. In a similar way they can be recorded on tracks of magnetic disk. To read or record information on a magnetic disk the recording-reading head moves to the correct track of the spinning disk so that the information on the track can be accessed.

Tape reels and disks can be removed from the machine and stored if you need to keep information for long periods of time. Small disk memories are often used on microcomputers where individual disks are inserted into the reader by the user. These disks are called **floppy disks** or **diskettes**. Diskettes are kept in paper envelopes to protect them. They are **not** removed from the envelope even during use.

Both tape and disk secondary memories require the movement of objects, a reel of tape, a spinning disk, and sometimes read-write heads. These mechanical devices can never give really high-speed access to information. We need memory devices with no moving parts so we can perform operations at rates of the order of a million a second. The only things that move in a really high-speed memory device are the electric signals. As you know, electric signals can move very rapidly, at nearly the speed of light. A very common form of high-speed memory uses large scale integrated circuits (LSI).

The main memory of the computer is a number of bits grouped into words; to find any particular word you must know where it is located in the array of words. You need to know its **address**. Every word (which, remember, is just a group of bits) has its own address which is a number. An address may, for example, be *125*. Words that are neighbors in the array have consecutive addresses, such as *125* and *126*, just like apartments in an apartment house. The addresses themselves do not have to be stored in the computer. You can tell what address a word has from its location in the array.

The information that is stored in main memory is quickly accessible; any one word can be accessed as speedily as any other. We say that the memory is a **random access memory** (RAM). A disk secondary memory allows you to access any one piece of information about as fast as any other, although at a much slower rate than does main memory. For this reason we call a disk a **random access device** or a **direct access device**. Magnetic tape is not a random access device. Sometimes parts of the main memory of a computer have been arranged so that the user can read information from it but cannot write information into it. This is called a **read only memory** (ROM). The information stored in a read only memory must be placed there by the supplier. For example, a compiler program might be stored in a read only memory.

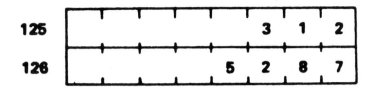

THE CONTENTS OF WORDS IN MEMORY

Since the development of microminiaturized electronic circuits on silicon chips, high-speed memory devices holding thousands of bits can be produced using as little as a single chip.

ARITHMETIC UNIT

All computers have a part where arithmetic can take place. This is the **arithmetic unit**. When a new number is written in a memory location, the old number stored there is automatically erased, just as any old recording is erased as a new recording is made on a magnetic tape recorder. Just reading a number, like playing an audio recording, does not damage the recording no matter how often you do it. If you want to combine numbers, say add them, it is usually done in one or more special locations in the arithmetic unit called **accumulators**. On some machines, the size of an accumulator is the same as the size of a word in memory. The information stored in memory locations, can be loaded into the accumulator. In a simple machine language, the instruction

load 125

would cause the number recorded in location *125* to be placed in the accumulator. Whatever was recorded in the accumulator before would be erased before the load takes place. If we want to add another number we would write

add 126

This would add the number stored in *126* to what was already in the accumulator and the sum of the two numbers would then be in the accumulator. This total could be recorded in the memory for later use by the instruction

store 127

The result of the addition would now be in location *127* but would also remain in the accumulator.

The accumulator can also be used for subtraction, multiplication, and division. In a high-level language like Fortran you never need to think about the accumulator. You merely indicate that you want numbers in two locations, say *a* and *b*, to be added and name the location, say *c*, where you want the answer to be stored. You write this all in one statement, namely

$$c = a + b$$

This Fortran statement says: add the number stored in location *a* to the number stored in location *b* and place the result in location *c*. In the machine all location addresses are numbers. In Fortran we give the locations names which are called **identifiers**. The compiler changes these names to numerical locations and changes the single Fortran instruction

$$c = a + b$$

to the three machine instructions.

> *load a*
> *add b*
> *store c*

The addition of two numbers can be accomplished through a combination of gates in a device called an **adder**. Multiplication is accomplished by a series of shifts and additions since shifting a number left one position is equivalent to multiplying the number by two.

CONTROL UNIT

You have just seen examples of machine language instructions. They each consist of two parts: the operation part, for example *load*, and the address part, *a*. Each part can be coded as a binary number, then the whole instruction will just be a string of bits. Suppose that you have a machine with a word length of 32 bits. Then an instruction might be itself stored in such a word with, say, 16 bits for the operation part and 16 bits for the address part. With 16 bits you can represent binary numbers that go from 1 up to 2 to the power 16, which is 65,536. The number of memory locations is a power of two and we often speak in terms of 1024 locations (which is 2^{10}) as K locations. The K is short for kilo which usually means one thousand. We say the memory has 32K or 64K locations.

Consecutive instructions in a machine language program are stored in consecutive locations in the memory and are to be executed one after the other. The control unit does two things. It uses a special location called the **instruction pointer** to keep track of what instruction is currently being executed. It places the instruction to be executed in a special location called the **control register**. In the control register the instruction is decoded and signals are issued to the different parts of the computer so that the operation requested is actually carried out. As each instruction is executed, the instruction pointer is increased by one to give the address of the next instruction in the program. This next instruction is then fetched from the memory, placed in the control register, and executed. This process continues, with instructions being executed sequentially unless a special instruction is encountered, which resets the instruction pointer and causes a **jump** from the normal sequence to a different part of the program.

In brief, the control unit controls the sequence of execution of instructions and determines the effect that execution has on the information stored in the memory.

Computers were originally referred to as **stored program calculators** because the instructions as well as the numbers or characters they operate on are stored in the memory. They were also referred to as **sequential machines**, because normally they followed a sequence of instructions one after another unless a jump instruction directed them to do otherwise.

We have said that the memory of a computer can be contained on a single silicon chip. This is true also of the parts of the computer that make up the central processing unit. If the CPU is all on a single chip we call the computer a **microprocessor**.

INPUT AND OUTPUT

We have spoken of putting both data and instructions in the memory of the machine and changing the data by the execution of instructions. But how do we get data or instructions into the computer, and how do we get data out of the machine after it has been operated on? That is the function of the **input** and **output units**. We must have instructions that cause the machine to **read** information into its memory and to **write** information out from its memory. And we must have parts of the computer, the input and output units, that respond to these instructions. Most computer systems use individual input-output terminals at which information can be entered through a keyboard and output is produced as a display on a cathode ray tube (CRT) screen. Microcomputers often have only one terminal; we say the system is a **single-user system** or a personal computer. Larger systems have many such terminals; the system is a **multi-user system**. There is also a printer for obtaining **hardcopy** of what can be seen on the screen. Because each user enters his program and data directly into the computer and receives the results rapidly, the system is often said to be an **interactive** system. If several people can simultaneously use a system interactively, we say it is a **time-sharing** computer system.

The keyboard of an input terminal is similar to that of a standard typewriter, so it helps if you can type. But hunt-and-peck methods will get you there too. In addition to the ordinary typewriter keys, there are special keys for indicating that you want the computer to take certain actions. These keys are not the same from one kind of terminal to another.

The hardcopy output units can be line-at-a-time printers or typewriters. Across a displayed page there are often positions to output 120, 132 or more characters although some printers output only 72 characters on a line. The paper is continuous but may be divided by perforations into pages, each capable of holding about 60 lines of output. Some printers form their characters out of an array of dots; these are called **matrix printers**.

PROGRAM TRANSLATION

We have said that three machine language instructions, namely,

> *load   a*
> *add   b*
> *store   c*

correspond to what is written in Fortran as

> *c = a + b*

Instructions in the high-level language Fortran are very much simpler to write than instructions in machine language. For one thing, you do not have to be aware of the accumulator; for another, the notation is very similar to the one used in simple mathematical expressions and should be easy for you to get used to. The Fortran language is more powerful in that a single Fortran instruction can correspond to many machine language instructions. We will see later that if you are working in a high-level language, the machine can detect when you make certain kinds of mistakes in your program.

In summary, high-level languages are designed to suit **you** rather than suit a computer. As a result, they make the job of programming less difficult.

A Fortran program cannot execute directly on a computer but must be translated into the language for the particular computer you have. This is accomplished after the Fortran program has been entered into the memory. The translation is performed by another program, called the compiler, that is already stored in the computer memory. The compiler scans your Fortran program and produces the appropriate sequence of machine language instructions from your Fortran statements. After compilation, execution of the machine language program can be initiated provided you have not made any errors in your Fortran program that the compiler can detect. The kind of errors that are detectable are mostly in the **form** of the statements. If they are not proper or grammatical statements in the Fortran language the compiler will report an error to you on your screen. Errors in grammar are called **syntax errors**. In English you know there is an error in the sentence,

> *The boys is walking.*

A machine can spot this kind of error but it cannot easily spot an error in meaning. It might never determine that the sentence,

> *The house is walking.*

is not a meaningful sentence; it would accept it as syntactically correct. We call an error in meaning a **semantic error**.

CHAPTER 2 SUMMARY

In this chapter we presented the main parts of a computer and showed how information is stored in the memory. We explained briefly how a high-level language such as Fortran is translated, or compiled, into machine language before being executed by a computer. The following important terms were introduced.

Pulse — an electric signal which is produced by turning on an electric voltage for a certain time, the pulse time, and then turning it off.

Clock — the timing device in the computer which determines the pulse rate. Typical clock rates are tens of megahertz.

Gate — a combination of transistors and their electric connectors which has certain logical properties.

Or gate — a gate from which there is an output pulse if there is an input pulse on either or both of the two incoming lines.

And gate — a gate from which there is an output pulse if there are input pulses on both of the two incoming lines.

Not gate — a gate from which there is no output pulse if there is an input pulse and vice versa.

Flip-flop — an interconnection of *and*, *not*, and *or* gates capable of storing one bit of information.

Memory — the part of a computer that stores information, such as data or a program. Magnetic tapes and disks are called secondary memory; they require mechanical motion to access information stored on them. Main memory can be immediately accessed by the computer; main memory is usually in the form of microminiaturized circuits on a silicon chip. We say the memory is a solid state one. Other forms of memory, such as bubble memories, are being developed. The computer can transfer information between secondary memory and main memory.

RAM — random access memory, a term used for main memory since any one word may be accessed as rapidly as any other.

Random access device — a term used for a secondary memory device, such as a disk, from which any one piece of information can be obtained approximately as rapidly as any other. The access time is much longer than from main memory.

ROM — read only memory, a term used for main memory which has been produced in such a way that information can be read from it but nothing can be written there by the user. The information in a ROM is generally prerecorded by the manufacturer.

CPU (central processing unit) — composed of the arithmetic unit and the control unit. The arithmetic unit carries out operations such as addition and multiplication. The control unit directs other parts of the computer, including the arithmetic unit, to carry out a sequence of instructions that is in the main memory. If the CPU is contained on a single silicon chip we call it a microprocessor.

Accumulator — the part of the CPU where numbers can be held during the performance of arithmetic operations.

Input and output — ways of getting information into and out of a computer. An output device called a printer takes information from main memory and outputs it on paper. This is referred to as hardcopy. An input-output device suitable for use by individual users is often a keyboard and a cathode ray tube (CRT) display screen attached to the computer.

Screen — a cathode ray tube used to display the output from a computer. This is also called a video display; the terminal with screen is referred to as a video display terminal (VDT).

Keyboard — the array of keys used to enter data and instructions into a computer.

Bit — a digit in the binary system of numbers, usually written as a 0 or a 1.

Byte — a sequence of bits treated as a unit, for example, the number of bits used to represent an alphabetic character. Bytes contain 8 bits on most computers.

Word — A number of bits grouped as a unit for holding information in the memory of a computer. Each word has an address which indicates its location in the array of words in memory. A word often consists of two or four bytes.

Coded information — before information can be entered into a computer, it
must be coded in a convenient form for the computer's circuitry.
The circuitry recognizes *off* and *on* which we can think of as the
binary digits 0 and 1.

Translation (or compilation) — before a program written in a language like
Fortran can be executed by a computer, it must be translated into a
language that can be interpreted by the computer. The program as
written in Fortran is called the source program. The translated program is placed in words in computer's memory and is executed by
the computer's CPU.

Microprocessor — a computer in which the CPU is contained on a single
silicon chip.

Syntax error — an error in the form (or grammar) of instructions.

Semantic error — an error in the meaning of a program.

Chapter 3

THE MINIMAL PROGRAM

In this chapter we will introduce the minimum number of elements of programming that you need in order to begin to program. Nothing very important will be programmed but you will be able to go through the motions of writing a complete program and enter the program into a computer using the command language of the operating system and have it executed. Also you will see what kind of output to expect. Things will happen, though what the computer is actually doing for you will not be very exciting yet. But remember you will go through the same motions as are necessary when your programs do have more content.

BASIC SYMBOLS OF THE FORTRAN LANGUAGE

We will be presenting the programming language Fortran a little bit at a time. Any language consists of words and the words are made up of symbols that we call characters. These characters are put together in strings. In English the word

elephant

is a string of characters of length eight. It contains only seven different characters, the character *e* being used twice. We can tell that it is a word because it has a blank in front of it and one at the end. In a way the blank is also a character, but a special character for separating words. We sometimes denote the blank by *b* when we show programs in this book so that you can see how many blanks are present.

In English, we group words into sentences and we can tell the end of a sentence because of a special mark, the period. We also have a different kind of sentence that ends with a question mark, don't we? In addition to periods and question marks, we have other **punctuation marks** which serve to make sentences in the language easier to read. They also serve to remove ambiguity in a sentence. There is some doubt about the meaning of the sentence,

The student claims the teacher understands.

The doubt is removed if it is written with commas, as,

The student, claims the teacher, understands.

It is important that statements in a programming language be **unambi-guous**, so punctuation is used a great deal. Instead of a sentence, the basic unit in the main part of a program is a **statement**. Statements are separated from each other by starting each statement on a new line for input. In some other high-level languages, statements are separated by having a semicolon between them. This serves to separate them just as periods separate sentences in English. In most high-level languages the comma is used to separate items in any list of similar items, and parentheses are used to enclose things that belong together.

We will have words in Fortran that are made up of letters of the alphabet and might also have digits in them. Although there are definite rules governing the way that Fortran statements are formed, we want them to be understandable. This means the words should be like English words. We use words like *name, cost, income, tax, sum*, or words like *page1, table6, item35*, and so on. Most of these words are invented by you. You are not allowed to use words that do not start with a letter. If the Fortran compiler sees a digit at the beginning of a word it assumes that it is a **number**. For example, the word 317 is taken as a number. This means that words like *3rd* are illegal and will not be accepted by the Fortran compiler. The words that you make up must not be longer than six characters. So words like *invoice, account, surname*, and *direction* are illegal.

Before we leave characters we should perhaps list them all. A **character** is a letter, or a digit, or a special character. The **letters** are the upper case letters

A B C D E F G H I J K L M N O P Q R S T U V W X Y Z

as well as lower case letters

a b c d e f g h i j k l m n o p q r s t u v w x y z

The **digits** are

0 1 2 3 4 5 6 7 8 9

The **special characters** are

+ - * / ( ) = . , $
b (blank)
' (apostrophe or single quote)

NUMBERS

When you learned arithmetic you first learned to handle numbers that are whole numbers, or integers. You learned that $5 + 6 = 11$ and $2 \times 3 = 6$. In Fortran numbers like 2, 3, 512, 809, and 46281 are called **integer constants**. Any string of digits is an integer constant. You will remember that we will be storing numbers in the computer and representing them as a string of bits in some coded representation. The largest integer we can represent will be limited by the length of the string of bits that are in a word in our computer. Word lengths vary from one computer to another and different Fortran compilers have different maximum lengths for the digit strings that represent integers. You will probably be safe in expecting at least nine decimal digits to be within the maximum.

If you have integers requiring longer digit strings, say for instance the population of the world, you must use the other form of numbers which is the **real** form. If you have a number like

635,642,000

where the zeros are not significant, you can write it as

6.35642×10^8

Perhaps you recognize this as what is called scientific notation. In Fortran the form of a **real constant** with an exponent such as our example is

.635642e9

The first part is called the **significant digits part**, the second part the **exponent part**. The exponent part is the letter *e* followed by the power of 10 that is to multiply the significant digits. Real numbers are more often numbers that are not integers. These are either **fractions** or **mixed numbers**. We write either of these in decimal notation where a point called the decimal point separates the integer from the fraction part. Examples of fractions are

.5 .0075 .0000023

Mixed numbers are

5.27 889.6 6.0216

When we write fractions or mixed numbers in scientific notation we usually standardize the form by giving the first non-zero digit followed by a decimal point then the remaining digits. Then the power of 10 is computed to make it right. The fraction .0000023 is written as 2.3×10^6. In Fortran we standardize the form as a decimal point followed by the significant digits so that our number would be .230000000e$-$05. This is the way it appears in the standard output form. For input, or in a program, it can also be written in various forms, for example, as .23e−5, or 23.e−7.

An integer constant must **not** have a decimal point; a real constant **must** have a decimal point, or an exponent, or both. The exponent part is the letter *e* followed by an optional plus or minus sign followed by one or more digits. Some compilers allow up to nine digits in the significant digits of a real number, and exponents up to e+76 and down to e−78. If the significant digits part of a real constant is an integer it need not have a decimal point provided that the exponent is present.

CHARACTER STRINGS

We have said that computers can handle both numbers and strings of characters. We have seen that there are two forms for numbers, the integer and the real.

A character string can consist of any of the characters that we have specified: letters, digits, and special characters. Very often, when outputting the results of a computer calculation, we want the results labelled. What we want is to output a string of characters. In the statement that specifies that we want the computer to output, we include the actual string that we want output enclosed in single quotation marks. These strings enclosed in quotation marks are called **literals** or **character string constants**.

Examples of literals are

'Bill Jones ', 'balance in account ', 'x = '

If the literal you want to give contains a single quotation mark or an apostrophe, which is the same character, then you must put two single quotes rather than one single quote. For example, the literal corresponding to the short form of 'cannot 'is 'can ''t '.

We will see how to use these literals in a program when we learn what the instruction is that causes output.

EXPRESSIONS

One of the important concepts we have in Fortran is that of an **expression**. The way that we explain what a word like expression means is basically to give examples and then generalize these examples.

First of all, 32, 5, 6.1e2 and 58.1e6 are all expressions. So the general statement is that integer constants and real constants are expressions. Any expression may be enclosed in parentheses and still be an expression. For example, (32) and (6.1e2) are also expressions. The expressions that are integer or real constants can be combined into compound expressions using the signs of arithmetic for adding, subtracting, multiplying, and dividing. These expressions are called **arithmetic expressions**. We use the standard signs for adding and subtracting, namely the plus and minus. For multiplication we use the asterisk (*). For division we use the slant or slash symbol (/). Examples of arithmetic expressions are

$$2 + 3, 5.2e1 * 7.8e5, 6. / 2., 10 - 15$$

Integer and real values may be combined in a single expression, and when they are the result is a real value. For example, 2 + 3.0e1 has the value 3.2e1.

If two numbers are to be divided, one of them must be a real number if you want the correct value for the result of division. Instead of writing 13/2, which will produce the result 6, you write 13/2. and get the correct result 6.5e0. Make a habit of using a decimal point to make the divisor a real number for the division in any integer division and all will be well.

A very complicated arithmetic expression is

$$2 * 5 + 8 - 3 * 5 / 2. + 6$$

In evaluating this you have to know what to do first because you really can only add, subtract, multiply, or divide numbers two at a time. The rule is to do the multiplications and divisions first, then the additions and subtractions. Also you start at the left-hand side of the expression and work to the right. We are using here **rules of precedence**: that the operations multiply and divide have precedence over add and subtract. Parentheses can be used to guide the sequence of evaluation. For example, you write 3 * (5 + 8) instead of 3 * 5 + 8 if you want the addition to take place before the multiplication. Expressions in parentheses take precedence.

Numbers may be raised to a power by means of the **exponentiation** operator which is written as **. For example, the value of 5 cubed is 5 ** 3, this being the same as 5 * 5 * 5. Non-integer powers may also be computed. For example, we can write 10. ** .5 to mean the square root of 10. We will later see that a more efficient way of computing square roots is to use the built-in function *sqrt* and write *sqrt(10.)* to get this same result.

The exponentiation operator has higher precedence than the other arithmetic operators so that in the expression

$$5 + 3 ** 2$$

the 3 is first squared to give 9 then added to 5 to give 14. If two or more exponentiation operators appear in the same expression they, unlike other arithmetic operators, are evaluated from the right to the left-hand side of the expression.

EXAMPLES OF ARITHMETIC EXPRESSIONS

The following examples illustrate the rules for performing arithmetic in the Fortran programming language.

72 + 16   Value is 88.

8 * 5 + 7   Value is 47. Note that * means multiply.

2 + 10 * 4   Value is 42. Note that multiplication is done before addition.

(2 + 10) * 4   Value is 48. The parentheses cause the addition to be done before the multiplication.

1 / 3   This division is not advisable because neither 1 nor 3 is a real number. Instead, you could write 1/3. (3. is the real equivalent of 3).

1 / 3.   Value is .333333333e0, which is approximately one third. Note that the result of combining an integer such as 1, and a real number, such as 3., is a real number. The value .333333333e0 can be written in other forms such as 3.33333333e−1 and 3.33333333e−01.

72.e0 + 16.e0   Value is 88.e0, which can be written in other forms such as 8.8e1 and 8.80000e+01.

(9.83e0 + 16.82e0)/ 2.935e0

This expression is equivalent to the following
$$\frac{9.83 + 16.82}{2.935}$$
The parentheses were used so the division would apply to the sum of 9.83e0 and 16.82e0 (and not just to 16.82e0).

OUTPUT

Our main purpose in this chapter is to introduce you to Fortran and to get you to write your first program. The program is not going to do very much but it has to do something so that you can see that it is working. The most it can do is to display numbers or character strings on the screen. Then you can see that some action is taking place.

The statement that we will use in the program is like this

> **print** *, 3, 5.1e1, 'Bill '

In the statement the keyword **print** is followed by an asterisk and a comma. Following the comma is a list of items to be displayed. The asterisk in the **print** statement tells the compiler that the format of the output is to be directed by the list of items. This is known as **list-directed format**. Output produced by the list-directed **print** statement is placed in successive fields across the line. The size of the field depends on the type of value that is being output. The output line has spaces for a certain number of characters. In some compilers an integer value is output on the right-hand side of a field the same size as the integer, a real value in a field of 15 characters. The items that are after the **print** are placed in fields going from left to right with a blank separating each pair of fields. The output line is also started with a blank. Literals are output, without the quotation marks, in fields that have the same number of character spaces as the literal has characters including blanks. When real numbers are output, their exponents are given, and they appear in a standard form with a fixed number of digits in the significant digits part, for example

> **.250000000e−01**

If two **print** statements are given one after another then the output of the second goes to a new line. A blank line can be left by using

> **print** *, ' '

since here the literal consists of a blank. Literals consisting of blanks are also useful for skipping character spaces.

Expressions other than integer and real constants and literals may also be placed in a **print** statement. The statement

> **print** *, 2 + 3, 4 / 2.

will result in a 5 being output in the first field followed by a blank and .200000000e+01 in the second which will be of width 15. The statement

> **print** *, '2 + 3 =', 2 + 3

would output

$$2 + 3 = 5$$

A blank separates the two fields. Note that the quotes are not output.

In output expressions, it is not legal to have a expression that begins with a parenthesis. It is illegal to write

print *,(2 + 3) * 5

Instead you write the legal expression

print *, + (2 + 3) * 5

It is not legal to have two arithmetic operators, together as in

print *, 5 /− 3.

Instead you write the legal expression

print *, 5 /(− 3.)

THE PROGRAM

Now that you know a statement that will give some action, you must learn what is necessary to make a complete program. Then you can try the computer for yourself. The shortest program you can write consists of one statement preceded by a statement beginning with the keyword **program** giving the program a name and followed by the two statements

stop
end

The name of the program is limited to six letters or digits and must begin with a letter. The keyword **end** indicates to the Fortran compiler that this is the end of the program during **translation**. The keyword **stop** causes control to return to the operating system at the end of the **execution** of your program. It is not absolutely necessary to have **stop** in your program but you must have **end**.

Now comes the big moment for a complete program.

program *addup*
print *, '2 + 3 = ',2 + 3
stop
end

There it is, our first Fortran program.

When you enter the statements of the program use columns 7-72 of the line. Information entered beyond column 72 is ignored by the Fortran compiler. Any number of blanks can be left after column 7 before the first word, or between words, in a statement. Later on we will be showing you how to indent the statements in your program to make it easier to read.

If a statement is too long to fit within the limit of column 72 it may be continued on the following line by placing a + sign (or any character other than blank or zero) in column 6.

EXAMPLE PROGRAMS

The following is a complete program for the computer. This program illustrates the use of several **print** statements. Line numbers are shown for the program so that we can refer to it. They are not part of the program.

```
1          program zigzag
2          print *,'z   g   z   g'
3          print *,'i a    i a '
4          print *,' gz      gz '
5          stop
6          end
```

The program causes the following pattern to be output.

```
z   g   z   g
 i a    i a
 gz      gz
```

As you can see, the top line of the pattern is output by the **print** statement numbered 2. Statements 3 and 4 cause the output of the second and third lines of the pattern. Line 1 begins with the Fortran keyword **program** and is followed by a name *zigzag* that we make up to identify this particular program. This name can be used as an identification of the file when the program is stored in the secondary (disk) memory of the computer. If you position the first character of the word **program** in column 7 it will provide a guide for typing the rest of your program statements. Remember statements must not start before column 7.

Here is a program that computes the kinetic energy in joules ($\frac{1}{2}mv^2$) and the momentum *mv* of a particle of mass 10 kg moving in a straight line with a velocity of 5 meters per second.

```
1          program motion
2          print *,'Particle of mass 10 kg, velocity 5 m/sec'
3          print *,'Kinetic energy is:',(1/2.) * 10 * 5**2,'joule'
4          print *,'Momentum is:',10 * 5,'kg— m/sec'
5          stop
6          end
```

Here is the output produced by this program:

Particle of mass 10 kg, velocity 5 m/sec
Kinetic energy is: .125000000e+03 joule
Momentum is: 50 kg−m/sec

Notice in line 3 that a decimal point is included after the 2 in the (1/2.) of the kinetic energy formula. This is because the division of two integers gives an integer result which for positive values results in the truncation of the fractional part. The result for (1/2) would be zero. Because 2. is a real number the final answer will be a real number and will be output in the exponent form. The momentum here has an integer value and is output as an integer. Notice how the calculated values are labelled in the output. This is done by putting literals in the list of items to be output by the **print** statements.

Notice that the name *motion* that we have chosen for this program and the name *zigzag* for this previous program are no longer than six characters. We try to choose names that are descriptive of what the program will do.

CHAPTER 3 SUMMARY

In this chapter, we explained how to write very simple Fortran programs. The following important terms were presented.

Character − is a letter: ABC...Z or abc...z, digit: 0123456789, or special character: +-*/()=.,$ and blank.

Integer constant − is an integer (whole number) such as 78 and 2931. There may be a minus sign in front of the integer. An integer constant must not contain commas or a decimal point. The following should **not** be used: 25,311 125.00.

Real constant − is a number such as 3.14159e0 (equal to 3.14159×10^0 or simply 3.14159). Real constants consist of a significant digits part (3.14159) and an optional exponent part (e0). The exponent part can be absent when there is a decimal point.

Literal (or character string constant) − is a sequence of characters enclosed in quotes, such as *'why not?'*.

Arithmetic expression − composed of either a single number or a collection of numbers combined using addition, subtraction, multiplication, division, and exponentiation (+,−,*,/, and **). Parentheses may enclose parts of the expression. If arithmetic expressions appear in a **print** statement they must not begin with a left parenthesis. Place a + sign in front of the parenthesis to avoid the problem. Two operators (*,− ,*,/,**) cannot appear next to each other.

Rules of precedence — specify the order for applying +,−, *, /, and ** to find the value of an arithmetic expression. Parenthesized expressions are evaluated first. Next, any ** operators are applied from right to left. Finally, proceeding from left to right, * and / are applied first, and then + and −.

print statement — this statement is of the form:

> **print** *, list of items separated by commas

The items to be output must be literals or arithmetic expressions. Each **print** statement starts a new output line. The asterisk after the keyword **print** indicates that the format of the output is to be directed by the list of items to be output. This is called list-directed formatting.

Field — the list-directed **print** statement causes output in fields across a line. The size of the fields depends on what is being output. The sizes of the fields may be different for different compilers. For some compilers, integers appear in fields just large enough to hold the integer, real numbers in 15-character fields, and literals in fields of their own length. Each pair of fields is separated by a blank. Some compilers output real numbers in the range between 1 and 10 without exponents.

Output — information which the computer displays at your request. The **print** statement produces output.

program — the first statement of all programs should begin with this keyword and be followed by a program name. The name must start with a letter and be no more than 6 letters (or digits) long.

end — the last statement of every Fortran program. It is used as a signal to stop compiling.

stop — the signal that the program's operation is to stop and control is to be returned to the operating system of the computer because the execution is finished.

sqrt — the built-in function for obtaining the square root of a number. For example to output the square root of 2 we write

> **print** *,*sqrt (2.)*

Note that the function *sqrt* gives the square root of a real number so that we must include the decimal point.

CHAPTER 3 EXERCISES

1. What will the following program cause the computer to output?

    ```
    program em
    print *,'*    *'
    print *,'** **'
    print *,'* * *'
    print *,'*    *'
    stop
    end
    ```

    Rearrange the lines in this program to display a different letter.

2. What do the following cause the computer to output?
    (a) **print** *, 2,'plus', 3,'is', 2 + 3
    (b) **print** *,'23424 + 19872 + 36218=',23424 + 19872 + 36218
    (c) **print** *,'2 formulas:', 2 + 3 * 5, + (2 + 3) * 5
    (d) **print** *,'subtraction', 20 − 10 − 5, 20 − (10 − 5)

3. Write statements to calculate and output the following:
    (a) The sum of 52181 and 10032.
    (b) 9213 take away 7918.
    (c) The sum of 9213, 487, 921, 2013 and 514.
    (d) The product of 21 times the sum of 816, 5 and 203.
    (e) 343 plus 916 all multiplied by 82.
    (f) 3.14159 (pi) times 8.94 divided by 2.
    (g) 3.14159 times the square of 8.94 (Note: x^2 can be written as $x*x$ or as $x**2$).

4. Write programs to calculate and output the following with the appropriate labels:

    (a) The area of a triangle whose base is 10.5 cm and whose altitude (or height) is 8.7 cm.

    (b) The volume a cylinder whose circumference is 9.2 cm and whose height is 5.3 cm.

    (c) The distance between two points in a plane whose co-ordinates are (3,2) and (5,8).

    (d) The value of the polynomial $y=x^2-2x+3$ at the three values $x=1,2,3$.

    (e) The resistances of two resistors of 5 and 10 ohms connected in serial and in parallel.

(f)   The wavelength of electromagnetic radiation of frequency 7 megahertz.

Chapter 4

BASIC CONCEPTS OF PROGRAMMING

In order to read numerical information into the computer, to perform arithmetic calculations on the numbers you read in, and to output the answers we must look at the concepts of: **variable, data type, declaration**, and **assignment statement**. We will, as well, introduce the statement for **input** and the idea of **program tracing**.

VARIABLES

We have said that a computer has a memory and that in the memory there are locations where information can be stored. Each location has its own unique address. In a high-level language like Fortran we do not ever refer to an actual machine address. Instead we use a name to identify a particular location. It is like referring to a house by the name of the owner rather than by its street address. We use the word **variable** to stand for the memory location. It is named by an **identifier**.

The identifier for a variable must begin with a letter and contain no blanks or special characters. If you think of the variable as the memory location and its name as the identifier then you will realize that the **value** of the variable will be the actual information that is stored in the memory location. Locations are arranged to hold only one type of information or data. We speak of the **data type** of a variable. A variable may hold integers, in which case we say it is an **integer variable**. It could also be a **real variable** or a **character variable**. If a variable is an integer variable its value can be any integer. The value may be changed from time to time in the program but its **type** can never change; once an integer variable, always an integer variable.

Examples of variable identifiers are

factor, tax, total, mark

Identifiers for variables can be up to 6 characters long.

It is **very** important to choose identifiers that relate to the kind of information that is stored in the corresponding locations. Well-chosen identifiers make a program easier to understand.

DECLARATIONS

We must make the words we want to use as variable identifiers known to the compiler and associate them with memory locations suitable for the particular data type they will hold. This is accomplished by means of **declarations** that are placed at the beginning of the program.

We will not, at the moment, show how character variables can be declared but look only at integer and real variables. To declare that *sum* is to be an integer variable we write

> **integer** *sum*

The identifier is placed after the keyword **integer**. This establishes *sum* as having the type **integer**. To declare *width* to be a real variable use

> **real** *width*

If a number of integer variables are required they can all be listed separated by commas, for example

> **integer** *sum, mark, number*

Putting declarations in a program is like phoning ahead for hotel reservations; when you need it, the space is there with the right name on it. Also the compiler can substitute the actual machine address whenever it encounters a variable identifier in the program. It does this by keeping a directory showing variable identifiers and corresponding memory locations. This directory is set up as the declarations are read by the compiler.

You should not use as variable identifiers any of the words that are Fortran keywords. These are **integer, real, print, stop, end**, and so on. It makes the programs confusing.

ASSIGNMENT STATEMENTS

In addition to declarations, you will be learning two kinds of Fortran statements that cause things to happen as the program is executed. We say that they are **executable statements**. The **print** statement is an executable statement; it causes output to take place. One of the two new executable types we will have is the statement that inputs data, the **read** statement, but first we will look at the **assignment statement**.

There are no keywords in an assignment statement but it has a very definite form. The form is

variable identifier = expression

There is an **equal sign** and on the left of it is a variable identifier. This identifier must have been declared to be either integer or real. On the right hand of the equal sign there is an expression. We have looked at expressions that contained integer or real constants; now expressions can also contain integer or real variable identifiers. We have expressions like

5 + 10 / 3.e0   (8 + 9) * 7

but now we can have expressions like

sum + *1*   *total* / *1.00e2*   *sum* − *mark*

We will not use variable identifiers in the expression on the right-hand side of an assignment statement to begin with but instead use a simple expression, an integer constant. For example,

age = *5*

is an assignment statement. It has the result of storing the number 5 in the memory location identified by the identifier *age*. If *age* has appeared in the declaration

integer *age*

then the number will be stored as an integer and would be output by

print **,age*

as 5. If, on the other hand, it were declared

real *age*

it would be stored and output as .500000000e+00.

Assignments look like equations and this is misleading. When we write

age = *5*

we are not stating something that is true when you encounter it in a program. You mean by the statement that the value 5 is to be assigned to the variable *age*. Some programming languages try to keep assignments from looking like equations by using an arrow pointing left instead of an equal sign, and write

age ← *5*

This way of writing the assignment indicates the action that is to take place. Other languages use := instead of =. We are stuck with Fortran's equal sign and you must just learn to think of the action.

So far the expression on the right-hand side of the assignment has just been an integer constant, but we can have more complicated expressions.

$$age = 1985 - 1966$$

Here we are subtracting the year of birth, 1966, from the year 1985 to get the age in 1985. This instruction would assign the value 19 to the variable *age*. We could get the same result as follows

$$born = 1966$$
$$now = 1985$$
$$age = now - born$$

Here we have two additional variables *born* and *now* which are given values in assignment statements and then used in an expression on the right-hand side of another assignment statement. We could have another statement

$$newage = age + 1$$

which would give the age the following year to the variable *newage*. Remember, if we use identifiers in a program they must **all** appear in declarations. We would need the declaration

integer *age, born, now, newage*

A variable may be assigned values over and over during a program. For example, we might have

$$sum = 2 + 3$$
print **, sum*
$$sum = 3 + 4$$
print **, sum*

and so on. Now we come to a somewhat confusing type of assignment statement. Suppose in a program you were making calculations year by year and needed to keep a variable *age* that held the value of the current age for the calculation. We might change the value at the end of the year by the assignment:

$$age = age + 1$$

Now you can see that the assignment statement is certainly **not** an equation, or this would be nonsense. What happens when this statement is executed is that the value stored in the variable *age* is added to the integer 1 and the result of the addition stored back in the same location.

TRACING EXECUTION

We have seen that variables are associated with locations in the memory of the computer. We can assign values to variables and, during a program, we can change the values as often as we want. The values can **vary** and that is why the locations are called variables. The location stays the same but the value can change.

Sometimes it is helpful when getting used to writing programs, to keep track of values stored in the memory locations corresponding to each variable. This can help us to understand the effect of each statement. Some statements change a value; others do not. We call this **tracing the execution** of instructions.

We do not need to know the numerical, or machine address of the locations. As far as we are concerned the identifier is the address of the variable. For example, if before execution of

$$age = age + 1$$

the value of *age* was 9 then after it would be 10.

We will trace now a slightly more complicated program by writing the values of all the variables involved after each instruction is executed. Here we will use some meaningless names like *x, y,* and *z* because the program has no particular meaning. We just want to learn to trace execution. We will write the tracing on the right-hand side of the page and the program on the left. The labels over the right-hand side give the names of the variables; their values after execution of the instruction are listed under the names, opposite each instruction. When the value of a particular variable has not yet been assigned we will write a dash.

line		*x*	*y*	*z*
1	**integer** *x, y, z*	—	—	—
2	*x = 5*	*5*	—	—
3	*y = 7*	*5*	*7*	—
4	*z = x + y*	*5*	*7*	*12*
5	*x = x + 5*	*10*	*7*	*12*
6	*x = z*	*12*	*7*	*12*
7	*y = z*	*12*	*12*	*12*
8	*x = x + y + z*	*36*	*12*	*12*
9	*y = y * z*	*36*	*144*	*12*
10	*z = (x + y)/12.*	*36*	*144*	*15*
11	*x = x/5.*	*7*	*144*	*15*
12	**print** **,x,y,z*	*7*	*144*	*15*
13	**stop**			
14	**end**			

The lines of the program are numbered so that we can make reference to them. The computer numbers lines so that it can refer to errors in specific lines. Lines can also be numbered by the line editor for editing purposes.

First notice that the locations *x, y,* and *z* do not get established until the declaration **integer** *x,y,z.* They have no values assigned at this point though. All is straightforward until line 5 when *x* appears on both sides of the assignment statement. The values shown at the right are, remember, the values after execution of the statement on that line. In line 10 note that we add a decimal point to the integer 12. The result of the division is exactly 11 so you do not notice that the fractional part is dropped when the result is assigned to the integer variable *z*. In line 11 you can see that the fractional part of this division is dropped. We say it is **truncated**. The answer is computed as 7.2 but only the integer 7 is stored in location *x* because it is of the type **integer**. To get the fractional part of the result in a division we must store the answer in a **real** variable location.

The output statement in line 12 is different from the output statements in previous programs because now we can include the names of variables in the list. We have

print **, x, y, z*

The machine can tell the difference between variable identifiers and literals in output statements because identifiers have no quotes. There is no possible confusion between numbers and identifiers because an identifier may not begin with a digit. You can see now why Fortran has this rule.

In this example we showed a division with truncation. Sometimes we want to round off the results of a division, say in determining costs to the nearest cent. If *cost* is the value in cents of a 2-kilogram package of soap flakes then the cost of one kilogram to the nearest cent *kgcost* is

$$kgcost = cost / 2. + .5$$

The variable *kgcost* has been declared to be integer so it will accept only whole number values. This method of rounding is to add .5 to the answer, which is computed with the proper fractional part. Then, after addition, the fractional part is truncated because the value is assigned to the integer variable *kgcost*. Adding .5 has the effect that if the right answer has a fractional part below .5 then it is rounded by truncation of the fraction. If it is .5 or over , it is rounded up to the next integer.

INPUT OF DATA

Now we will learn how to input data from the keyboard into the computer. We did not learn this at the same time as we learned to output data because the idea of a variable is essential to input. It is not essential to output because we can have numbers and literals, that is, integer and real constants and constant character strings. If we write

> **read** *$^*,x,y,z$*

we will read three numbers from the keyboard and store them in the three variables x, y, and z. As the data is entered the numbers need not be arranged in any set fields, but must be separated from each other by at least one blank. Here is a program that reads and outputs information.

```
program total
integer x,y,z
print *, 'Enter x and y '
read *,x,y
z = x + y
print *,z, y, x
stop
end
```

A sample display for this program might be

> **Enter x and y**
> *5   7*
> **12 7 5**

The first line of the display appears on the screen and the cursor is positioned at the beginning of the second line. We will show what the computer displays in **boldface** type; what you type is in *italics*. In an actual display all the characters are the same. After the display of the first line the computer waits for you to enter the data. On input, the first number entered, namely 5, is associated with the first variable x and stored in that location. The number 7 is stored in location y.

The numbers are separated by at least one blank. After you have entered the 7 you must press the enter (or return) key so that the numbers can be accepted by the **read** statement of the program and the sum computed. When this happens the last line of the display, giving the sum, appears. When a program reaches the end of execution this display will remain on the screen and the computer will indicate that control has passed back to the operating system.

When inputting real numbers, you do not have to put any more significant figures than necessary in either the significant digits part or exponent; you need not enter

.2000000e +01

You can have only .2e1. If the exponent is zero, you may omit it completely as long as a decimal point is present. Thus numbers like

35.8   3.14159   0.025   2.

are all acceptable as real numbers.

CONVERSION BETWEEN INTEGER AND REAL

In assignments, conversions between integer and real form will occur automatically whenever required by the type of the variable that is to hold the number. If a data item is entered as an integer and is read into a location defined by a variable that has been declared as **real**, then it will be converted to real. A real constant cannot be read into a location defined by a variable that has been declared as **integer**. For example:

```
program convrt
integer x, y
real z
print *, 'Input values for x, y, and z '
read *, x, y, z
print *, x, y, z
print *, 'Input values for x, y, and z '
read *, x, y, z
print *, x, y, z
stop
end
```

The display for this program might be

Input values for x, y, and z
22 36 25
22 36 .250000000e+02
Input values for x, y, and z
2 181 5.e4
2 181 .500000000e+05

In this display remember we show what the program outputs in **boldface type** and what you input in *italic type*. This is so you can see which is which. On the actual display all the characters look the same.

Within a program it is often necessary to convert between integer and real. This can be accomplished by assigning the integer to a real variable and vice versa. For example, suppose that *avmark* is a real variable holding the average mark in a term examination. You would like the average to the nearest mark. Declare another variable *mark* as integer and write in the program

$$mark = avmark + .5$$

mark will then be an integer, the rounded average mark. Another way of rounding is to use the built-in function *nint.* Then you can produce the same result by the statement

$$mark = nint(avmark)$$

If instead of rounding you wanted the fractional part of *avmark* to be truncated you can use either

$$mark = avmark$$

or

$$mark = int(avmark)$$

An integer can be converted to a real by using the built-in function **real**.

COMMENTS

One of the main aims of structured programming is that your programs be easily understood by yourself and by others. Choosing variable names that suggest what is being stored is an excellent way to make programs readable. We have shown several programs with just *x, y,* and *z* as variable names. This is because these are meant to show you what happens in assignment statements and **read** or **print** statements and are not about real applications. It is not advisable to use such meaningless names. Your programs should look more like English than like algebra when you are finished. Unfortunately the six character limitation on variable names leads to some unavoidable abbreviating.

One other thing that you can do to make a program understandable is to include comments in English along with the program. We have been providing comments to some of our examples in the accompanying text but you can write comments right into the program. To accomplish this, simply precede the comment by a *c* in column 1 of the input line. For example

    c   *This is a comment*

could be placed at the beginning of a program or between statements or between declarations **anywhere** in the program. A blank line is accepted as a comment and will result in a blank line in the program listing.

Comments should not be split between lines, or be put in the data. From now on we will be including comments in our examples.

EXAMPLE PROGRAMS

We now give a program which illustrates the use of variables, assignment statements, **read** statements, and comments. The program reads in the length, width, and height of a box (as given in inches) and then outputs the area of the base of the box (in square centimeters) and the volume of the box (in cubic centimeters).

```
1              program box
2    c         Read box length, width, and height in inches
3    c             then convert to centimeters and calculate
4    c             the box's base area and volume
5              real length, width, height, area, volume, intocm
6              parameter (intocm = 2.54)
7              print *,'Enter length and width in inches'
8              read *,length, width
9              length = intocm*length
10             width = intocm*width
11             area = length*width
12             print *,'area = ',area,'square centimeters'
13             print *,'Enter height'
14             read *,height
15             height = intocm*height
16             volume = height*area
17             print *,'volume = ',volume,'cubic centimeters'
18             stop
19             end
```

This program might display the following

Enter length and width in inches
2.6 1.2
area =   .201289932e+02 square centimeters
Enter height
6.92
volume =   .353803271e+04 cubic centimeters

The area and volume output depend on the three values of the data input; the data values 2.6, 1.2, and 6.92 could be replaced by the dimensions of a different box.

Lines 2, 3, and 4 are comments intended for the reader of the program, and are ignored by the computer. Line 5 of the program sets up memory locations for variables called *length, width, height, area, volume*, and *intocm* (the conversion factor from inches *(in)* to centimeters *(cm)*). These variables have the **real** type, instead of the **integer** type, because they have non-integer values (such as 2.6). Line 6 sets the value of *intocm* to 2.54. This assignment is enclosed in parentheses and preceded by the keyword **parameter** which insures that it remains a constant throughout the program. Line 7 cuases the data values 2.6 and 1.2 to be read into variables *length* and *width*.

Line 9 takes the value 2.6 from the *length* variable, multiplies it by *intocm*, and then returns the result to *length*. The multiplication sign (*) is required; we could **not** write simply

$$length \ = \ intocm \ length$$

Line 10 is similar to line 9. Line 11 takes the values in *length* and *width*, multiplies them together, and places the result in *area*. Line 12 then outputs:

area $=$ .201289932e$+$02 square centimeters

As of line 11, the variables *height* and *volume* have not been used. An attempt to output *height* or *volume* in line 12 would be an error because those variables have not yet been given a value.

Since the **read** statement of line 8 reads the first data entered, 2.6 and 1.2, the **read** statement of line 14 reads the value 6.92 into *height*. The computer does not know that 6.92 represents the height of a box. It only knows that it is instructed to read the next data value into the variable named *height*. Line 15 converts to centimeters, line 16 computes the volume and line 17 outputs the volume. Line 18 tells the computer to stop working on this program.

This program would output the same thing if we made the following changes:

(1) Replace line 8 by the two assignment statements:

$$length \ = \ 2.6$$
$$width \ = \ 1.2$$

(2) Replace line 13 by the assignment statement:

$$height \ = \ 6.92$$

(3) No data values are entered.

These three changes result in a program which is given the dimensions of the box by assignment statements rather than by input statements (**read** statements). The advantage of the original program, which uses **read** statements, is that the program will work for a new box simply by entering different data.

Here is a program that will compute the equivalent electrical resistance *r* of three resistances, *r1, r2,* and *r3*, connected in parallel.

```
          program resist
c         Read values for three resistances
c             and compute the resistance of the three in parallel
          real r,r1,r2,r3, recip
          print *,'Enter values in ohms of three resistances'
          read *,r1,r2,r3
          recip = (1/r1) + (1/r2) + (1/r3)
          r = (1/recip)
          print *,'Equivalent resistance is:',r,'ohms'
          stop
          end
```

Here is a sample display:

Enter values in ohms of three resistances
500 1000 200
Equivalent resistance is: .124999992e + 03 ohms

Notice that we prompt the user of the program to enter the values for *r1*, *r2*, and *r3*. These are entered in the sample as integers; they might be mixed numbers such as 1.5 or 9.25. The reciprocal of the equivalent resistance *r* is the sum of the reciprocals of the individual resistances. Notice how we introduced the additional variable *recip* to calculate *r*.

We could have put *1/recip* instead of *r* in the output list of the second **print** statement but the program would not have been as understandable. Remember we want our programs to be as easy to read as possible.

LABELLING OF OUTPUT

Just as comments help to make a program more understandable, output that is properly identified by labels is self-explanatory. What you are trying to do is to prepare a program that need no further explanation from you when you show it to others. The output data should be labelled so the reader is in no doubt about what the numbers are, without reading the program.

There are two basic ways to label results. If different values of the same set of variables are listed in columns on the output display, then a label can be placed at top of each column. For example, the display for comparing costs of boxes of soap flakes might be

cost (cents) weight (kgs) cost per kg
125	*1*	
		125
200	*2*	

100

260   *3*

87

There is no reason to use exactly the same labels as the variable names, since the literals output at the top of the columns can be longer and contain blanks. If you are labelling columns the labels should fit over the columns. Blanks can be inserted in the output to make them come out to the right length. The program that produces this table might be

```
        program soap
c       Compute and tabulate cost per kg
        integer cost, weight, kgcost
c       Print headings of table
        print *,'cost (cents)','weight (kgs)','cost per kg'
c       Process data for first box
        read *,cost, weight
        kgcost = cost/(weight*1.) + .5
        print *,'            ','            ',kgcost
c       Process data for second box
        read *,cost, weight
        kgcost = cost/(weight*1.) + .5
        print *,'            ','            ',kgcost
c       Process data for third box
        read *,cost, weight
        kgcost = cost/(weight*1.) + .5
        print *,'            ','            ',kgcost
        stop
        end
```

You can see how comments can be inserted, how the column headings are output, and how each line of the table is calculated and output. In order to get the computer to read the cost and weight that you enter you must press the return key. This means that the cost per kg will be on the next line. We get it to line up with the column heading by putting two literals ahead of *kgcost* in the output list. Each literal consists of 12 blanks. We multiplied *weight* by the real constant 1. because this produces the real number equivalent of *weight*; this is done to avoid dividing an integer by another integer. In the program we have repeated three statements, without change, one set of three for each box. If we had 100 boxes, this would have been a little monotonous. When we want to repeat statements we do **not** do it this way; a more convenient way is possible with a new kind of statement that will cause this repetition. But that comes in the next chapter.

A second kind of output labelling was already used in the previous example but can be illustrated by a program segment

```
cost = 5
print *, 'cost = ', cost
```

This would result in the output

cost = 5

This method is easier than column headings when just a few numbers are being output, and saves the problem of making labels of a precise number of characters.

MATHEMATICAL FUNCTIONS

So far in our calculations we have had arithmetic expressions with addition, subtraction, multiplication, division, and exponentiation. As well, we introduced the idea of a mathematical function, giving as an example the square root *sqrt.* If in a program we had the statement

print *,sqrt(100.)

the output would be

.100000000e+02

which is the standard exponent form for 10 (the square root of 100). We had to put a decimal point after the 100 because the square root function *sqrt* requires an **argument** which is real.

There are other mathematical functions that are built-in to the Fortran compiler. Among these are the trigonometric functions for sine, cosine, and arctan, called *sin, cos,* and *atan.* The functions *sin* and *cos* require as an argument an angle in radians, and atan gives the angle in radians that has a particular tangent.

Here is a program that computes the force along and perpendicular to a tilted plane produced by a block of mass *m* kg sitting on the plane. If the plane is at an angle *A* to the horizontal then the force along the plane will be *mg sin A*, perpendicular to the plane is *mg cos A*, where *g* is the acceleration due to gravity, namely 9.8 m$-$sec^{-2}.

```
        program slide
c       Computes components of force
        real angle,mass,g,pi,A
        print *,'Enter angle in degrees and mass in kg'
        read *,angle,mass
        parameter (g = 9.8, pi = 3.14159)
c       Compute A the size of the angle in radians
```

```
        A = angle * pi/180
        print *, 'Force along plane:',mass * g * sin (A), 'newton'
        print *, 'Force perpendicular to plane:',mass * g *cos (A), 'newton'
        stop
        end
```

This program repeats the calculation of $m*g$. It might be made more efficient by having an auxiliary variable called *mg* which is assigned the value $m*g$ then used in both force components. Notice the **parameter** statement that assigns values to the constants *g* and *pi*.

Other built-in functions requiring real arguments are *abs* for find the absolute value of a number, *exp* for finding the value of *e* to a power and *alog* for giving the natural logarithm of a number. The function *alog10* gives the logarithm to the base 10.

The function *mod(a,b)*, where *a* and *b* have integer values, has an integer value which is the remainder when *a* is divided by *b*. For example, *mod(13,5)* has a value 3.

Here is an example using *exp* and *alog*. The number of atoms N_t of a radioactive material at time *t* is related to the number N_0 at time 0 by the formula

$$N_t = N_0 e^{-\lambda t}$$

where λ is the decay constant. Usually this constant is given in terms of the half-life. The relationship between λ and the half-life is

$$\lambda = (\log_e 2)/half-life$$

For radiocarbon 14 the half-life is 5760 years. Here is a program to determine the fraction left undecayed after time *t*, namely N_t/N_0.

```
        program decay
c       Computes fraction of radiocarbon left after time t
        real t,left,lambda,log2
        print *, 'Enter time in years since start'
        read *,t
        parameter (log2 = alog(2.))
        lambda = log2/5760
        left = exp(- lambda * t)
        print *, 'Fraction left after',t,'years is',left
        stop
        end
```

Notice that *alog* requires a real argument so that to find $\log_e 2$ we put a period after the 2. We have designated *log2* as a constant.

Here is an example using *mod.* The program reduces any angle to one between 0 and 360 degrees.

```
      program cycle
c     Computes the equivalent angle less than 360 degrees
      integer angle
      print *,'Enter angle in degrees'
      read *,angle
      print *,'Equivalent angle is:',mod(angle,360)
      stop
      end
```

PROGRAM TESTING

It is easy to make mistakes in programming. The first thing you should do to test a program is to read over your program carefully to spot errors. It is valuable to trace the execution yourself before you submit it to the computer. Your goal should always be to produce programs that you **know** are correct without testing, but this is not always possible. You could ask someone else to read it too. If they cannot understand your program it may show that your program is poorly written or has errors. Next you put your program into the computer and proofread it on the screen to see that it matches your intentions. Then you should request a compilation and execution.

If you have made errors in your program that involve the form of statements, the compiler spots these during compilation and reports them on the output. It refers to an error of a certain type in line so and so of the program. It gives numbers to each line so that it can make these references. Errors in form are called **syntax errors**. Examples of common syntax errors are

1.   leaving out the comma after **read** * or **print** *

2.   forgetting the **end**

3.   misspelling a keyword

In a way, a syntax error is a good error since it is detected for you by the computer. But it is frustrating to have to correct it and recompile the program. It wastes time. Some people say that having syntax errors is a symptom of sloppy programming and a sure indication that there are other errors.

When there are simple syntax errors, some compilers attempt to repair them and go on. Their repairs are just guesses at what you intended and some of the guesses are pretty wild. They always give the programmer a warning if a repair has been attempted. Some errors cannot be repaired and, as a result, no execution takes place. Your output has only the error messages. Very sad! Back to the drawing board. Errors that are detected during compilation are called **compile-time errors**.

If there are no unrepairable syntax errors, execution can take place right after compilation.

If answers are output, they should be checked against hand calculated answers. If they agree, it is possible that your program is correct. If they disagree it is possible that your hand calculations are incorrect or that your program has errors. The errors now are usually of a kind called **semantic errors**. You are asking for a calculation that you did not mean to ask for. It has a different **meaning** from your intentions. These errors which are not detected until the program is executed are also called **run-time errors**.

To find semantic errors you must look at the program again and try to trace what it must be doing rather than what you thought it would do. To help in the tracing it is often good to insert additional **print** instructions between other statements and output the current value of variables that are changing. In this way you can follow the machine's activity. These extra **print** instructions can be removed after the errors have been found.

Sometimes there is no output from the **print** instructions that give the final results. It is important that the data items match the variables in the **read** statements, or answers can be ridiculous. Usually the computer will give you a run-time error message when you enter unacceptable data. Care must be taken about the **integer** and **real** distinction between numbers as the computer converts automatically and will not warn you if things are going wrong.

When you try running a program on a computer, the computer may detect other kinds of errors in your program. As a result, error messages will be output. Since the computer does not understand the purpose of your program, its error messages are limited to describing the specific illegalities which it detects. Unfortunately, the computer's error messages usually do not tell you how to correct your program so that it will solve the problem you have in mind.

In order to help you avoid errors, we list some of the errors which commonly occur in beginners' programs.

Missing commas — Do not forget to put commas after the **read** * and **print** * keywords.

Too many commas — Do not put commas after the keywords **integer** or **real**.

Parentheses — For every left parenthesis in a expression there must be a balancing right parenthesis.

Missing **end** at the end of the program.

Missing quotes, especially the last quote, for example

> **print** *, 'cost of living*

Uninitialized variables — When a variable is declared, a memory location is set aside, but no special value is placed in the location, that is, it has not yet been initialized. A variable must be given a value, via an assignment statement or a **read** statement, before an attempt is made to use the value of the variable in a **print** statement or in an expression.

Mistaking *i* for 1 — The characters *i* and 1 look similar, but are entirely different to the computer.

Mistaking *o* for 0 — The characters *o* (oh) and 0 (zero) look similar, but are entirely different to the computer.

Mistaking 1 (one) for l (the letter "ell").

CHAPTER 4 SUMMARY

This chapter introduced variables, as they are used in programming languages. Essentially, a variable is a memory location which can hold a value. Suppose x is the name of a variable; then x denotes a memory location. If x is a variable having the **integer** type, then the location for x can hold an integer value such as 9, 291, 0, or -11.

The following important terms were discussed .

Identifier — can be used as the name of a variable. An identifier must begin with a letter; this letter can be followed by additional letters or digits. It cannot be longer than six characters. The following are examples of identifiers: *x, i, width, income,* and *a1.*

Type — Each variable has a type; in this chapter we introduced the **integer** and **real** types. The type of a variable is determined by its declaration.

Declaration — establishes variables for use in a program. For example, the declaration

integer *i*

creates a variable called *i* which can be given integer values. Declarations must be at the beginning of a program before any **read, print**, or assignment statements. A declaration can be one of the forms:

integer list of identifiers separated by commas

real list of identifiers separated by commas

Assignment — means a value is assigned to a variable. For example, the following is an assignment statement which gives the value 52 to the variable *i*:

i = *52*

Truncation — throwing away the fractional part of a number. When a real number is assigned to a variable with type **integer**, the variable is given the truncated value.

Number conversion — changing an integer number to a real number or vice versa. Conversion from real to integer causes truncation of the result.

Data (or input data) — values which a program can read.

read statement — this statement is of the form:

read *, list of variable names separated by commas

If a **read** statement contains a list of several variables, reading will automatically proceed to the next data line when the values of one line have all been read. Each new **read** statement will start reading a new line.

Comments — information in a program which is intended to assist a person reading the program. The following is a comment which could appear in a Fortran program:

c *This program outputs gas bills*

The initial *c* of a comment must be in column one. Comments do not affect the execution of a program. A blank line is accepted as a comment resulting in a blank line in the listing of a program.

Documentation — written explanation of a program. Comments are used in a program to document its actions.

Keyword — a word, such as **read** or **stop**, which is an inherent part of the programming language. Keywords should not be used as identifiers.

parameter — the keyword used before an assignment of a value to a constant in the program. The form of the statement is

> **parameter**(name of constant = value)

The name of the constant must appear in a previous type declaration.

Mathematical functions — built into Fortran are a number of mathematical functions. The function *sin(x)* and *cos(x)* give the sine and cosine of an angle in radians. The function *alog(x)* gives the natural logarithm of *x*, exp(x) gives the value of *e* to the power *x*. The function *atan(x)* gives the angle in radians with a tangent *x*. The function *abs(x)* gives the absolute value of *x*. The function *sqrt(x)* gives the square root of *x*. All these functions require *x* to have a real value and produce a real value. The function *mod(a,b)* requires two integer values and produces an integer value, the remainder when *a* is divided by *b*.

Errors — improper parts of, or actions of, a program. For example, the statement

> **print** *, 5 *(2 + 3*

has an error in that a right parenthesis is missing. If the computer detects an error in your program, it will output an error message.

CHAPTER 4 EXERCISES

1. Suppose that *i, j,* and *k* are variables with the integer type and they presently have the values 5, 7, and 10. What will be output as a result of the following statements?

    > **print** *,i,i + 1,i + j,i + j * k*
    > *k = i + j*
    > **print** *,k*
    > *j = j + 1*
    > **print** *,j*
    > *i = 3 * i + j*
    > **print** *,i*

2. The variables *radius, diamtr, circum,* and *area* are **real** variables. A value has been read into *radius* via a **read** statement. Write statements which do each of the following.

(a) Give to *diamtr* the product of 2 and *radius*.

(b) Give to *circum* the product of pi (3.14159) and *diamtr*.

(c) Give to *area* the product of pi and *radius* squared. (*radius* squared can be written as *radius* * *radius* or *radius* ** 2.)

(d) Output the values of *radius, diamtr, circum*, and *area*.

3. Suppose *i*, a variable with the **integer** type, has already been given a value via an assignment statement. Write statements to do the following.

(a) Without changing *i*, output twice the value of *i*.

(b) Increase *i* by 1.

(c) Double the value of *i*.

(d) Decrease *i* by 5.

4. The variables *m, n*, and *p* are of integer type. What will the following statements cause the computer to output?

```
m = 43
n = 211
p = m
m = n
n = p
print *,m,n
```

5. What might be output by the following program?

```
program pairs
integer first, second
print *,'Enter two integers'
read *,first, second
print *,first + second
print *,'Enter two more integers'
read *,first, second
print *,first + second
stop
end
```

The input data are: 6 7 21 12

6. What might be output by the following program?

```
program avrage
c       Calculate term mark
real grade1, grade2
integer mark
print *,'Input two grades'
```

```
read *,grade1, grade2
mark = (grade1 + grade2)/2 + .5
print *,grade1, grade2, mark
stop
end
```

The input data are:

81.7
85.9

7. Trace the execution of the following program. That is, give the values of the variables *size, length, width,* and *about* and give any output after each line of the program.

```
         program area
         real size, length, width
         integer about
c        Read sizes and convert feet to yards
         print *,'Enter width'
         read *,size
         width = size/3.
         print *,'Enter length'
         read *,size
         length = size/3.
         about = width*length + .5
         print *,'length and width are:',length, width
         print *,'area is:',length *width,'this is about:',about,'(square yards)'
         stop
         end
```

The input data are:

9.60
15.9

8. Write a program which reads three values and outputs their average, rounded to the nearest whole number. For example, if 20, 16, and 25 are entered then your program should output 20. Make up your own data for your program. Try using the built-in function *nint.*

9. Write a program which reads a weight given in pounds and then outputs the weight in (1) pounds, (2) ounces, (3) kilograms and (4) grams. Note: 16 ounces equal one pound, 2.2046 pounds equal one kilogram, and 1000 grams equal one kilogram.

10.   Write a program which reads a distance given in miles and outputs the distance in (1) miles, (2) yards, (3) feet, (4) inches, and (5) meters. Note: 1760 yards equal one mile and 1 kilometer equals 0.62137 miles.

11.   Write a program that reads in a temperature in Fahrenheit degrees and converts it to one in degrees Celsius. Remember 32 degrees F corresponds to 0 degrees Celsius and a Fahrenheit degree is (5/9) of a Celsius degree.

12.   Write a program to compute the energy of photons of electromagnetic radiation of a given wavelength that is to be input to the program. The energy in joules of a photon is hf where h is Planck's constant 6.63×10^{-34} joule-sec and f is the frequency in hertz. The wavelength in meters is given by (c/f) where c is the speed of electromagnetic radiation, 3.00×10^8 m/sec. Introduce as many auxiliary variables as are necessary to make your program understandable.

13.   Write a program to compute the mass m of an electron that has been accelerated by a voltage V volts in an electron gun. The formula for m can be obtained from this relation for its kinetic energy

$$Ve = mc^2 - m_0c^2$$

where e is the charge of the electron which is 1.60×10^{-19} coulomb, m_0 is the rest mass of the electron which is 9.11×10^{-31} kg and c is the speed of light which is 3.00×10^8 m/sec.

14.   Write a program to compute the speed of an electron of mass m given the relation $m/m_0 = (1-(v/c)^2)^{-1/2}$.

15.   Put the two programs (of question 13 and 14) together to find the speed of an electron accelerated by a voltage V volts.

Chapter 5

CONTROL STRUCTURE

In all programs we have examined so far the statements were executed in sequence until the **stop** was reached, at which time the program execution was terminated. In this chapter we will learn two ways in which the sequence of statements may be altered. One involves the repetitious use of statements; the other involves a selection between alternate sets of statements. The first is called a **loop** or **repetition**, the second a **selection**. We speak of the **flow of control** since it is the control unit of the computer that determines which statement is to be executed next by the computer.

COUNTED LOOPS

The normal flow of control in a program is in a straight line. We can, however, give a statement that will cause a set of statements to be repeated. In the last chapter, in the example where we were reading information about boxes of soap flakes, we had to write the statements over and over to get repetition. A statement that will produce repetition is the **counted do loop**. For our example we could have written

```
        do label i = 1,3
            read *,cost,weight
            kgcost = cost/(weight*1.)+.5
            print *,'          ',' ','          ',kgcost
label       continue
```

The three statements that we had to repeat three times are prefaced by

```
        do label i = 1,3
```

and followed by **continue**. The word "label" in non-italic letters appears twice; for the moment we will ignore it.

The variable *i* is an index, is usually an integer variable, and counts the number of repetitions. First the index *i* is set to 1, then the three statements are executed. When the **continue** is reached, control is sent back to the **do**. At this time the index *i* is increased by 1, making it 2. A test is made to see if this value of the index is greater than the 3 which appears in the **do** statement. The 3 is called the test value. Since 2 is not greater than 3 we will proceed. The three statements are again executed and, at **continue**, back we go to the **do**. This time *i* becomes 3 which is not greater than the test value and a third execution of the three statements in the **do** loop takes place. When control returns to the **do**, this time *i* would become 4 and this is found to be larger than the 3 which is the upper limit of the count. When this happens, control goes out of the loop to the next statement after the **continue**.

We must now look at the "labels" that we have ignored so far. In order that the computer may perform the looping operation it is necessary in Fortran to tell, at the beginning of the counted **do** loop, where the end of the loop is located in the program. This is done by giving to the **continue** statement, which is the end of the loop, a label. The label of a statement is any integer from 1 to 99999. The label of a statement must be placed in columns 1 to 5 of the input line. We always start the label in column 1. The **continue** statement is the only statement we have looked at so far that needs a label. We can choose any number we like in the allowed range. Of course if there are several **continue** statements in the same program each must have its own individual label.

Suppose we choose (in an arbitrary way) to use 10 for the label, our program would be written as

```
      do 10 i = 1,3
          read *,cost,weight
          kgcost = cost/(weight*1.)+.5
          print *,'          ',          ',kgcost
10        continue
```

A counted or **indexed do** loop is used whenever we know exactly how many repetitions we want to take place. We do not need to count by ones or start the count at 1. We could, have for example,

```
      do label count = 12, 24, 2
```

Here we have called the index *count* and are starting at 12 and going by 2s up to, and to include, 24. If the increment by which you are counting is not 1 it is included in the **do** following the test value. So far each of the initial value, the test value, and the increment have been positive integers or variables which have positive integer values. We can also count backwards by using a negative increment or have expressions having integer values for any of the initial, test, or increment. As well it is possible, though not advisable, to use real expressions. When a **do** loop is first entered, the expressions for the initial, test, and increment are evaluated and the number of iterations of the loop is determined. For a positive increment the number of iterations is zero if the test is less than the initial value. Sometimes the initial, test, and increment will be referred to as start, limit, and step respectively.

The other kind of loop statement is the conditional loop statement but we cannot introduce it until we look at **conditions**.

CONDITIONS

There are expressions in Fortran that are called conditions or **logical expressions** and these have values that are either **true** or **false**. The following is a list of logical expressions with their value written on the same line. The symbol **.gt.** means greater than, **.le.** means less than or equal to, **.ge.** means greater than or equal to, and **.ne.** means not equal to.

logical expression	value
5.eq. 2 + 3	*true*
7.gt. 5	*true*
2.lt. 6	*true*
5 + 3.lt. 2 + 1	*false*
6.ne. 10	*true*
5.gt. 5	*false*
5.ge. 5	*true*

You can see how these work.

There are compound conditions formed by taking two single conditions and putting either the **logical operator .and.** or the logical operator **.or.** between them. With **.and.** both conditions must be true or else the compound condition is false. For example, *(8.gt. 7.and. 6.lt. 3)* is false since *(6.lt. 3)* is false. With **.or.**, if either or both of the single conditions is true, the compound condition is true. For example, *(8.gt. 7.or. 6.lt. 3)* is true since *(8.gt. 7)* is true. It is possible to have multiple compoundings. For example,

$$(8.gt.\ 7.and.\ 2.eq.\ 1+1).and.\ (6.gt.\ 7.or.\ 5.gt.\ 1)$$

is true. The parentheses here show the sequence of the operations. There is a rule of precedence if there are no parentheses, namely, the **.and.** operator has higher precedence than the **.or.** operator. This means that **.and.** operations are done before **.or.** operations. The operator **.not.** placed in front of a condition reverses it; it changes false to true and true to false.

CONDITIONAL LOOPS

We have introduced the notion of a condition; now we will actually use it. One of the major uses of conditions is in the conditional loop. There is no construct in Fortran 77 for the conditional loop so that we must create one using the **if** statement. The form we will use in this book is

label1	**if**(condition) **goto** label2
	statements
	go to label1
label2	**continue**

The repetition of the statements in the body of the loop is to take place as long as the condition stated in parentheses after the keyword **if** is false. Once it is true, the control goes to the **continue** that terminates the loop and from there to the statements that follow the **continue**. The counted **do** loop was also terminated by a **continue** but in that case the control was set back to the beginning of the loop at the **continue**.

So far we have discussed only conditions involving integer constants. These we labelled as true or false. The condition in the **if**(condition)**go to** loop cannot be like this, because if it is always false we would loop forever and if always true we would not loop at all. The condition must involve a variable whose value changes during the looping.

In the following program segment the **if**(condition)**go to** is used to accomplish exactly what the counted **do** loop did for the soap flakes boxes.

```
1              i = 1
2     5        if (i.gt. 3)go to 10
3                  read *,cost,weight
4                  kgcost = cost/(weight*1.) +.5
5                  print *,'         ','          ',kgcost
6                  i = i + 1
7                  go to 5
8     10       continue
9              print *,i
```

In statement 1 the value of the variable i appearing in the condition is set initially to 1. This stage is called **initialization** and is always necessary in conditional loops. In line 2 we begin the loop. If the condition following the **if** were true, control would **go to** the **continue** which terminates the loop. This is because the label of the **continue** namely 10, is given as the location to **go to**. Control would then pass immediately to the **print** statement in line 9 as the **continue** itself produces no effect unless it is in a **do** loop. But the fact is that the condition in parentheses is false since i is 1, which is less than 3. Thus the next four statements are executed. These constitute the **body** of the loop. In the body, statement 6 **alters** the value of the variable appearing in the condition. This means that it is changing each time around the loop. At the end of the first loop it becomes $1 + 1 = 2$. The **go to** 5 causes control to return to the start of the loop because the **if** has a label 5. The condition is then examined and since it is false, (2.**gt**.3) is false, the body is executed a second time. It will be false also on the third time but on the fourth round, *i* will be 4 and (4.**gt**.3) is true. When *i* is output by statement 9 it is 4. This output is not part of the original example, but was included here to show you what happens to the index *i*. It is best not to concern yourself with the value of a counting variable outside the loop since for a counted **do** the value of the index is undefined outside the loop.

The various phases of an **if**(condition)**go to...continue** loop are:

    Phase 1. Initialization, especially of the variable in the condition.

    Phase 2. Testing of condition and if false then going to the next line, if true going to the **continue**.

    Phase 3. Execution of the body of loop which includes altering the variable in the condition.

    Phase 4. At the **go to** preceding the **continue** returning to phase 2.

In the presentation of Fortran 77 in this book the **go to** will only be used as it is in the **if...go to...continue** statement, an example of which has been shown here. It will **never** be used outside of this context. Sometimes it has been said that structured programming is **go to**less programming. Certainly the use of a **go to** must be strictly controlled.

READING LINES OF DATA

As an example of the two types of loops we will look at a very simple example of reading data for student marks and computing an average for the class. The number of students in the class is not known at the time the program is prepared. The only real problem will be to stop when we reach the last student and compute the average. There are two distinct ways of doing this. One is to count the lines of data and enter this count before the data lines. Then we use a counted **do** loop to read them. The other method is to place an entry at the end of the data lines with a piece of data that is impossible as an actual entry. We call it a **dummy entry**. Sometimes it is called an **end-of-file marker**. Suppose, to talk specifically, that each data line has on it a student number and a grade received in an examination. To illustrate we will have only three data lines.

Method 1. Counting lines

```
        program marks1
        integer ident,mark,count, sum,i
        print *,'Enter number of students'
        read *,count
        print *,'Give',count,'student numbers with mark'
        sum = 0
c       Print headings for data entries
        print *,'student no. ','      ','mark in exam'
        do 25 i = 1,count
            read *,ident,mark
            sum = sum + mark
25          continue
        print *,'average = ',nint(sum/(count * 1.))
        print *,'count = ',count
        stop
        end
```

Here is a sample display:

```
Enter number of students
3
Give 3 student numbers with marks
student no.        mark in exam
1026               86
2051               90
3163               71
average = 82
count = 3
```

Notice that we took the trouble to label the output. In the second method we will place a dummy data entry with two zeros on it after the last valid line of data.

Method 2. Testing for the dummy entry

```
        program marks2
        integer ident,mark,sum,count
        print *,'Give student numbers and marks, end with 0'
c       Print headings for data entries
        print *,'student no. ','      ','mark in exam'
        sum = 0
        count = 0
        read *,ident,mark
5       if (ident.eq. 0)go to 10
```

```
                count  =  count + 1
                sum  =  sum + mark
                read *,ident,mark
                go to 5
        10      continue
             print *,'average=',nint(sum/(count * 1.))
             print *,'count=',count
             stop
             end
```

The display is very much like the one for the first method. Here it is:

Give student numbers and marks, end with 0

student no.	mark in exam
1026	*86*
2051	*90*
3163	*71*
0	*0*

average= 82

count= 3

In this example you will notice that the initialization involves reading the first data line outside the loop, in order to get a value for the variable *ident* appearing in the condition of the **if...go to**. Since the first mark has already been read, it must be added to the sum before a new line is read. This means that the sequence is add to *sum* then **read**, rather than the way it is in the first method. As soon as the new line has been read, we return to the **if...go to** where the condition is tested. These two techniques for dealing with a variable number of items, like data entries, are used again and again in programming. The **if...go to** is more difficult to program but probably more useful, since if there are many data entries, it is easier for the user to stick in an end-of-file entry than to count entries. Notice that both the **continue** of the counted **do** and the **continue** of the **if...go to** both need labels. At the **continue** of a counted **do**, control is automatically returned to the **do** where in the **if...go to**, a specific **go to** must be placed before the **continue** to return control to the start of the loop.

SELECTION

We have learned how to change from a flow of control in a straight line, or **sequential** control, to flow in a loop, either counted or conditional. Now we must look at a different kind of structure of control called **selection**. The basic form of the selection statement is

```
if (condition) then
        statements
    else
        statements
    end if
```

When the condition following the keyword **if** is true the statements following the keyword **then** (call the **then** clause) are executed and if the condition is false the statements following the keyword **else** (called the **else** clause) are executed. Only one of the two sets of statements is executed; we select one or the other. If no statements are to be executed after the **else** then the keyword **else** is also omitted.

After one or other of the two sets of statements has been executed, control goes to the statement after the keywords **end if**. Suppose that there is a variable called *classa* which contains the number of students in a class called *a*. Students are to be assigned to Class *a* if their mark in computer science *(csmark)* is over 80; otherwise they are to be assigned to Class *b* *(classb)*. The statement that decides which class to place the student in, and counts the number going into each class, is

```
if (csmark.gt. 80) then
    classa = classa + 1
else
    classb = classb + 1
end if
```

Notice that the **if...then...else** has after it **end if**. This terminates the statement just as **continue** terminates the counted **do**. In Fortran 77 the **if...then...else** is sometimes referred to as the block **if** to distinguish it from the **if** that we used for the conditional loop.

Notice that in the **if...then...else** there are parentheses around the condition just as there are in the **if...go to** we used for the conditional loop.

You must always have at least one statement after the **then**. As we said, if there is nothing that you want to do in the **else** clause you must leave out the **else** entirely. For instance, you may have the statement which would eliminate the balance in a bank account if it were less than or equal to 10 cents.

```
if (balnce.le. 10)then
    balnce = 0
end if
```

Here there is no **else** clause, but this just means that if the balance is larger than 10 cents we do **not** make it zero.

THREE-WAY SELECTION

We have presented a statement which selects between two alternatives. We will now show how you can select among three alternatives.

As an example, we will write a program that counts votes in an election. Suppose that there are three political parties called Right, Left, and Middle, and that to vote for one of these parties you enter a 1, or a 2, or a 3 respectively on a data line. Here is the program that reads the vote entries and counts each party and the total. The last entry is the dummy entry −1.

```
        program voting
c       This program counts votes
        integer vote,right,left,middle,count
        right = 0
        left = 0
        middle = 0
        print *,'Enter votes one to a line, finish with − 1'
        read *,vote
25      if (vote.eq. − 1) go to 40
            if (vote.eq. 1) then
                right = right + 1
            else
                if (vote.eq. 2) then
                    left = left + 1
                else
                    if (vote.eq. 3) then
                        middle = middle + 1
                    end if
                end if
            end if
            read *,vote
            go to 25
40      continue
        count = right + left + middle
        print *,'right =',right,'left =',left,'middle =',middle,'total =',count
        stop
        end
```

In this program we have two different things happening. One is a three-way selection, which is accomplished by a series of three **if...then** statements, one for each value of *vote*. It may startle you to see the three **end ifs** one after the other. Each **if...then** requires its own **end if**. You will notice that an invalid vote does not get counted anywhere. If we wanted notification that there was an invalid vote we could have inserted the following in the program right after *middle = middle + 1*

>**else**
>>**print** *, 'invalid vote ', vote*

This then makes it a four-way selection.

In Fortran 77 there is an **else if** structure that gets around the sequence of **end if**s. The program *voting* could be written this way, replacing the conditional loop by:

```
25      if (vote.eq. − 1) go to 40
            if (vote.eq. 1) then
                right = right + 1
            else if (vote.eq. 2) then
                left = left + 1
            else if (vote.eq. 3) then
                middle = middle + 1
            else
                print *, 'invalid vote', vote
            end if
            read *, vote
            go to 25
40          continue
```

The **if** in the *voting* program with the **go to** which has the label 25 does not have an **end if** because it is not a block **if**. It is used to begin a conditional loop whose body is terminated by the **continue** labelled 40. Whenever you see an **if** with a **go to** rather than a **then** after the condition you know it is a loop rather than a selection construct.

EXAMPLE if...then...else STATEMENTS

We will now give a series of examples of **if...then...else** statements which might be used in a government program for handling income tax. Let us suppose that the program is to write notices to people telling them whether they owe tax or they are to receive a tax refund. The amount of tax is calculated and then the following is executed.

```
if (tax.gt. 0) then
    print *, tax due is', tax, 'dollars'
else
    print *, 'refund is', − tax, 'dollars'
end if
```

Notice that it was necessary to change the sign of *tax* when outputting the refund.

Unfortunately, our program, like too many programs, is not quite right. If the calculated tax is exactly zero, then the program will output *refund is 0 dollars.* We could fix this problem by the following.

```
if (tax.gt. 0)then
      print *,'tax due is',tax,'dollars'
else if (tax.eq. 0)then
      print *,'you owe nothing'
else
      print *,'refund is',— tax,'dollars'
end if
```

We have used an **else if** to solve the problem.

Now suppose that when tax is due we wish to tell the taxpayer where to send his check. We can expand the program as follows:

```
if (tax.gt. 0)then
      print *,'tax due is',tax,'dollars'
      print *,'Send check to district office'
else if (tax.eq. 0)then
      print *,'you owe nothing'
else
      print *,'refund is',— tax,'dollars'
end if
```

PARAGRAPHING THE PROGRAM

In order to follow the **structure** of **if...then...else** statements we have indented the program so that the **if, else if, else,** and **end if** that belong to each other are lined up vertically. The statements in the **then** and the **else** clauses are indented. This is called **paragraphing** the program, and is analogous to the way we indent paragraphs of prose to indicate groupings of thoughts. Paragraphing makes a valuable contribution to understandability and is a **must** in structured programming.

Also, if you examine the programs with loops you will see that the loop has been indented starting right after the beginning **do** or **if...go to** and going down to the **continue** that belongs with it.

In the next chapter we will be examining the situation where loops are nested and then we will use two levels of indentation.

There are no set rules about how much indentation you should use or exactly how, for instance, an **if...then...else** statement should be indented; but it is clear that being systematic is an enormous help. When you are writing programs, decide how many blanks you will use for each level of indentation and stick to this. We use three blanks for indentation.

LOGICAL VARIABLES

Conditions are either true or false. It is possible in Fortran to have variables which have these two values. They are called **logical variables**. Logical variables can then be used in place of conditions in conditional loops or **if...then...else** constructs. To declare a variable as being a logical variable we use a declaration of the form:

logical name of variable

A value can be assigned to the variable by an assignment statement or an input statement. The constant value true is written as *.true.*; the value false is written as *.false.* in assignment statements.

On output, the value of a logical variable is displayed as *t* for true or *f* for false. On input, the value true is written as any word beginning with *t*, false as any word beginning with *f*.

Here is an example program using a logical variable.

```
       program movie
c      Computes admission price to a restricted movie
       logical adult, senior
       print *, 'I am over 18 years old (t or f)'
       read *,adult
       print *, 'I am over 65 years old (t or f)'
       read *,senior
       if (adult .and. (.not. senior)) then
           print *,'Please pay $5.00'
       else if (senior) then
           print *,'Please pay $2.50'
       else
           print *,'Sorry you cannot see this movie'
       end if
       stop
       end
```

AN ALTERNATIVE CONDITIONAL LOOP

There are two types of non-linear control structures: repetition and selection. Conditional repetition is not part of Fortran 77. We have tried to implement conditional repetition by a construct that did not look like a selection construct. Many Fortran programmers prefer to use a different form. The form we have used is

```
label1      if(condition)go to label2
                statements
                go to label1
label2      continue
```

An alternative form is this:

```
label1      if(condition)then
                statements
                go to label1
            end if
```

It has the advantage that there is only one labelled instruction and one **go to** but it has the disadvantage that because of the **end if** it looks more like a selection **if...then...else** construct.

Obviously it is a matter of taste; we have chosen to stick by the first method. One thing that you must observe is that the conditions after the **if** in the two versions are not the same. The condition we use in method 1 is the **termination condition**. If it is true you exit the loop. The condition in method 2 is the **continuation condition**; if it is true you continue to execute the body of the loop. The second condition is the negative of the first; when the second is true the first is false and vice versa.

CHAPTER 5 SUMMARY

In this chapter we introduced statements which allow for (a) repetition of statements and (b) selection between different possibilities. We introduced conditions which are used to terminate the repetition of statements and to choose between different possibilities. Comparisons and logical operators are used in specifying conditions. The following important terms were discussed in this chapter.

Loop — a programming language construct which causes repeated execution of statements. The loops we showed are either counted **do** loops or **if...go to** conditional loops.

Counted **do** loop — has the following form:

> **do** label index variable $=$initial,test [,increment]
>   statements
> label   **continue**

The index variable, or counting variable, usually has the **integer** type. The square brackets shown around increment indicate that it can be omitted. If it is omitted, an increment of 1 is assumed. Sometimes we refer to start, limit, and step instead of initial, test, and increment. These are usually integer expressions and their value is calculated as the loop begins. If the initial value is larger than the test value when the increment is positive the loop will be executed zero times.

if...go to conditional loop — has the following form:

> label1   **if**(condition)**go to** label 2
>   statements
>   **go to** label1
> label2   **continue**

The condition is tested at the beginning of each pass through the loop. If it is found to be false, the statements inside the loop are executed; the **go to** label1 sends control back to the beginning of the loop and then the condition is again tested. When the condition finally is found to be true, control is passed to the **continue** and thus to the statement which follows the **continue** since the **continue** here itself produces no result. Any variables which appear in the condition must be given values before the loop begins. Notice that the condition is in parentheses.

Loop body — the statements that appear inside a loop.

Comparisons — used in conditions. For example, comparisons can be used in a condition to determine whether or not to execute a loop body. The following are used to specify comparisons.

> **.lt.**   less than
> **.gt.**   greater than
> **.le.**   less than or equal
> **.ge.**   greater than or equal
> **.eq.**   equal
> **.ne.**   not equal

Conditions — are either true or false. Conditions can be made up of comparisons and the following three logical operators.

> **.and.**
> **.or.**

.not.

End-of-file (or end-of-data) detection — When a loop is reading a series of data items, it must determine when the last data item has been read. This can be accomplished by first reading in the number of items to be read and then counting the items in the series as they are read. It can also be accomplished by following the last data item by a special dummy entry which contains special, or dummy data. The program knows to stop when it reads the dummy data.

if...then...else statement — has the following form:

> **if**(condition)**then**
>   statements
> {**else if**(condition)**then**
>   statements}
> [**else**
>   statements]
> **end if**

The curly brackets around the **else if** clause indicate that there may be any number of such clauses, or none at all. The square brackets are shown around the **else** clause to show that it can be omitted. If the condition is true, the statement or statements after the **then** are executed. If the condition is false, the condition after the first **else if**, if present, is tested. If the condition is true the statements of that **else if** clause are executed. If false the next **else if** is executed, and so on to the **else**. If all conditions have been false the statement or statements after the **else**, if present, are executed. In any case, if the statements of any clause are executed control then goes to the next statement after the **end if**.

Paragraphing — indenting a program so that its structure is easily seen by people. The statements inside loops and inside **if...then...else** statements are indented to make the overall program organization obvious. The computer ignores paragraphing when translating and executing programs.

Logical variables — variables whose only values are true and false. A variable is declared as being of logical type by a declaration of the form

> **logical** variable identifier

CHAPTER 5 EXERCISES

1. Suppose *i* and *j* are variables with values 6 and 12. Which of the following conditions are true?

   (a)   *2*i.le.j*
   (b)   *2*i— 1.lt.j*
   (c)   *i.le. 6.and.j.le. 6*
   (d)   *i.le. 6.or.j.le. 6*
   (e)   *i.gt. 0.and.i.le. 10*
   (f)   *i.le. 12.or.j.le. 12*
   (g)   *i.gt. 25.or. (i.lt. 50.and.j.lt. 50)*
   (h)   *i.ne. 4.and.i.ne. 5*
   (i)   *i.lt. 4.or.i.gt. 5*
   (j)   *.not. (i.gt. 6)*

2. The following program predicts the population of a family of wallalumps over a 2-year period, based on the assumption of an initial population of 2 and a doubling of population each 2 months. What does the program output?

   ```
         program births
   c      Shows population explosion
         integer month,number
         number = 2
         print *,'month','population'
         do 12 month = 2,24,2
             print *,month,'      ',number
             number = 2*number
   12       continue
         stop
         end
   ```

3. Suppose you have hidden away 50 dollars to be used for some future emergency. Assuming an inflation rate of 6 per cent per year, write a program to compute how much money, to the nearest dollar, you would need at the end of each of the next 15 years to be equivalent to the buying power of 50 dollars at the time you hid it.

4. Trace the following program. That is, give the values of the variables together with any output after the execution of each statement.

   ```
         program class
   c      Handles examination marks
         integer number,grade,sum
         sum = 0
         print *,'Enter grades, one to a line, — 1 at end'
   ```

```
          read *,grade
          sum = 0
          number = 0
20        if (grade.eq. − 1)go to 30
              if (grade.ge. 0.and. grade.le. 100)then
                  sum = sum + grade
                  number = number + 1
              else
                  print *,'**error: grade = ',grade
              end if
              read *,grade
              go to 20
30            continue
          print *,'average is', 1. *sum/number
          stop
          end
```

The input data is:

```
86
120
71
−1
```

5. Write a program that reads the following data and calculates the average of (a) each of the two columns of data, and (b) each row of the data. You should either precede the data with a number giving the count of the following lines of data or add a dummy entry following these data lines.

92	88
75	62
81	75
80	80
55	60
64	60
81	80

6. Write a program which reads in a sequence of grades (0 to 100) and outputs the average grade (rounded to the nearest whole number), the number of grades and the number of failing grades (failing is less than 50). Assume that a dummy grade of 999 will follow the last grade. See that your output is clearly labelled.

Test your program using the following data:

85 74 44 62 93 41 69 73 999

7.   Write a program which determines the unit price (cents per ounce) of different boxes of laundry soap. Round the unit price to the nearest penny. Each box will be described by a line of data of the form:

pounds	ounces	price in cents
5	0	125

This box of soap has a rounded unit price of 2 cents per ounce. Make up about 10 data lines describing soap boxes; if you like, use real examples from a supermarket. You are to precede these entries a single integer giving the number of soap box entries. Do not use a dummy entry to mark the end of the data. Output a nicely labelled table giving weights, prices in cents, and unit costs.

8.   Write a program that tabulates y for values of $x = .1, .2, ... 1.0$ given that y is the sum of terms for $n = 1, 2, ... 10$ where the term for $n = 3$ is x/3!. The 3! is factorial 3, namely 3*2*1. Remember that 0! has a value 1.

9.   A mortgage is taken out for a house at a rate of interest of 10%. The mortgage is for $100,000. Write a program to read in various annual payments and calculate how long it would take to pay off the mortgage. Change the program so that it reads in the face value of the mortgage and the interest rate as well as the annual payment. Have it output a table year by year of the amount paid as interest and the amount paid on the principal for the life of the mortgage. Note: the annual payment must exceed $10,000 for the mortgage we described.

10.   Write a program to find and output the integers from 1 to 100 that are perfect squares.

11.   Write a program that will read real values for the lengths of the three sides of a triangle, calling them A, B and C, and determine which of the following is true:

(a) no triangle is possible,
(b) triangle is isosceles,
(c) triangle is equilateral,
(d) triangle is right-angled,
(e) triangle is neither isosceles, nor equilateral, nor right-angled.

12. The Fibonacci series of integers can be generated by the relationship that the next member of the series is the sum of the two previous members and that the first two members are 1 and 1. Write a program to generate the first 25 members of the Fibonacci series.

13. Write a program that will read in any amount (under $20), given in dollars and cents, and determine the way that this can be made up of bills ($10, $5, $1) and coins (25, 10, 5, 1 cents). This is an automatic changemaker and should give the minimum number of bills and coins possible.

14. Write a program that will count the number of digits in a positive integer that is input.

15. Write a program that will tell whether an integer is a palindrome, that is, has the same value with the digits reversed. Examples of integer palindromes are 11, 323, and 7667.

16. Convert a series of angles in degrees that are read in to radians and output the results properly labelled along with the values of their sines, cosines, and tangents.

17. Compound logical conditions are made by combining simple conditions with the **and** and **or** operators. If *A* and *B* are logical conditions a pair of relationships holds which are called de Morgan's laws. These are:

$$(not\ A)\ and\ (not\ B)\ =\ not\ (A\ or\ B)$$
$$(not\ A)\ or\ (not\ B)\ =\ not\ (A\ and\ B)$$

Write a program that will test de Morgan's laws for combinations of conditions *A* and *B* that are both true, one false and one true, and both false.

Chapter 6

COMPLEX CONTROL STRUCTURES

In the last chapter we introduced the two kinds of statements that cause an alteration from the linear flow of control in a program. One type caused looping, the counted loop or the conditional loop; the other caused selective execution, the **if...then...else**. Learning to handle these two kinds of instructions is absolutely essential to programming. And learning to handle them in a systematic way is essential to structured programming.

BASIC STRUCTURE OF LOOPS

It is hard to appreciate, when you first learn a concept like loops, that all loops are basically the same. They consist of a sequence of statements in the program that:

1. initialize the values of certain variables that are to be used in the loop. These consist of assigning values to:

    (a) variables that appear in the condition of an **if** (condition) **go to**

    (b) variables that appear in the body of the loop on the right-hand side of assignment statements.

2. indicate that a loop is to commence and give the information that is to control the number of repetitions. Both types of loops contain a control phrase. The control phrase may be of two types:

    (a) for the counted **do**, it is, for example

    $i = 1, 20, 1$

    (b) for the conditional loop, it is, for example

    if $(i.\text{gt}. 20)$

The condition should contain at least one variable.

3. give the list of statements, called the body of the loop, that are to be executed each time the loop is repeated. If the loop is controlled by an **if** (condition), then within the body of the loop there must be some statements that assign new values to the variables appearing in the condition. Usually there is only one variable and its value may be changed by either

    (a)   an assignment or

    (b)   a **read** statement.

4. indicate the end of the loop. This is the **continue** for a counted **do** or the **go to** preceding the **continue** for a conditional loop. At this point control is returned to the beginning of the loop with its control phrase.

5. give the next statement to be executed once the looping has been carried out the required numbers of times. Control goes from the beginning of the loop to this statement when

    (a)   the condition of the **if** (condition) **go to** is found to be true or

    (b)   the value of the index controlling the counted **do** plus the increment is beyond the test value indicated after the first comma in the **do**.

It is to be noted very carefully that there is no **exit** from either kind of loop, except from the beginning of the loop itself, and this exit goes to the statement immediately after the **continue**. In this way we keep track of control flow and never have the possibility of getting confused about its path. The complete Fortran 77 language offers unrestricted use of the **go to** statement for altering the path of control. It permits you to send control anywhere in your program. Since computer scientists came to recognize the importance of proper structuring in a program, the freedom offered by the unrestricted use of the **go to** statement has been recognized as not in keeping with the idea of structures in control flow. For this reason we will **never** use it that way.

Many good programmers also use the **go to** to leave the body of a counted **do** loop somewhere in the middle, exiting to the statement following the end of the loop. An exit inside the body is usually related to a second condition. This second condition can be incorporated in the condition of an **if**(condition) **go to** loop by having a compound condition. We will look at examples of this later in the chapter.

FLOW CHARTS

A flow chart is a diagram made up of boxes of various shapes: rectangular, circular, diamond, and so on, connected by lines with directional arrows on the lines. The boxes contain a description of the statements of a program and the directed lines indicate the flow of control among the statements. The main purpose of drawing a flow chart is to exhibit the flow of control clearly, so that it is evident both to the programmer and to a reader who might want to alter the program.

A method of programming that preceded the present method of structured programming found that drawing a flow chart helped in the programming process. It was suggested that a first step in writing any program was to draw a flow chart. It was a way of controlling complexity.

When we limit ourselves to the two standard forms of altering control flow, the loop and the **if...then...else**, there is little need to draw these flow charts. In a sense, especially if it is properly paragraphed, the program is its own flow chart; it is built of completely standard building blocks.

Perhaps it would be helpful to show what the flow charts of our two basic building blocks would be like in case you wanted to draw a flow chart for your whole program.

The flow chart for an **if...then...else** statement is shown.

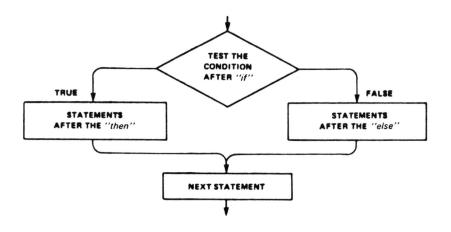

FLOW CHART FOR **if...then...else**

For the **if** (condition) **go to** loop that we described, the flow chart would be as shown. The various phases are numbered.

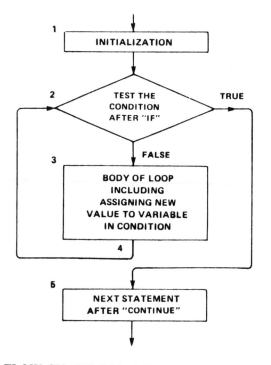

FLOW CHART FOR CONDITIONAL LOOP

The flow chart for the counted **do** would be similar except that box 2 would initialize the index to its first value, then on successive repetitions increment it by the required amount and test to see if it has gone beyond the test value.

With these basic diagrams and the ordinary straight line sequence, flow charts for all Fortran programs that we will show can be built. In a way, because they are so obviously related to the program, they do not really need to be drawn. Any one of the rectangular boxes in these diagrams may be replaced by a sequence of rectangular boxes, or either one of the two basic diagrams themselves.

An important thing to notice is that into each of these elementary blocks there is a single entrance and, from each, a single exit. This is critical to maintaining good structure. A fact worth noticing is that if you drew the flow chart for a properly structured program no two lines of flow need cross over each other.

PROBLEMS WITH LOOPS

Certain errors are very common with loops. With counted loops the likelihood of errors is much smaller, since the initialization and alteration of the index are done by the **do** itself. You can, however, forget to initialize a variable that is used in the body of the loop. Another problem comes if by chance the index that is used to count the loop is altered in the loop body. This is strictly illegal in Fortran. The letters i, j, and k are often used as indexes, and you might forget to declare them or accidentally use them again. This can happen when one **do** loop is nested inside another and the index i is used by mistake for both loops. You might on the other hand write

do label $i = 1 , n$

and forget to initialize n. You should trace the execution of all loops by hand to see if the first iteration is working alright. Then you should also check the last one.

We mentioned that you might forget to declare the index variable. In Fortran if a variable is not declared, its type is taken implicitly from the first letter of its identifier. If that letter is i, j, k, l, m, or n an undeclared variable is typed as an integer variable. If the identifier begins with another letter and is undeclared, it is typed as a real variable. We have made a practice of declaring all variables.

NESTED LOOPS

We will now look at more complicated loops. In the following example, the program sums the marks of students in 4 subjects and outputs these with the average, to the nearest mark. The marks of the 4 subjects are entered on separate lines and these are preceded by the student's identification. A line with the total number of students precedes all the other lines. Since we were not certain that our program was correct we tested it first on a sample containing only three students.

```
         program class
c        Computes the overall average for each student
         integer number,i,sum,avrage,mark,j,ident
         print *,'Enter number of students'
         read *,number
         print *,'Enter',number,'sets of student number and 4 marks, one to a line'
         do 50 i = 1, number
              sum = 0
              read *,ident
              do 40 j = 1,4
                   read *,mark
                   sum = sum + mark
40                 continue
              avrage = sum/ 4. +.5
              print *,'average = ',avrage
50            continue
         stop
         end
```

Here is the display:

Enter number of students
3
Enter 3 sets of student number and 4 marks, one to a line
205	*55*	*60*	*65*	*70* (one to a line)
average＝63
| *208* | *83* | *81* | *96* | *90* (one to a line) |

average＝88
| *209* | *72* | *68* | *78* | *81* (one to a line) |

average＝75

You will notice that when we have one **do** loop nested inside another we use two levels of indentation to indicate the control structure. Since the average cannot be computed until all four marks have been entered the average must appear on the next line of the display. It would be a good thing if we could have entered the student number and marks on a single line, but in that case in Fortran they would have had to be read by a single **read** statement rather than by four **read** statements as they are in this program. Each **read** starts a new data line.

LOOPS WITH COMPOUND CONDITIONS

Sometimes we must terminate a loop if something happens that is unusual. One of the conditions controlling the loop is the standard one; the other is the unusual one. All loops with double-headed conditions must be **if** (condition) **go to** loops, since the counted loop does not allow for the possibility of a second condition. We have seen that compound conditions can be formed from two or more simple conditions using the **.and.** and **.or.** operators.

As an example, we will write a program to look for a certain number in a list of numbers. If you find it in the list, output the position it occupies in the list; if it is not in the list, output *not in list*. The list will be positive integers terminated by an end-of-file marker -1.

```
        program hunt
c       Looks for a certain number in a list
        integer number,listno,i
        print *,'Enter number you are looking for'
        read *,number
        print *,'Start typing in list, one number to a line; finish with − 1'
        read *,listno
        i = 1
50      if (listno.eq.number.or.listno.eq. − 1)go to 60
            read *,listno
            i = i + 1
            go to 50
60          continue
        if (listno.eq.number)then
            print *,'position = ',i
        else
            print *,'not in list'
        end if
        stop
        end
```

Here is a sample display:

```
Enter number you are looking for
35
Start typing in list, one number to a line; finish with −1
12
16
25
35
position = 4
```

Notice that in the body of the loop the variable *listno* in the condition can be changed by the **read** statement; it is initialized outside the loop. Since an index *i* is required to give the position of the number in the list, it must be incremented in the statement $i = i + 1$ and initialized to *1* outside the loop.

if...then...else STATEMENTS WITH COMPOUND CONDITIONS

Just as **if...go to** statements can have multiple conditions for looping, so also can **if...then...else** statements. These can be used very effectively to avoid nesting of **if...then...else** statements. Suppose you want to count people in a list who fall into a particular age group, say 18−65, as adults. The following program will count the number in the category *adult* in the list. The list of ages is terminated by a − *1*.

```
        program worker
c       Counts the number of adults in a list
        integer adult,age
        print *,'Start typing list of ages, one to a line; finish with − 1'
        read *,age
        adult = 0
20      if (age.eq. − 1)go to 30
            if (age.ge. 18.and.age.le. 65)then
                adult = adult + 1
            end if
            read *,age
            go to 20
30      continue
        print *,'number of adults =',adult
        stop
        end
```

The **if** with the compound condition could have been replaced by the more awkward construction with a nested **if** statement:

```
        if (age.ge. 18)then
            if (age.le. 65)then
                adult = adult + 1
            end if
        end if
```

but this is not nearly as understandable.

CHAPTER 6 SUMMARY

In this chapter we have taken a closer look at loops and **if...then...else** constructs. We discussed flow charts and the **go to** as they relate to our use of Fortran 77. We presented more complex examples of loops and conditions. The following important terms were discussed.

Flow chart — a graphic representation of a program. A flow chart consists of boxes of various shapes interconnected by arrows indicating flow of control. Fortran programs can be represented by flow charts.

Exit from a loop — means stopping the execution of a loop. Exit from an **if...go to** loop occurs when the loop's condition is found to be true.

go to — transfers control to another part of a program. The **go to** is an integral part of the **if...go to...continue** statement used for conditional loops. It is not a statement in its own right in the Fortran 77 we present in this book. In the full Fortran 77 language **go to** is a statement. Careless use of **go to** statements leads to complex program structures which are difficult to understand and to make correct. That is why we do not use it except in conditional loops.

Nested statements — means statements inside statements. For example, **do** loops can be nested inside **do** loops.

Compound conditions — conditions which use the **.and.** or **.or.** logical operators. Both **if...go to** loops and **if...then...else** statements can have compound conditions; counted **do** loops may not.

CHAPTER 6 EXERCISES

We will base all the exercises for this chapter on the same problem, which we now describe. A meteorologist keeps records of the weather for each month. The first line of the data gives the number of days of the month, its length. The following line give the rainfall, low temperature, high temperature, and pollution count for each day of the month. For example, the data for a month could be as follows:

```
31
0    33   37   3
1.2  34   39   3
0    35   40   .5
0    34   38   2
etc.
```

Each of the following exercises requires writing a program which reads one month's weather and answers some questions about the month's weather. To make things easier for you, answers for the first two exercises are given. You may want to prepare the data as a file using the editor of the operating system and redirect the normal keyboard input to be taken from that file.

1. Find the first rainy day of the month. (The following program finds the required day.)

```
        program wetday
c       Finds the first wet day of the month
        real rain,low,high,pollut
        integer day,length
        print *,'Enter length of month'
        read *,length
        day = 0
        rain = 0
        print *,'rain  low  high  pollution'
10      if (rain.ne.0.or.day.ge.length)go to 20
            read *,rain,low,high,pollut
            day = day + 1
            go to 10
20          continue
        if (rain.gt.0)then
            print *,'day',day,'was rainy'
        else
            print *,'no rainy days'
        end if
        stop
        end
```

2. See if the data for the days of the month are reasonable. Verify that the rainfall does not exceed 100 and is not negative. Verify that the temperature lies between -100 and 200 and that the high is at least as large as the low. Verify that the pollution count is neither above 25 nor below zero. (The following program validates the month's data and is a solution for this exercise.)

```
        program verify
c       Validates the weather data
        real rain,low,high,pollut
        integer day,length
        print *,'Enter length of month'
        read *,length
        print *,'rain  low  high  pollution'
        do 10 day = 1, length
```

```
          read *,rain,low,high,pollut
          if (rain.lt. 0.or.rain.gt. 100) then
              print *,'day',day,'has wrong rain:',rain
          end if
          if (low.lt. − 100.or.low.gt.high.or.high.gt. 200) then
              print *,'day',day,'has wrong temperatures:',low,high
          end if
          if (pollut.lt. 0.or.pollut.gt. 25) then
              print *,'day',day,'has wrong pollution:',pollut
          end if
10        continue
      stop
      end
```

3. What was the warmest day of the month, based on the high?

4. What was the first rainy day having a high temperature above 38?

5. What were the days of the month with more than a 5-degree difference between the high and low temperatures?

6. What were the two warmest days of the month?

7. Did the pollution count ever exceed 5 on a day when the temperature stayed above 35?

8. What three consecutive days had the most total rainfall?

9. Was it true that every rainless day following a rainy day had a lower pollution count than the rainy day?

10. Using the first 10 days' data, "predict" the weather for the 11th day. Compare (either by hand or within the program) the prediction with the data for the 11th day.

Chapter 7

CHARACTER STRING HANDLING

We have said that computers can handle character information as well as perform numerical calculations. But most of the emphasis so far, except for labelling our tables of numerical output, has had very little to do with character string handling. It is true that we have been dealing with words, like identifiers, but these have been in the Fortran programs rather than being handled by them as data. We have, in fact, never had anything but numbers, either real or integer, as data, In this chapter we will learn how to read in character data, how to move it from one place to another in the memory of the computer, and how to search for a particular piece of information.

CHARACTER STRINGS

The term alphabetic information is sometimes used to describe what we will learn to handle in this chapter. It is true that we will be able to handle what you normally mean by alphabetic information, things like people's names

Sarah Marie Wood

but we also want to handle things like street addresses. For example, an address like

2156 Cypress Avenue

includes digits as well as letters of the alphabet. This kind of information we call **alphanumeric** or **alphameric** for short. But that is not all; we want to handle any kind of English text with words, numbers, and punctuation marks, like commas, semicolons, and question marks.

This text contains 7 words; doesn't it ?

We have defined a word as being a string of one or more characters preceded and followed by a blank or a punctuation mark, other than an apostrophe. This definition makes 7 a word.

The information we want to handle is any string of characters that may be letters, digits, punctuations marks, or blanks.   We tend to think of a blank as being not a character, but a string of blanks is quite different from a string with no characters at all.   We call the special string with no characters at all a **null string**.   We often write *b* for the blank character so that you can count how many blank characters are in a string.

herebisbabcharacterbstringbshowingbthebblanksbexplicitly.

In Chapter 3 we introduced the characters in the Fortran language. In that listing there are more than we have referred to so far in this chapter.   The list of special characters includes symbols we need for arithmetic operations $+$, $-$, $/$, $*$, as well as the equal sign, comma, and parentheses.

One reason we want to be able to handle strings of any of these characters is to be able to work with Fortran programs themselves as data.   This is the kind of job a compiler must do, and a programming language similar to Fortran should be suitable for writing a compiler program.   This is one of the reasons it has been extended as it was in Fortran 77 to include the ability to handle character strings.

CHARACTER STRING VARIABLES

Just as we had to set aside space in the computer memory for storing real and integer numbers, we must have space for storing strings of characters.   Character strings can be declared with different lengths.

We might declare a character string variable named *text* by the declaration

character **50 text*

We know it is a character string variable because of the keyword **character**. The amount of memory reserved for the variable *text* is 50 character spaces.   This will be a number of machine words as each character requires a number of bits to represent it.   When a character string of less than 50 characters in length is placed in this character string variable it is placed on the left-hand side of the available space and padded on the right with blanks.   If an attempt is made to place a longer string into the space it is truncated on the right.

READING AND OUTPUTTING STRINGS

We learned earlier how to output a string of characters that was in the form of a literal such as *'cost='*, and we have been using this for putting labels on our numeric output. We just put the literal, which is a string of characters enclosed in single quotes, in the list of a **print** statement. The string would be output, in a field of its own size and with the quotation marks removed.

Now that we can have character string variables we can read information into them from the keyboard and output them. For example, this program reads and outputs character strings.

```
        program getput
c       Read and output a text
        character *78 text
        print *,'Enter text in quotes'
        read *,text
        print *,text
        stop
        end
```

Here is a sample display:

Enter text in quotes
'Here is a sample text'
Here is a sample text

Notice that the input data must have quotes around the character string and that these quotes are not output since they are not part of the string. The largest string that can be put on an 80 character data line is 78 characters, since the quotation marks take two columns. It is best to limit variables that are input to those that will fit on to a line. On output the size is limited by the length of an output line. Variables that go from line to line are difficult to manage. Some compilers limit string variables to being at most 255 characters.

Character string variables may also be given values in an assignment statement. In the example

```
        character *10 name
        name = 'Philip Langtry'
        print *, name
```

the character string to be assigned to *name* has more characters than the maximum 10 that are declared. This means that the leftmost 10 characters are stored in *name* and the rest are lost. The output would be

> *Philip Lan*

This is a string of length 10. Remember the blank is a character. Character variables that are output by a list-directed **print** statement are output in a field the same size as what appears in the declaration of the character variable. Remember lower and upper case letters are different.

COMPARISON OF STRINGS FOR RECOGNITION

We need to be able to compare one string with another for two purposes. One purpose is for the **recognition** of strings. In this we are concerned with whether two strings are the same or not. String comparisons are made in logical conditions since their result is either true or false; the strings are the same or they are not. Here is a program that reads words until it reaches the word **stop** and gives the number of words:

```
        program readin
c       Stops when it is told
        character *10 word
        integer count
        count = 0
        print *,'Enter words one to a line, ending with stop'
        read *,word
5       if (word.eq. 'stop')go to 10
            count = count + 1
            read *,word
            go to 5
10          continue
        print *,count,' words read before stop'
        stop
        end
```

Here is a sample display:

Enter words one to a line, ending with stop
'soup'
'slow'
'slop'
'stop'
3 words read before stop

The logical condition *(word.eq. 'stop')* controls the **if...go to**. It is false until the *word* read is *stop*. If there were no word *stop* in the input data the computer would just sit waiting for another word.

SEQUENCING STRINGS

The other use of string comparisons is to sequence strings, to put them in order. Usually we speak of alphabetic order for alphabetic strings.

ABCDEFGHIJKLMNOPQRSTUVWXYZ

The alphabet and digits have the normal order among themselves: 0 comes before 9, *A* comes before *Z*, *a* comes before *z*. Blanks have the lowest value. The operators **.gt.** and **.lt.** are used to compare the strings. If the two strings being compared are of unequal lengths, blanks are added on the right of the shorter string to make them equal in length. The following comparisons are labelled as true or false:

Comparison	*Value*
('John' .gt. 'Jim')	true
('John' .lt. 'Johnston')	true
(' a' .lt. 'a')	true because blank.**lt.** *'a '*
('McLeod' .gt. 'MacKay')	true
('22' .gt. '156')	true because *'2 '.gt. '1 '*

The following program reads in 10 names and outputs the one that is the last alphabetically.

```
        program last
c       Look for alphabetically last name
        character *15, name,last
        integer i,number
        last = 'AAAAA'
        print *,'Enter number of names'
        read *,number
        print *,'Enter',number, 'names, one to line'
        do 18 i = 1,number
            read *,name
            if (name.gt.last)then
                last = name
            end if
18          continue
        print *,'Alphabetically last is:',last
        stop
        end
```

Here is a sample display:

> **Enter number of names**
> *4*
> **Enter 4 names, one to a line**
> *'Hopper'*
> *'Turing'*
> *'Backus'*
> *'Chomsky'*
> **Alphabetically last is: Turing**

Notice that the variable *last* is initialized to the string *AAAAA*. This is to provide a beginning value for use in the **if...then** statement. Because it is alphabetically low in value it will undoubtedly be replaced by the first name read. We could instead have read the first name into *last* and reduced the count in the **do** loop by one.

OPERATIONS WITH CHARACTER STRINGS

In Fortran, character strings are stored in such a way that their lengths are always the same. If a string is read into or assigned to the location that is shorter than this length, it is padded on the right with blanks. If it is longer, it is truncated. There is a built-in function in Fortran 77 which will give you the length of a character string. It is called *len*. But it really is of little use. For example, the statement

> **print** *,len ('Harriet')*

will output the integer 7, the length of the string. This is a fact you already know. If instead we have the statement

> **print** *,len (word)*

where the character variable *word* has been declared by

> **character** **20 word*

the result output will be 20; again a fact we already know.

For the same reason the operator for joining strings together, which in Fortran is two slashes / /, is of little use. For example, the statement

> **print** *,'up' / / 'stairs'*

will produce the output

> *upstairs*

This is interesting but useless. If we try to concatenate string variables we are stuck with all the padding blanks. For instance, if we have this program:

```
program cat
character *10 word1,word2
word1 ='up'
word2 ='stairs'
print *,word1// word2
stop
end
```

The result will be

up   stairs

There will be eight blanks between the *p* and the *s*.

In Fortran 77 there is also a way of obtaining a substring of a character string variable. For example if *word* is a character string variable the substring

word (3: 5)

is a string of characters which runs from the third character to the fifth character inclusive. For example,

```
character *10 word
word = 'splendid'
print *,word(6: 8)
```

will result in the output

did

We output the substring from the 6th to the 8th character. We can also assign strings to substrings. For example, if we added these statements to the previous ones

```
word (9: 10) ='ly'
print *,word
```

the result would be

splendidly

Whenever we assign to a substring whatever is there before is replaced.

In substrings, if the first position and the last position are the same, the substring has only one character. If the last position is omitted it is assumed to be the last position of the string. For example, if we add this statement

```
print *,word(2: )
```

the output would be

plendidly

If the first position is omitted, it is assumed to be the first position of the string. This

print *, *word(: 4)*

will produce the output

splen

Just as programs can be constructed using the three basic control structures: linear, repetition, and selection, all string manipulations can be accomplished using three basic operations. These are joining strings together (catenation), selecting part of a string (substring), or finding the length of a string. In Fortran 77 the substring facility is adequate for this purpose but neither the *len* function or the catenation operation are useful because string variables were always fixed in length. Catenation is useful with substrings. Often we use substrings of single characters. Strings can also be handled as arrays of single characters. As a result of the generally unsatisfactory nature of the present Fortran 77 in regard to string handling we will to use single character arrays for storing strings to operate on; but that must wait until we have discussed arrays in the next chapter.

CHAPTER 7 SUMMARY

In this chapter we have given methods of manipulating strings of characters. We introduced character string variables and showed how they can be used to read and output strings, recognize strings, or sequence them alphabetically. The following important terms were presented:

Length of a literal — a literal (character string constant) must have a length of at least one, as in *'q'*. Note that the literal *'don''t'* has length 5 because it represents *don't*.

Length of a character string variable — given in the declaration of the variable. The length of the variable never changes. If a character string shorter than the declared length is assigned to the variable then the string is padded with blanks on the right up to the declared length.

Null string — The string of length zero, that is, the string with no characters.

String truncation (or chopping) — throwing away characters from the right-hand end of a character string. Suppose a character string is assigned to a character string variable *s*, and the length of the string exceeds the length of *s*; then *s* takes the value of the string as truncated to the length of *s*. (An error message may be output.)

String comparisons — used to test character strings for equality and for ordering. Strings can be compared using the following operators:

>.lt. comes before (less than)
>
>.gt. comes after (greater than)
>
>.le. comes before or is equal (less than or equal)
>
>.ge. comes after or is equal (greater than or equal)
>
>.eq. equal
>
>.ne. not equal

Capital letters and little letters do not have the same value. The condition *'A '*.eq.*'a '* is false. The precise relation between these depends on the machine code used to represent them.

Blank padding — extending a character string on the right with blanks so it can be compared with or assigned to a longer string. For example, in Fortran, the comparison

>*'Jones'*.eq.*'Jones   '*

is true because the shorter string is temporarily extended on the right with blanks.

len — a built-in function for determining the length of a string. Since all character string variables in Fortran 77 have a fixed length, this function is of little use. It is of some use in subprograms.

Catenation — joining strings together. Strings can be joined by using the operator / / between them. We will not use this operator much in this book because strings can also be treated as arrays of single characters more conveniently.

Substring — a part of a string. To obtain a substring, place in parentheses after the name of the string the first character position of the substring, a colon, and the last character position of the substring. We will not use substrings very much in this book although they are possibly useful for catenation.

CHAPTER 7 EXERCISES

1. Which of the following comparisons of strings are true? Can you tell?
   (a) *'David Barnard'*.eq.*'David Barnard   '*
   (b) *'E. Wong'*.eq.*'Edmund Wong'*
   (c) *'Mark Fox'*.eq.*'Mark Fox'*

(d)   *'Johnston'* **.gt.** *'Johnson'*

(e)   *'416 Elm St'.***lt.** *'414 Elm Street'*

(f)   *'Hume,Pat'* **.gt.** *'Holt,Ric'*

(g)   *'Allen'* **.ne.** *'Alan'*

2.   Write a program that reads a list such as the following and outputs a list of all persons named Jones:

> *'Jones, A.B.'*
> *'Young, A.C.'*
> *'Jones, R.M.'*
> *'Collins, R.A.'*
> *'ZZZZ'* (dummy value)

Hint: Use one string that is **.le.** the alphabetically first Jones and another string that is **.ge.** the alphabetically last Jones.

3.   Write a program that reads in ratings for movies and outputs titles for those rated *'x'*. For example, the data might be:

'Thor and the Amazon Women'	*'adults only'*
'Bullets, Gore and Sex'	*'x'*
'Alice in Wonderland'	*'children'*
'The Godfather, part VIII'	*'x'*
'ZZZ'	*'none'*

4.   Write a program which looks up Nancy Wong's telephone number and outputs it. You are given a set of lines of data each containing a name and a phone number. For example, the first line of the set might be

> *'John Abel'*   *'443– 2162'*

The last data line is the dummy entry

> *'ZZZ'*   *'000– 0000'*

5.   You are to write a program which prints personalized appeals for contributions to the annual fund drive of the Loyal Order of Wallalumps, an exclusive men's club.

Each member is to be sent a letter of the following form:

Dear XXXXXX,

Thank you so much for your last year's contribution of CCCCCCC dollars.

Since your contribution last year was PPPPPPPPPPPP to help us meet our quota this year.

Yours sincerely,

Each record contains the member's last name, his nickname if known (if not, '?' is used), his last year's contribution and his estimated salary.

In the letter XXXXXX should be filled in with the member's nickname, if known, but otherwise with Mr. YYYYYY, where YYYYYY is the member's last name. The phrase PPPPPPPPPPPP should be either

> so generous, we are counting on you

or

> not as large as hoped, we need you

Phrase PPPPPPPPPPPP is picked according to whether last year's contribution was more or less than .1% of the member's estimated salary.

The following is an example data entry:

'Lazowska' 'Ed'   15   12000

Chapter 8

ARRAYS

So far in our programming, each memory location for data had its own special name; each variable had a unique identifier. In this chapter we will introduce the idea that groups of data will share a common name and be differentiated from each other by numbering each one uniquely.

Suppose that we have a list of names of persons. We could give the list the name *person* and identify the first name as *person(1)*, the second as *person(2)*, and so on. We call the number that is enclosed in parentheses the index of the **list** or **array**. The reason why we should use this method of identifying variables is not clear. We will have to do an example so that you can see the power of the new method. As an example, suppose you wanted to read in a list of names of 50 persons and output them in reverse order, that is, last first. We would need to read in the entire list before we could begin the output. This means we must have a memory location for each name. We must be able to reserve this space by a declaration.

DECLARATION OF ARRAYS

For the list of names of persons we would use a declaration

character **20 person(50)*

Each name is a character string variable whose length is 20. The fact that the variable identifier *person* is a list is shown by having something in parentheses after it. And what is shown is the fact that it is a list numbered, or indexed, from 1 to 50. What actually is shown in parentheses is the number of entries in the list.

If we want the fifty entries to be indexed say from 51 to 100 we would write the declaration as

character **20 person(51: 100)*

Most arrays have an **index** starting at *1*.

HANDLING LISTS

We are now ready for the program that reverses the order of a list of names. Here the array index is an integer variable *i.*

```
        program redo
c       Reverse the order of a list of names
        character *20 person(50)
        integer i,j
        print *, 'Enter 50 names in quotes, one to a line'
c       Read list of names
        do 5 i = 1,50
            read *,person(i)
5           continue
        print *, 'Here is reversed list'
c       Output reversed list
        do 15 i = 50,1,-1
            print *,person(i)
15          continue
        stop
        end
```

The data input is a list of 50 names, each in quotes, one to a line.

Now, perhaps, you can see what a powerful programming tool the indexed variable can be. In the **do** loops the index *i* that is counting the loops can be used to refer to the different members of the list. In the first **do** loop the names are read; the first is stored in the variable *person(1)*, the second in *person(2)*, and so on. In contrast, we want the output loop to output *person(50)*, next *person(49)*, and so on. We use a negative step size.

When an array such as *person* is being read into the computer we do not need to write out a do loop; we can use a shorter form in which a **do** loop is **implied**. Instead of writing

```
        do 5 i = 1, 50
            read *, person(i)
        continue
```

we can write the single statement

```
        read *, (person(i), i = 1, 50)
```

As it happens we can write a shorter form still when the complete array is being read in normal order. We could have

```
        read *, person
```

This short form is possible for the output of an array as well. If we wanted to output the *person* array in the normal order perwson(1), person(2),..., person(50) we could use the statement

> **print** *, *person*

To output it in the reversed order we could use an implied **do**.

> **print** *, *(person(i), i = 50, 1, − 1)*

We will not often use these short forms because they are not as easily understood as the full **do** loops.

Suppose, as a second example, we had a list of 50 integers and we wanted the sum of all the numbers. Here is the program:

```
        program total
c       Sums 50 numbers
        integer number(50),sum,i
        print *,'Enter 50 integers, one to a line'
c       Read in numbers
        do 40 i = 1,50
            read *,number(i)
40          continue
c       Sum the numbers
        sum = 0
        do 80 i = 1,50
            sum = sum + number(i)
80          continue
        print *,'sum = ',sum
        stop
        end
```

In this example, it is not necessary to read all the numbers and then add them up but we did it that way just to show what is necessary for reading or summing a list. We could have written only one loop, combining the two operations.

```
c       Read and sum the numbers
        sum = 0
        do 50 i = 1,50
            read *,number(i)
            sum = sum + number(i)
50          continue
        print *,'sum = ',sum
```

In this program there is no need to use an array at all; the same result could be accomplished by this program:

```
        program total2
c       Sums 50 numbers
        integer number, sum, i
        print *, 'Enter 50 integers'
c       Read and sum numbers
        sum = 0
        do 50 i = 1, 50
             read *, number
             sum = sum + number
50           continue
        print *, 'sum = ',sum
        stop
        end
```

Each number is added to *sum* as it is read and is not kept in the memory. Usually, there is more to be done that requires having the complete list of numbers still present. For instance, we could think of dividing each member of the list by the sum and multiplying by 100. This would express each entry as a percentage of the group. To do this we would add these statements before the **stop** of the *total* program:

```
c       Compute percentages
        do 60 i = 1,50
             number(i) = (number(i)*100.)/ sum +.5
             print *,number(i)
60           continue
```

in the **do** loop the assignment statement with the index *i* results in each member of the list being operated on and changed to a percentage.

AN EXAMPLE PROGRAM

Arrays can be used in manipulating various kinds of tables. We will now give an example which uses three lists to store a timetable for teachers in a high school. The timetable has been prepared as a set of lines of data. Each line has a teacher's name, a period(1 to 6), and a room number. The data lines look like the following:

(teacher)	(period)	(room)
'Ms. Weber'	1	216
'Mrs. Miao'	6	214
'Mrs. Reid'	1	103
'Ms. Weber'	4	200
'Ms. Buday'	2	216

...

'xxx'	0	0 (dummy entry)

A program is needed to output the timetable in order of periods. First, all teachers with their classrooms for the first period should be output; then all teachers with their classrooms for period 2, and so on up to period 6. The output from the program should begin this way:

Period   **1**
Ms. Weber   **216**
Mrs. Reid   **103**

    ...

The following program produces this output:

```
                    program teach
 1   c              Shows teacher room assignments by period
 2                  character *20 teachr(50)
 3                  integer period(50),room(50)
 4                  integer i,now,number
 5   c              Initialize for reading timetable
 6                  i = 1
 7                  read *,teachr(i),period(i),room(i)
 8   c              Read the timetable
 9   2              if (teachr(i).eq.'xxx')go to 3
10                     i = i + 1
11                     read *,teachr(i),period(i),room(i)
12                     go to 2
13   3              continue
14                  number = i - 1
15   c              Output the timetable by periods
16                  do 14 now = 1,6
17                     print *,'Period      ',now
18                     do 8 i = 1,number
19                        if (period(i).eq.now)then
20                           print *,teachr(i),'      ',room(i)
21                        end if
22   8                 continue
23   14             continue
24                  stop
25                  end
```

The first loop in this program reads in the data representing the timetable. In lines 6 and 7, the initialization for this loop sets the count to 1 and reads the first element of the *teacher, period,* and *room* arrays.

Our program is able to read in a timetable consisting of at most 50 classes, including the dummy entry. If there are more than 50 classes in the timetable, then line 10 will eventually set *i* to 51; this value of *i* will be used in line 11 as an index for the *teachr, period*, and *room* arrays. This would be an error, because the declarations specify that 50 is the largest allowed array index. The problem is that the index is **out of bounds** in line 11 when *i* exceeds 50.

You should take care that array indexes in your programs stay within their declared bounds. In our example program, we can prevent bounds errors by changing line 9 to the following.

> *2*   **if** *(i*.**gt.** *49*.**or.** *teachr(i)*.**eq.** *'xxx'*)**go to** *3*

Our change guarantees that no more than 50 lines will be read.

INITIALIZATION OF ARRAYS

In the next example we will show a program that is given a year, say 1984, and a day in the year, say 69, and outputs the corresponding date namely Mar 9, 1984. We will use an array of 12 character string variables of length 5 called *month* to hold the names of the months and an array of 12 integer variables called *monlen* to hold the lengths of the months. These two arrays can be declared and initialized by these statements:

> **character** **5 month(12)*
> **integer** *monlen(12),i*
> **data** *(month(i),monlen(i),i = 1,12)/ 'Jan',31,'Feb',28,'Mar',31,*
> +*'April',30,'May',31,'June',30,'July',31,'Aug',31,*
> +*'Sept',30,'Oct',31,'Nov',30,'Dec',31/*

In the **data** statement the list of values following the slash / are put into correspondence with *month(1),monlen(1),month(2),monlen(2)*, and so on. There is an implied **do** in the **data** statement. This is the main use we will make of the implied **do**. We are initializing the array *monlen* for a non-leap year.

Here is the program that will find the date for five different pairs of year and day entries

> **program** *date*
> *c*   *Finds the date in a given year of a day*
> **integer** *day,year,monno*
> **character** **5 month(12)*
> **integer** *monlen(12),1*
> **data** *(month(i),monlen(i),i = 1,12)/ 'Jan',31,'Feb',28'Mar',31,*
> +*'April',30,'May',31,'June',30,'July',31,'Aug',31,*

```
      +'Sept',30,'Oct',31,'Nov',30,'Dec',31/
          do 50 i = 1,5
              print *,'Enter year and day'
              read *,year,day
c             Test for leap year or not
              if (mod(year,4).eq.0) then
                  monlen(2) = 29
              else
                  monlen(2) = 28
              end if
c             Find month for day
              monno = 1
10            if (day.le.0) go to 20
                  day = day - monlen(monno)
                  monno = monno + 1
                  go to 10
20            continue
c             Set to actual month number
              monno = monno - 1
c             Restore last month so day is positive
              day = day + monlen(monno)
              print *,'Date is',month(monno),',',day,',',year
50            continue
      stop
      end
```

TWO-DIMENSIONAL ARRAYS

It is possible to have arrays that are two-dimensional that correspond to entries in a **table** provided all the entries are of the same data type. For instance, a table of distances in miles between 4 cities might be

	1	2	3	4
1	0	20	30	46
2	20	0	12	20
3	30	12	0	15
4	46	20	15	0

We could call this array *miles* and *miles(1,4)* is 46; *miles(3,4)* is 15. The first number in the parentheses refers to the row in the table, the second to the column. You can see that *miles(3,1)* has the same value as *miles(1,3)*; the table is symmetric in this case about the diagonal line running from top left to bottom right. All entries on this diagonal are zero; the distance from a city to itself is zero.

We must learn how to declare such a two-dimensional array. All that is necessary is to write

integer *miles(4,4)*

The first index is the number of rows, the second the number of columns. As an example, we will read in this table and store it in the memory. On each input data line we will enter one element of the table. We will enter the elements of the first row from left to right, then go to the next row.

```
        integer miles(4,4),i,j
        do 10 i = 1,4
            do 5 j = 1,4
                read *,miles(i,j)
    5           continue
    10      continue
```

In this program segment there is one **do** loop nested inside another. We have used two indexes, *i* to give the row number, *j* to give the column number. When *i = 1* the inner loop has *j* go from 1 to 4. This means the first four elements of the array are stored in these variables:

miles(1,1) miles(1,2) miles(1,3) miles(1,4)

These are the elements in row 1 of the table. Since our table is symmetric it does not matter if we interchange rows and columns, because we get exactly the same result. For most tables it **does** matter, and you must be careful.

Again an implied **do** form is possible for a two-dimensional array. We could use the single statement

read *,((miles(i,j),j = 1,4),i = 1,4)*

to read the array row by row.

ANOTHER EXAMPLE PROGRAM

We will illustrate the use of two-dimensional arrays in terms of a set of data collected by a consumers' group. This group has been alarmed about the recent rapid rise in price of processed wallalumps. They sampled grocery store prices of processed wallalumps on a monthly basis throughout 1982, 1983, and 1984 and observed that prices varied from 75 cents to 155 cents as the following table shows:

Month

	1	2	3	4	5	6	7	8	9	10	11	12
1982	87	89	89	89	85	85	85	75	90	100	100	100
1983	95	95	95	95	90	90	85	90	100	110	120	110
1984	110	110	115	115	115	100	100	110	120	140	145	155

The following program reads in the data and determines the average price for 1983:

```
        program cost
c       Computes average price over a year
        integer price(3,12)
        integer month,year,total
        print *,'Enter prices month by month for year, one to a line'
        do 16 year = 1,3
c              Read in prices for one year
               do 7 month = 1,12
                      read *,price(year,month)
7              continue
16             continue
c       Determine the average price in 1983
        total = 0
        do 19 month = 1,12
               total = total + price(2,month)
19             continue
        print *,'average 1983 price:',total/ 12.
c       Add statements here to calculate other averages
        stop
        end
```

In this program, the array *price* is declared so it can have a first index which can range from 1 to 3 which corresponds to 1982 to 1984 and a second index which can range from 1 to 12 corresponding to the columns in the table. Effectively, the *price* array is a table in which entries can be looked up by month and year if you subtract 1981 from the year. The first part of the program uses the data to fill up the *price* array. The second part of the program sums the prices for each month during 1983 and calculates the average 1983 price. The value 2 of the first array index corresponds to the year 1983.

We could as well calculate the average price for a particular month. For example, the following calculates the average price in February:

```
        total = 0
        do 25 year = 1,3
```

```
                 total = total + price(year,2)
   25            continue
          print *,'average Feb. price:',total/ 3.
```

We could calculate the average price for the entire three-year period as follows.

```
          total = 0
          do 50 year = 1,3
              do 40 month = 1,12
                  total = total + price(year,month)
   40             continue
   50         continue
          print *,'overall average:',total/ 36.
```

This example has illustrated the use of two-dimensional arrays. It is also possible to use arrays with three dimensions. For example, our consumers' group might want to record prices for five grades of processed wallalumps (that makes one dimension), each month (that makes two dimensions), for three years (that makes three dimensions). The array declaration

integer *price(3, 12, 5)*

would set up a table to hold all this data.

A two-dimensional array such as the price array can be initialized using a **data** statement instead of by reading in the data from the keyboard. This is done by the following

integer *price(3,12),i,j*
data *((price(i,j),i = 1,3),j = 1,12)/ 87,95,110,89,95,110...,155/*

Notice that the *price* table is listed a column at a time. This **data** statement has the same effect as a **do** loop going from 1 to 3 nested inside a **do** loop going from 1 to 12.

In the discussion of arrays we have limited ourselves to arrays whose index started at 1 and went up to the maximum dimension. Sometimes it is more convenient to start at some other lower bound. For example, for the *cost* program we could have had the index of the *price* array have *year* start at 1982, and go to 1984 rather than from 1 to 3. In that case we would have declared it as

integer *price(1982: 1984, 12)*

When the lower bound of the index is 1 we do not need to mention it. That is the default value.

ARRAYS AS DATA STRUCTURES

We have spoken of structured programming and shown how control flow is structured in a program. Now we can speak of the structure of data. Giving variables identifiers that are meaningful has been the only way we could systematize data so far. But with arrays we find that data can be structured or organized into one-dimensional forms called lists, or two-dimensional forms called tables. We could also use three-dimensional arrays. If all the entries of a table are of the same data type we can use a two-dimensional Fortran array otherwise we must use a set of one-dimensional arrays, usually one for each column of the table.

When we approach a problem and want to solve it by creating a computer program we must decide on the data structures we will use. We must decide in particular whether or not we need to establish arrays for any of the data, or whether single variables will serve us well enough.

Arrays will be useful whenever we must store groups of similar pieces of information. They are not necessary when small amounts of information come in, are processed, and then go out.

CHAPTER 8 SUMMARY

This chapter has introduced array variables, which are used for manipulating quantities of similar data. An array is made up of a number of elements, each of which acts as a simple, non-array variable. The following terms are used in describing arrays and their uses.

Array declaration — sets aside memory space for an array. For example, the declaration

> **real** *cost(4)*

sets aside space for the array elements *cost(1)*, *cost(2)*, *cost(3)*, and *cost(4)*. Each of these elements can be used like a simple, non-array, **real** variable.

Array index (sometimes called array subscript) — used to designate a particular element of array. For example, in *cost(i)*, the variable *i* is an array index. An array index can be any arithmetic expression. It must have an integer value.

Array bounds — the range over which array indexes may vary. The range is written as

> [lower bound:] upper bound

The lower bound and the colon can be omitted (which is what is indicated by the square brackets) and, if they are, the default lower bound is 1. For example, given the declaration

    integer *price(12, 1982: 1984)*

an array element of *price* can be specified by *price(m,y)*, where *m* can range from 1 to 12 and *y* can range from 1982 to 1984. The bounds need not be positive. For example, the declaration of an array of real elements.

    x(− 5),x(− 4),x(− 3)...x(10)

would be written as

    real *x(− 5: 10)*

This indicates that the lower bound of the array is −5; the upper bound is 10. There are 16 elements in all.

Out-of-bounds index − an array index which is outside the bounds specified in the array's declaration. This is an error.

Multiply-dimensioned arrays − arrays requiring more than one index, such as the *price* array.

Implied **do** loops − arrays may be input or output an element at a time by using a **do** loop. An abbreviated form of this is possible when all that is in the **do** loop is the input or output instructions. The main use of the implied **do** in this book is in the **data** statement.

data statement − used in a program to initialize the values of an array.

CHAPTER 8 EXERCISES

1.   What does the following program output?

```
               program flower
    c          Talks about flowers
               character *6 poem(2)
               integer part,repeat
               poem(1) = 'a rose'
               poem(2) = 'is'
               do 5 repeat = 1,3
                   do 3 part = 1,2
                       print *,poem(part)
    3               continue
    5           continue
               print *,poem(1)
               stop
               end
```

2. What does the following program output?

```
        program rumors
c       Starts rumors
        character *6 he(4),she(4)
        integer who
        print *,'Here they are'
        do 8 who = 1,4
            read *,he(who),she(who)
8           continue
        print *,he(1),'says',she(2),'loves',he(2)
        print *,'however--'
        do 12 who = 2,3
            print *,she(who),'says',he(who+1),'says'
12          continue
        print *,she(2),'is just shopping around'
        stop
        end
```

This is to be input:

```
'John' 'Ann'
'Fred' 'Judy'
'Ed' 'Alice'
'Bill' 'Jane'
```

3. What does this program output?

```
        program polish
c       Looks at furniture polish
        character *10 name(50)
        integer price(50)
        integer i,p,n
        print *,'Input data'
        read *,n
        read *,(name(i),price(i),i = 1, n)
        read *,p
        do 15 i = 1,n
            if (price(i).gt.p)then
                print *,name(i)
            end if
15          continue
        stop
        end
```

The input data is:

3
'Johnsons' 518
'Lemon Oil' 211
'Domino'   341
300

4. Write a program which reads yesterday's and today's stock-market selling prices and outputs lists of rapidly rising and rapidly falling stocks. A typical data entry line will look like this:

> *'General Electric' 93.50 81.00*

The line gives you the company's name followed by yesterday's price, followed by today's price. Your program should output a list of companies whose stock declined by more than 10 per cent, and then a list of companies whose stock rose by more than 10 per cent.

5. You can determine whether or not an integer n is a prime number by dividing it in turn by all the prime numbers less that its square root. If on each division the remainder is non-zero, the number is a prime. Write a program to generate an array of the first 50 prime numbers using members of the list up to the current entry to produce that entry.

6. A classic method of generating prime numbers is the sieve of Eratosthenes. You can use this method to find all the primes up to an integer n but setting up a one-dimensional integer array of dimension n. Begin by setting the first element to zero and all the rest of the elements of the array to 1. Starting at 2, the lowest prime, set the elements whose indexes are multiples of 2 to zero to indicate that they could not be a prime. Then scan the array beyond the second element to find the next highest element whose value is one. This is the next prime. Now repeat the process until you reach the end of the array. Finally, output the prime numbers. Develop a program to do this to produce a list of all primes up to 500.

7. Write a program to get the transpose B of a square matrix A given the relation that for all i, j:

$$A(i,j) = B(j,i)$$

8. The sum C of two matrices A and B of the same dimensions is obtained by adding corresponding elements so that

$$C(i,j) = A(i,j) + B(i,j)$$

Write a program to add such matrices.

9.   What will the following program output? What error would occur if the data item *'germ '* is inserted just before *'all done '?* Explain how this error can be avoided by changing one declaration. Add statements so that if more than six objects are read in, the program will output *Thank you, you have been a wonderful audience,* and quit.

```
              program sing
c             Outputs the words of a song
              character *10 object(8)
              integer verse,v
              print *,'Song of the green grass'
              print *,' '
              verse = 1
              object(verse)='tree'
5             if (object(verse).eq.'all done')go to 10
                  if (verse.eq.1)then
                      print *,'There was a tree'
                  else
                      print *,'And on that',object(verse − 1)
                      print *,'There was a',object(verse)
                      print *,'The prettiest',object(verse)
                      print *,'That you ever did see'
                      v = verse
6                     if (v.le.1)go to 8
                          print *,'And the',object(v),'was on the',object(v − 1)
                          v = v − 1
                          go to 6
8                     continue
                  end if
                  print *,'and the tree was in the ground'
c             Belt out the chorus
              print *,'and the green grass grew all around, all around'
              print *,'and the green grass grew all around'
              print *,' '
              verse = verse + 1
              read *,object(verse)
              go to 5
10            continue
          stop
          end
```

The following strings of input data should be on separate lines:

'branch' 'nest' 'bird' 'wing' 'feather' 'flea' 'all done'

10. Do you know the song about the old lady who swallowed a fly? If so, write a program to output its words. Otherwise, if you know the song "Alouette", write a program to output its words. Otherwise, if you know the song "The Twelve Days of Christmas", write a program to output its words. Otherwise learn one of these three songs and repeat this exercise.

11. You work for the Police Department and you are to write a program to try to determine criminals' identities based on victims' descriptions of the criminals. The police have records describing known criminals. These records have the form

>   *name   height   weight   address*

Here is an example:

'Joey MacLunk' 67   125   '24 Main St.'

There is another set of records giving descriptions of criminals participating in unsolved crimes. Here is such a set:

'14 Dec: Shop Lifting'	*72*	*190*
' 9 Nov: Purse Snatching'	*66*	*130*
' 6 Nov: Bicycle Thievery'	*67*	*135*
'xxx'	*0*	*0*

The two numbers give the criminal's estimated height and weight. Write a program which first reads in the records describing the unsolved crimes. Then it reads the file records giving the known criminals' names, descriptions, and addresses. Each known criminal's height and weight should be compared with the corresponding measurements for each unsolved crime. If the height is within 2 inches and the weight is within 10 pounds, your program should output a message saying the criminal is a possible suspect for the crime. (Note: Joey MacLunk is not a real person])

12. Write a program that has a taxtable for income tax and computes the tax when a certain taxable income is read in. Make the taxtable a part of the program by initializing two one-dimensional arrays called *income* and *rate*.

Here is a table

Taxable income	Tax rate
$1,112.	6%
2,224.	16%
4,448.	17%
6,672.	18%
11,120.	20%
15,568.	23%
20,016.	25%
31,136.	30%
53,376.	34%

The tax rate is the rate that applies to income between the last tabulated income level and the one corresponding to the rate. For example, you would pay 18% tax on any income above $4,448. but below $6,672.

Chapter 9

DESIGN OF PROGRAMS

STEP-BY-STEP REFINEMENT

Most of the examples of programming so far have been short examples. Nevertheless we have emphasized **some** of the aspects of good programming. These were:

1. choosing meaningful words as identifiers,

2. placing comments in the program to increase the understandability,

3. paragraphing loops and **if...then...else** statements to reveal the structure of control flow,

4. choosing appropriate data structures,

5. reading programs and tracing execution by hand, to strive for correctness before machine testing.

All of these are important even in small programs, but it is only when we attempt larger programs that our good habits will really start to pay off.

And when we work on larger programs we will find that we have something else to structure, and that is our attack on the problem. To solve a problem we must move from a statement of what the problem to be solved is, to a solution, which is a well-structured program for a computer. The language of our program will be Fortran 77.

The original statement of a problem will be in English, with perhaps some mathematical statements. The solution will be in Fortran. What we will look at first in this chapter is the way we move from one of these to the other. We will be discussing a method whereby we go step by step from one to the other. This **systematic method** we will refer to as **step-by-step refinement**. Sometimes we say that we are starting at the top, the English-language statement of the problem, and moving down in steps to the bottom level, which is the Fortran program for the solution. We speak of the **top-down approach** to program development.

TREE STRUCTURE TO PROGRAM DEVELOPMENT

To illustrate the technique of structuring the design of programs by the step-by-step refinement, or the top-down approach, we need a problem as an example. We need a problem that is large or difficult enough to show the technique, but not so large as to be too long to follow. If a program is too long and involved we will use another technique that divides the job into modules and does one module at a time. This is called **modular programming**. It is another form of structured programming. But it must wait until we have learned about subprograms.

The example we choose is sorting a list of names alphabetically. We will now start the solution by drawing a diagram in the form called a tree which represents the structure of our attack. The root of the tree is the statement of the problem. In the first move we show how this is divided into three branches:

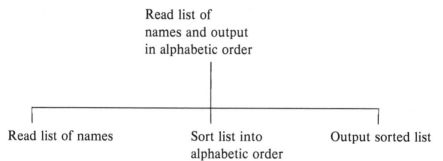

At each of the three nodes that descend from the root we have an English statement. These statements are still "what-to-do" statements, not "how-to-do-it."

We will be moving down each branch of the solution tree replacing a statement of "what to do" by an algorithm for doing it. The algorithms will not necessarily be in the Fortran language. We will use a mixture of English and Fortran at each node until, in the nodes farthest from the tree root, we have a Fortran program.

CHOOSING DATA STRUCTURES

Before we try to add more branches to the solution tree, we should decide on some data structures for the problem of sorting the list of names. We need not make all the decisions at this stage, but we can make a start.

We will use a one-dimensional array called *name* to hold the list of names to be sorted. The length of this list we will call *n* and we will allow names up to 30 characters in length. What we are deciding on is really the declarations for the Fortran program, and for now we have decided that we need

> **character** **30 name(50)*
>
> **integer** *n,i*

In these declarations we are allowing a maximum size for the list of 50 names. The actual list will have *n* names, and we must read this number in as part of the input. For indexing the list we clearly will need an index *i*. We will assume for the moment that we will keep the sorted list in the same locations as the original list. The names will have to be rearranged, and this means some swapping will be needed. We will need a single variable *temp* with type **character** **30* to do this swapping. You cannot interchange two names on the list without having a temporary location of the same type.

GROWING THE SOLUTION TREE

Having decided on at least some of the data structures, we are prepared to continue the process of structuring the solution tree. We can see how to develop the left and right branches now, even as far as transforming them into Fortran program segments. The middle branch can be refined a little by saying that sorting will be accomplished by element swapping. Here is the tree now:

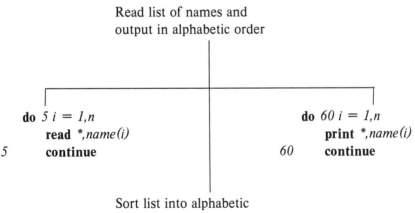

We could use the implied **do** for the input and output and have for input in the left branch of the solution tree

> **read** *, *(name(i),i = 1,n)*

and for output in the right branch

> **print** *, *(name(i),i = 1,n)*

At this stage we must obviously face up to designing an algorithm for producing a sorted list by swapping.

DEVELOPING AN ALGORITHM

We want the names to be in the sorted list so that each name has a smaller value than the name ahead of it in the list.

In the sorted list

> *Holt*
> *Horning*
> *Hull*

we see   *('Horning'.**gt.** 'Holt')*
            *('Hull'.**gt.** 'Horning')*

are both true conditions.

In our solution tree one branch must be developed further; this is, "Sort list into alphabetic order by swapping". We have seen from the example that a sorted list has the largest value in the last position. This is also true of the list if an element is removed from the end. The new last element is the largest one of the smaller list. So our next refinement in the solution is to arrange the list in this way. We write:

> **do** with *last* varying from *n* to second,
>   Swap elements so largest is in *last* element

Fortran 77 permits counting backwards so we could write

> **do** *15 last = n, 2, −1*

We must still refine the part,

> Swap elements so largest is in *last* element

This becomes:

> **do** with *i* varying from first to *(last − 1)*,
>   **if** (element *(i)*.**gt.**element *(i + 1)*)**then**
>   Swap elements
>   **end if**

The first two parts of this can now become Fortran; this produces the next refinement

```
        do 25 i = 1,last— 1
            if (name(i).gt.name(i + 1))then
                Swap elements
            end if
25          continue
```

We must now refine the statement "Swap elements". It is

```
        temp = name(i)
        name(i) = name(i + 1)
        name(i + 1) = temp
```

Now we can assemble the complete program.

```
        program sort
c       Sort list of n names alphabetically
        character *30 name(50),temp
        integer i,last,n
c       Read list of names
        print *,'Enter number of names in list'
        read *,n
        print *,'Enter',n,'names, one to a line'
        read *,(name(i),i = 1,n)
c       Swap elements of list until sorted;
c       do with last varying from n to second
c       Swap elements so largest value is in last element
        do 30 last = n, 2, — 1
c           do with i varying from first to last — 1
c               if (element(i).gt.element(i + 1)) then
c                   Swap elements
            do 25 i = 1,last — 1
                if (name(i).gt.name(i + 1))then
                    temp = name(i)
                    name(i) = name(i + 1)
                    name(i + 1) = temp
                end if
25          continue
30      continue
c       Output sorted list
        print *,'Here is sorted list'
        print *,(name(i),i = 1,n)
        stop
        end
```

Here is a sample display:

Enter number of names in list
5
Enter 5 names, one to a line
'Mendell'
'Perlegut'
'Cordy'
'Bregman'
'Venus'
Here is sorted list
Bregman
Cordy
Mendell
Perlegut
Venus

Notice that the English parts of the solution tree remain as comments in the final program. Comments are not added after a program is written, so that it can be understood at a later date, but are an integral part of the program construction process.

ASSESSING EFFICIENCY

In this approach to problem solution we have moved step by step to refine the statement of the problem in English into a program in a language that is acceptable to a computer, namely Fortran. In the process, as we constructed the solution tree, we gradually replaced statements of what is to be done by statements of how it is to be done; we devised an algorithm for performing the process. The algorithm was expressed in English, or a mixture of English and Fortran. Finally we had a Fortran program.

Nowhere during this process have we spoken about the efficiency of the method that we have chosen, that is, the efficiency of our algorithm. This is because the issue of efficiency complicates the solution. Since in structured programming we are trying to control complexity, we have in this first attempt eliminated efficiency from our considerations.

This means that to now add the refinement of a more efficient algorithm will require us to back up to an earlier point in the solution tree and redo certain portions. In the step-by-step refinement method of problem solution we do not always move from the top down in the solution tree. In practice this would be impractical, as afterthoughts must be allowed to improve a method of solution. The only reason to reject afterthoughts is that the work in incorporating them is not justified, considering the gain that would result.

In our particular example you can see that it is possible, at a certain stage, that the list might be sorted and that there is no need to keep on to the bitter end. What we should incorporate is a way of recognizing that the list is sorted so that the mechanical sorting process can stop.

A BETTER ALGORITHM

What we must do is to back up in the solution tree to the point where we had in the middle branch the words, "Swap elements of *name* until sorted." We have translated this essentially by the statement, "Swap elements of *name* in such a way that at the end of the swapping process the list is sure to be sorted."

We are going to change now to the statement, "Swap elements of *name* in such a way that at the end of the swapping process the list would be sorted, and stop either when the list **is** sorted or when the normal end of the swapping process is reached." You can see that we are going to have a loop now with two conditions. The condition of the swapping process's being finished is the same as what we have now. What we must add is the second condition

if (list is sorted) **go to**

But how do we know when the list is sorted? We must devise an algorithm to test whether or not the list is sorted. You will notice that if in any iteration of the inner loop there are no names swapped, the list **must** be sorted. We should have a logical variable called *sorted* that can be set to *.true.* to indicate that the list is sorted or *.false.* to indicate that the list is not sorted. The outer loop would then be

10   **if** *(sorted.***or.***last.***lt.** *2)***go to** *30*

We would have to initialize this loop by having this precede it.

sorted = .false.
last = n

These set the logical variable and start the count. Inside the loop just before the end we must perform the adjustment in the index *last* by -1. This would mean we need the instruction

last = last − 1

just before the end of the loop. We want *sorted* to be changed to *.true.* if **no** swapping takes place in the inner loop. This can be accomplished if we set it to *.true.* just before we enter the inner loop and return it to *.false.*

if any swapping does take place.   The altered part of the program is as follows.

```
c          Swap elements of list until
c                  either swapping process is completed
c                  or the list is sorted as indicated
c                  by 'sorted' being true
           sorted = .false.
           last = n
10         if (sorted.or.last.lt.2)go to 30
               sorted = .true.
               do 25 i = 1, last − 1
                   if (name(i).gt.name(i + 1))then
                       sorted = .false.
                       temp = name(i)
                       name(i) = name(i + 1)
                       name(i + 1) = temp
                   end if
25                 continue
               last  = last − 1
               go to 10
30             continue
c          Output sorted list
           (as before)
```

The variable *sorted* must be declared **logical**.

BETTER ALGORITHMS

In our example we could see that an improvement in the efficiency of the sorting algorithm could be achieved, and we backed up the solution tree and redid a portion to incorporate the improvement. This was an easier job than trying to think about efficiency in the first place. This is why in the step-by-step refinement method we do not consider efficiency at first. In a way we were lucky that our algorithm could be modified so readily.   We might have done the swapping in an entirely different way, in which we would not be able to detect a sorted list by the absence of swapping on any iteration of the process.

To see how this might be, suppose that to sort this list each element were compared with the first element. If it were smaller, the two would be swapped. With the smallest in the first position the list would be shortened by one and the process repeated.   The difficulty here is that the fact that no swapping occurs in any round only means that the smallest is already in the first position, not that the list is sorted. We have no way of seeing that the list is sorted unless we compare each list member with its next-door neighbor. And this is what we did in our sorting method.

So our method is more suited to this particular improvement than a method that involves swapping by comparison of each element with one particular element. If we had started this way we would have had to revise completely. To say that efficiency considerations are left until after a first algorithm is programmed produces disadvantages. For many standard processes like sorting, various algorithms have been explored, their efficiencies evaluated, and a best algorithm determined. The method we have developed is certainly not the best that has been devised.

This best, or optimal, algorithm often depends on the problem itself. For instance, one algorithm may be best for short lists, another for long lists.

The method we have used is known as the **bubble sort**. We have shown how it can be improved by testing to see if at any stage the list happens to be sorted. If the list is reasonably long a more efficient method is one devised by Donald Shell, know as the **Shell sort**. The Shell sort is really a series of bubble sorts in which the distance *space* between elements being compared, and swapped if necessary, is large to begin and is decreased until at last next-door neighbors are being compared. This results in many fewer swaps. Here is the program segment which does this. The variable *space* must be declared as an integer variable.

```
c        Sort list by Shell sort method
c        Set initial space between elements being compared
         space = n/ 2.
10       if (space.le. 0) go to 50
              do 40 i = space + 1,n
                 j = i − space
20            if (j.le. 0) go to 30
                 if (name (j).gt. name (j + space)) then
c                    Swap elements
                     temp = name (j)
                     name (j) = name (j + space)
                     name (j + space) = temp
                     j = j − space
                 else
                     j = 0
                 end if
```

```
                               go to 20
30                          continue
40                        continue
c               Divide space in half and repeat process
                space = space/ 2.
                               go to 10
50                          continue
c               Output sorted list
                (as before)
```

Try tracing this algorithm to see how it operates.

Establishing the best method is very difficult and depends on circumstances. Always try to pick a good algorithm if you are programming a standard process. At least avoid bad algorithms. Very often, programs are already written using good algorithms and you can use them directly in your own program. But that is something we will discuss in the chapter on subprograms. We can create programs using modules that are already made for us. Then one of the branches of your solution tree is filled by a **prefabricated module**. We need only learn how to hook it up to our own program. We can also create modules of our own. This technique is called **modular programming** and it is an additional way to conquer problem solving, by dividing the problem into parts.

PROGRAM SPECIFICATIONS

The **specifications** for a program tell what the program must do to solve a problem. These must be provided by the person who is requesting that the program be prepared. Before starting to write a program, the programmer needs the detailed specifications for the program. Suppose the problem is to output pay checks for the employees of a company; there is a record giving each employee's name and amount of payment. The programmer needs to know the format of the data entries as well as the format for the pay checks. These formats are part of the specifications for the program to output pay checks.

Sometimes the program specifications are not completely agreed upon and written down. If an employee's record indicates an amount of $0.00, this may mean that the employee is on leave and is to receive no pay check. If the programmer does not know the special significance of $0.00 - because the specifications are not complete - a program that outputs hundreds of worthless pay checks may result. All too often programs fail to handle special situations such as $0.00 correctly. If the programmer is in doubt about such a situation, the specifications should be checked to make sure they are complete.

DEFENSIVE PROGRAMMING

Errors are sometimes made in the entry of data for a program. The method of handling data errors may be given in the program specifications, or it may be left to the discretion of the programmer. Sometimes a programmer can write a program so that it detects and reports bad data. This is called **defensive programming**. Some programs are written to accept absolutely any data; after reporting a bad data item, the program ignores the item or attempts to give it a reasonable interpretation. If a program is written assuming no data errors, bad data items may prevent the program from doing its job. It is the programmer's responsibility to make the program sufficiently defensive to solve the problem at hand.

The quality of a computer program is determined largely by the attitudes and work habits of the programmer. Some programmers underestimate the programming task. They write programs too quickly; they do not test their programs sufficiently and they are too willing to believe that their programs are correct.

Most programs, when first written, contain some errors. This is not surprising when you consider the vast number of possible programming errors and the fallibility of every programmer. The programmer should take the attitude that a program is not correct until it is shown to be correct.

One good method of preparing computer programs is to write them using a soft lead pencil. This allows easy corrections and improvements by erasing and replacing lines. The program should be entered into the computer only when the programmer feels confident that no more changes are required. This method of program preparation can save the programmer a lot of time. The savings come because it is easy to change a program when it is still on paper and fresh in the programmer's mind. Each later change requires the programmer to relearn the program before modifications can be made confidently. A few minutes of desk-checking a program can save hours of debugging time. The programmer who tries to do it right the first time comes out ahead, saving time and writing programs with fewer errors.

PROGRAM CORRECTNESS

The most effective way to make sure a program works correctly is to study the program thoroughly. It should be read again and again until the programmer is thoroughly convinced that it is right.

It helps if a second programmer reads and approves the program. Ideally, the second programmer should read the program after its author feels that it is correct, but before it is entered into the computer. The second reader provides a new point of view and may be able to find typical errors such as incorrect loop initialization.

This process of studying programs to make as sure as you can that they are correct is extremely important. Sometimes programs can be proven correct using a mathematical approach; proving that a program is correct is similar to proving that a theorem in geometry is true. More often, programs are accepted as being correct by a non-mathematical, common-sense approach. But any program should be considered to have errors until proven correct. When one or more programmers study a program until they understand it and are convinced it is correct, we often have to be satisfied since formal proof is a difficult process.

PROGRAMMING STYLE

A program should be easy to read and understand; otherwise the job of studying it to attempt to verify its correctness will be hopeless. The programmer should strive for a good **programming style**, remembering that other readers will be in a hurry and will be critical of sloppiness or unnecessary confusion in the program. It commonly happens that as a programmer makes a program clearer and easier to understand, ways are discovered to improve or correct the program.

It takes work to write programs that are easy to read — just as it takes work to write clear English. Good writing requires care and practice. One way of making programs readable and understandable is to give them a simple organization — so the reader can easily learn the relationship among program parts. We have previously presented step-by-step refinement as a technique for designing programs. As well as aiding in the writing of programs, this technique helps make programs easier to read.

One of the rules of good programming style is this: comments and identifiers should be chosen to help make a program understandable. Comments should record the programmer's intentions for the parts of the program. It is a good idea to write comments as the program is being written. We have shown how the English parts of the step-by-step refinement process can become comments in the final program.

Good programs do not require many comments, because the program text closely reflects the intentions of the programmer. Programs become more difficult to read if they are cluttered with obvious comments such as

c   *increase n by 1*
        n = n + 1

Comments are usually needed to record:

- **Overall purpose of a program**. What problem the program is to solve. As well, comments may be used to record the program's author and its date of writing.

- **Purpose of each module**. Similar to the comments for an overall program.

- **Purpose of a collection of statements**. Such a comment might give the purpose of a loop.

- **Assumptions and restrictions**. At certain points in a program, certain assumptions and restrictions may apply to variables and the data. For example, one program part may assume that another program part has set *size* to a positive number less than 20 to indicate the number of customer accounts.

- **Obscure or unusual statements**. As a rule, such statements should be avoided. If they are required they should be explained. Here is an example:

c   *Round cents to nearest dollar*
        dollrs = (cents + 50)/ 100.0
        cents = 100*dollrs

Well-chosen identifiers make a program easier to read. Each identifier should record the function of the named object. For example, an array used to save credit limits should be named *limit* and not *array*. A subprogram used to input accounts should be named *input* and not *p1* or *Fred*.

If a variable has a very simple purpose, such as indexing through an array, a one-letter name such as *i, j,* or *n* may be appropriate. This is because these letters are commonly used for indexing in mathematics. But if the index variable has some additional meaning, such as counting lines of input data a longer name may help the reader.

Avoid obscure abbreviations, such as *tbntr* for table entry. Avoid acronyms, such as *sax* for sales tax. Unless abbreviations or acronyms are well known to the reader before seeing the program, they impose an extra memorization task that interferes with understanding the program. Unfortunately, Fortran variables can be at most six characters long, so some abbreviations are inevitable; choose these to have maximum readability.

Avoid meaningless identifiers such as *a, b, c, d,* and *temp1.* A single-letter identifier such as *d* is sometimes appropriate for a simply-used variable when the name *d* is relevant, for example, it stands for diameter. Adding a digit such as 1 or 2 to the end of an identifier, as in *temp1*, can be confusing unless it explains the purpose of the named object.

TESTING

After the program has been written and studied to verify its correctness, it should be tested. The purpose of testing is to run the program to attempt to demonstrate that the program is correct.

The tests must be chosen with care because only a limited number of them can be run. Consider a program designed to sort any list of 100 names into alphabetic order. Certainly we could not test it exhaustively by trying every possible list of 100 names. We would be testing for years! Rather than exhaustive testing we need to design tests which try every type of situation the program is to handle.

Well-designed tests should point out any errors in the program. Ultimately, testing demonstrates errors better than it demonstrates program correctness.

When testing reveals an error, that is, a **bug**, in the program, the programmer is faced with a **debugging** task. We shall present debugging techniques later. Right now, we will give techniques for testing.

The programmer will need to study the program in order to design good tests. The tests should make each statement execute at least once — but this is not enough. Suppose the statement

   avrage = total/ count

is tested and computes the desired average. This does not demonstrate that all is well; it may be that in some situations *count* can become zero. If this statement is executed with *count* set to zero, the statement does not make sense. So, not only should every statement be executed, but it should be executed for the type of situation it is expected to handle. Care should be taken to:

— **Test end conditions**. See that each loop is executed correctly the first time and last time through. Test situations in which indexes to arrays reach their smallest and largest possible values. Pay particular attention to counters which may take on the value zero.

— **Test special conditions**. See that data which rarely occurs is handled properly. If the program outputs error messages, see that each situation requiring such a message is tested.

Designing tests to exercise all end conditions and special conditions is not easy — but it is worthwhile in terms of program reliability.

The programmer should be able to tell from test results if the program is executing correctly. Sometimes this is easy because the program outputs intermediate results as it progresses. Sometimes the programmer will need to add special output statements to verify that the program is running correctly. These statements can:

Output messages to record the statements being executed. For example, a message might say *input subroutine entered.*

Output values of variables. This allows the programmer to verify by hand that the values are correct. The best time to output variables is when modules start and when they finish, so the programmer can verify that variables were modified correctly.

Output warnings of violated assumptions. Suppose a subroutine is used to set *where* to the index of the smallest number in a list of 12 numbers. The assumption that *where* receives a value from 1 to 12 can be tested by

```
if (where.lt. 1.or. where.gt. 12)then
    print *,'error:where = ',where
end if
```

Care must be taken to design appropriate output statements for testing. Too much output will confuse the programmer; too little output will not give the programmer sufficient information about the execution of the program.

Ideally, tests should be designed before the program is entered into the computer. With the program still fresh in mind, the programmer can more easily invent tests that try out every statement. Sometimes a programmer discovers that parts of a program are difficult to test; a slight change in the program may overcome this difficulty. It is best to make these changes when the program is still on paper, before time has been invested in entering the program and compiling it. Designing tests requires the programmer to read the program with a new point of view. It sometimes happens that this point of view uncovers errors in the program. The best time to fix these errors is when the program is still on paper.

As programs become larger, it becomes increasingly difficult to test them thoroughly. Large programs can be tested by first testing the modules individually. Then the modules are combined into larger modules and these are tested and so on. The process is called **bottom-up testing**. This method of testing uses specially-written test programs.

Whenever a program is modified, it should be retested. All the changed parts should be tested. In addition, it is a good idea to test the entire module containing changes, or even the entire program. The reason is that modifications often require a precise understanding of the surrounding program, and this understanding is sometimes not attained. Very commonly, program modifications introduce errors.

DEBUGGING

A program has bugs (errors) when it fails to solve the problem it is supposed to solve. When a program misbehaves we are faced with the problem of debugging — correcting the error. The program's misbehavior is a symptom of a disease and we must find a cure. Sometimes the symptom is far removed from the source of the problem; erroneous statements in one part of a program may set variables' values incorrectly and trigger a series of unpredicted actions by the program. When the symptoms appear via incorrect program output, the program may be executing in a different part. The programmer is left with a few clues: the incorrect output, and must solve the mystery and cure the disease. Solving these debugging mysteries can take more time than writing the program.

When a program contains a bug, this means that the programmer made at least one mistake. We can categorize programmer errors as follows:

Errors in entering the program. **return** might be mis-typed as **retrun**. These are typing errors.

Errors in using the programming language. The programmer did not understand a language construct.

Errors in writing program parts. Although a particular program part was properly designed, it was not correctly written in Fortran. For example, a loop designed to read in account entries might always execute zero times because of writing the loop's terminating condition incorrectly.

Errors in program design. The program parts and their interactions might be improperly designed. The program designer might forget to provide for the initialization of variables.

Solving the wrong problem. The programmer did not understand the nature of the problem to be solved, that is the program specifications. Perhaps the specifications were not correct or complete.

This list of possible errors has proceeded from the least serious to the most disastrous. The first type of errors, such as typing errors, can be corrected easily once detected. The last type of error, misunderstanding the purpose of the program, may require scrapping the entire program and starting over again.

Some programmers are overly optimistic and immediately conclude that any bugs in their programs are not very serious. Such a programmer is quick to make little changes in the program to try to make the symptoms of the problem disappear. The wise programmer knows that program misbehavior is an indication of sloppiness and that sloppiness leads easily to disastrous errors. Program misbehavior is taken as a sign that the program is sick — a checkup by study is required.

The overly optimistic programmer is forever saying, "I just found the last bug." When the wise programmer finds a bug, it is assumed that there are more.

Many of the least serious errors, such as misspelled keywords, are automatically pointed out by error messages, because the error results in an illegal Fortran program. These errors are usually easy to fix. Some errors are particularly treacherous; they seem to defy attempts to correct them. Here is some advice — some of it repeated from earlier parts of this book — to help you track down treacherous bugs.

Read all error messages. In their hurry to read their program's output, some programmers fail to notice error messages. These messages may pinpoint a bug.

Beware of automatic error repair. Some compilers try to make it easier to get programs working by "repairing" errors. For example, the programmer might carelessly write $x = 2y$. The compiler might repair this to $x = 2$. Such repairs can save time by allowing more of the program to be compiled and executed on one run. However, these repairs should not be taken as intelligent advice; remember, the compiler has no idea what problem you are trying to solve.

The first error messages may help more than later ones. This is because the first messages are closer to the source of the problem. Later messages may simply indicate that a previous error is still causing trouble.

Beware of confusion between *i* **and 1**. Some people can consistently read $x = x + i$ to mean increase x by one. Errors like this can be found by reading the program character by character — as a computer does! In general, the human tendency to read what we want to be there, rather what is actually there makes debugging difficult.

Beware of misspellings. Some words are easily misspelled. A person who is concentrating on understanding a program may overlook *weight* occasionally spelled as *wieght*. In Fortran 77 new identifiers are automatically declared to be variables. Hence, Fortran 77 would not warn us that *wieght* suspiciously did not appear in a declaration.

If everything else fails in the debugging effort, the programmer is forced to rerun the program to gain more information about the errors. The programmer may add statements to output variables or to trace the program's execution. These statements are designed using the same techniques used in testing to show programs work properly. If the original tests had been carefully enough designed, there is a good chance they would have pinpointed the error and eliminated later time-consuming debugging.

CHAPTER 9 SUMMARY

In previous chapters we concentrated primarily on learning a programming language; we have covered variables, loops, character strings, arrays, and so on. In this chapter, the focus has been on the development of slightly larger programs and discussed ways of improving program reliability.

The method of program development which we described is based on the idea of dividing the problem into parts — the divide-and-conquer strategy. Each of these parts in turn is divided into smaller parts. This continues until eventually the solution to the problem has been broken into small parts which can be written in a programming language like Fortran. We will review this method of program design using these:

Top-down approach to programming. When using a computer to solve a problem, you should start by understanding the problem thoroughly. You start at the "top" by figuring out what your program is supposed to do. Next you split your prospective program into parts, for example, into a reading phase, a computation phase, and an output phase. These phases represent the next level in the design of your program. You may continue by defining the data which these phases use for passing information among themselves, and then by writing Fortran statements for each of the phases. The Fortran statements are the bottom level of your design; they make up a program which should solve your problem. In larger programs, there may be many intermediate levels between the top - understanding the problem completely - and the bottom - a program which solves the problem. (Beware: top-down program design does **not** mean writing declarations at the top of the page, followed by statements! The top level in top-down design means gaining an understanding of the problem to be solved, rather than writing the first line of Fortran.)

Step-by-step refinement. When you are writing a program, you should start with an overall understanding of the program's purpose. You should proceed step by step toward the writing of this program. These steps should each refine the proposed program into a more detailed method of solving the problem. The last step refines the method to the level where the computer can carry out the required operations. This means that the final refinement results in a program which can be executed by the computer. As you can see, the idea behind top-down programming is step-by-step refinement leading from the problem statement to the final program.

Tree structures to program design. In this chapter we have illustrated top-down programming by drawing pictures of trees. The root, or base, of the tree is labelled by the statement of the problem. Once the problem has been refined into subproblems, we have our tree grow a branch for each subproblem. In turn, each subproblem can be divided, resulting in sub-branches, and so on. When you are actually solving problems, you will probably not actually draw such a tree. However, you may well use the idea behind drawing this tree, namely, step-by-step refinement leading from problem statement to computer program.

Use of comments. One of the purposes of comments in a program is to remind us of the structure of the program. This means that comments are used to remind us that a particular sequence of Fortran statements has been written to solve one particular part of the problem. The English language parts used in the development of a program can become comments in the final program.

Program specifications — explanation of what a program is to do. This should include the forms of the input and output data and the type of calculation or data manipulation to be performed. Essentially, program specifications explain how the computer is to be used to solve a particular problem.

Programming habits — the way a programmer goes about work. Ideally, the slow but sure approach is best, completing a program in pencil and thoroughly studying it before submitting it to the computer.

Proving program correctness — studying a program to verify that it satisfies its specifications. This verification would usually involve mathematical techniques if a formal proof of correctness is expected. Usually we must be satisfied to stop short of formal proof.

Programming style — if the style is good, then the program can be easily read and understood.

Use of identifiers — good programming style requires that identifiers be chosen to make a program understandable. Identifiers should record the function or use of the named object.

Testing — running a program to demonstrate that it is correct. Tests should be designed to try every type of situation the program is to handle. Ultimately, testing is better at demonstrating bugs than demonstrating program correctness.

Debugging — correcting errors in a program. Debugging can be the most difficult and time-consuming part of trying to make a program work. These difficulties can be minimized by using the techniques listed in this chapter.

CHAPTER 9 EXERCISES

1. You are to have the computer read a list of names, followed by the dummy name 'zzz', and output the names in reverse order. In your top-down approach to writing your program, you first decided your program should have the overall form:

    (a) Read in all of the names;

(b)   Output the names in reverse order;

Next, you decided that the names will be passed from part (a) to part (b) via an array declared by

character **10 name(50)*

The index of the last valid name read into this array will be passed to part (b) in an integer variable called *number*. Making no changes to this overall form, you must now complete the program. Include comments at the appropriate places to record the purpose of the two parts of your program. Answer the following questions about your completed program.

— Can you think of another way to write part (a) of your program without changing part (b)? How?

— Can you think of another way to write part (b) of your program without changing part (a)? How?

2. The school office wants a list of all *A* students and a list of all *B* students. There is a data entry line for each student giving his grade, for example:

    'David Tilbrook' 'A'

Each grade is *A, B, C, D,* or *F*. The names and grades are followed by the dummy entry

    'zzz' 'z'

The school's programmer has designed the following three possible structures for a program to read these data and the two required lists.

First program structure:

(a)   Read names and grades and save all of them in arrays.

(b)   Output names having *A* grades.

(c)   Output names having *B* grades.

Second program structure:

(a)   Read names and grades and save only those with *A*s or *B*s in arrays.

(b)   Output names having *A* grades.

(c)   Output names having *B* grades.

Third program structure:

(a) Read names and grades, outputting names with *A*s and saving only names with *B*s.

(b) Output names having *B*s.

Suppose the final program will have room in arrays to save at most 50 students' names. What advantage does the second program structure have over the first one? What advantages does the third program structure have over the second one? You do not need to write a program to answer these questions.

3. A company wants to know the percentage of its sales due to each salesman. Each salesman has a record giving his name and the dollar value of his sales. The last salesman's record is followed by a record giving the dummy name *'nobody '* and sales of zero dollars. The top-down design of a program to output the desired percentages has resulted in this program structure:

(a) Read in salesmen and sales and add up total sales.

(b) Calculate each salesman's percentage of the total sales.

(c) Output the salesmen's names and percentages.

Parts (a) and (c) have been written in Fortran. You are to write part (b) in Fortran, add declarations and complete the program. Here is part (a) written in Fortran:

```
c        Read in salesmen and sales and add up total sales
         total = 0
         i = 1
         read *,man(i),sales(i)
5        if (man(i).eq. 'nobody')go to 10
            total = total + sales(i)
            i = i + 1
            read *,man(i),sales(i)
            go to 5
10       continue
```

Here is part (c) written in Fortran:

```
c        Output salesmen's names and percentages
         print *,'salesman    ','percent'
         i = 1
30       if (man(i).eq. 'nobody')go to 40
            print *,man(i),prcent(i)
            i = i + 1
            go to 30
```

40   **continue**

You are to complete the program without changing parts (a) and (c).

4.   Design and develop a program to handle cash register accounts of purchases in a supermarket. Certain items are taxable, others are not. The cashier enters the amount of the purchase and the status of the purchase: taxable *T* or non-taxable *NT*. Assuming there is a sales tax of 7% on the taxable items, prepare a bill showing the items purchased, the taxable total, the tax, rounded to the nearest cent, and the final total including tax.

5.   Assemble the complete *sort* program incorporating the Shell sorting method and test it on a reasonably long list. How could you test it to see if it is more efficient than the bubble sort method?

6.   Design and write a sorting program that uses the method of **selection**. In this method the list is scanned to find the lowest element. This is placed as the first element of a second list, which will be the sorted list when you are finished. The entry selected is changed in the original list to a dummy entry and the process is repeated until all the entries in the original list are dummy entries. Compare the efficiency of the method of selection with a bubble sort.

7.   Design and write a sorting program that uses the method of **insertion**. In this method the elements of the unsorted list are examined in sequence and inserted into their proper position in a second list, which when you finish will be the sorted list. As each element of the unsorted list is to be inserted you must find out where it belongs and move all higher elements along one position to make room for the insertion to take place.

8.   In this exercise you are to use defensive programming. Modify the following program so that it will handle errors in the data gracefully. The program reads a list of names and outputs the list in reverse order. You have no control over the data, but if you wish, you can add a redundant dummy data entry to the end of the data.

```
        program revrse
c       Print names in reverse order
        character *15 name(10)
        integer size,i
        print *,'Enter length of list'
        read 10,size
10      format (i3)
        print *,'Enter',size,'names one to a line'
```

```
          do 20 i = 1,size
            read *,name(i)
20          continue
          i = size
30        if (i.lt. 1)go to 40
            print *,name(i)
            i = i − 1
            go to 30
40        continue
          stop
          end
```

9.   You are to debug the following program. It is supposed to read strings and determine if they are palindromes. A string is a palindrome if reversing it yields the same string again; for example, each of the following are palindromes: *'mom '*, *'oh ho '*, and *'deed '*. Do **not** submit the corrected program to be run by the computer.

```
          program poor
c         This program is full of bugs
          character *1 string(10),revrse(10)
          character *20 reply
          integer count,i,j,half,r
          print *,'Enter number of strings'
          read *,count
          print *,'test',count,'strings'
          read 10,string
10        format (10a1)
          do 40 i = 1,count
            i = 10
12          if (string(i).eq.' ')go to 13
              i = i − 1
              go to 12
13            continue
          half=i/ 2.0
          r = 1
14          if (i.gt.half)go to 15
              revrse(r) = string(i)
              r = r + 1
              i = i − 1
              go to 14
15            continue
            do 20 j = 1,half
```

```
                         if (string (j).eq. revrse (j))then
                               reply = 'is a palindrome'
                         else
                               reply = 'is not a palindrome'
                         end if
     20                  continue
                   print 30,string,reply
     30            format (' ',10a1,a20)
     40            continue
            stop
            end
```

Here is a desired sample display:

> **Enter number of strings**
> *4*
> **test 4 strings**
> *'deed'*
> **deed is a palindrome**
> *'oh ho '*
> **oh ho is a palindrome**

10. Try to write a program that is completely correct before you submit it to the computer. Have a friend help you by studying your program for errors after you are convinced that it is free of errors. Record the time you spend preparing the program and record any programming errors you make. Your program should perform one of the following tasks:

   (a) The program should read a series of integers followed by the dummy value 99999. Output the sum of the positive integers and the number of negative integers.

   (b) The program should read and output a list of alphabetically ordered names. If a name is repeated in the data, it should be output only once.

11. The following program reads employees' names, hours worked in a week and hourly rates of pay. It computes each employee's pay based on his rate and number of hours, with one and a half times the rate for overtime hours (hours beyond the first 40 hours). Make the program readable by adding appropriate comments, by improving the format, and by choosing meaningful variable names. No other changes to the program are required.

```fortran
        program opaque
c       Has poor identifiers and needs comments
        character *11 b1
        integer b,a,c,b2
        print *,'employee   ','regular hrs','overtime   ','payment'
        read *,b1,a,b
5       if (b1.eq. 'zzz')go to 10
            c = 0
            if (a.gt. 40)then
                c = a - 40
                a = 40
            end if
            b2 = b*(a + 1.5*c) + 0.5
            print *,b1,a,c,b2
            read *,b1,a,b
            go to 5
10          continue
        stop
        end
```

Chapter 10

CONTROLLING INPUT AND OUTPUT

So far we have had one statement for input, the **read** statement, and one statement for output, the **print** statement. These statements were list-directed, or format-free, **read** and **print** statements. These allowed us to read data from the keyboard, or display data on the screen. Often we would like to arrange the format of output in a way that is different from the standard format provided by the list-directed **print** statement. Input has been more flexible; we have been able to accept **real** numbers either in the form without an exponent, such as 25.32, or the form with an exponent, such as 2.532e1. As well, we could arrange the input numbers in any columns of the line that we wanted, as long as each pair of numbers was separated by at least one blank; there were no standard widths for **fields** on the input line as there were on the output line.

In this chapter we will introduce new versions of the **read** and **print** statements that use **format items** to specify exactly how each data item is to be read or output. The **read** and **print** statements that are format-free are easier for the beginning programmer. The fact that they are format-free can be told from the fact that there is an asterisk in the position that is normally occupied by a format identifier. The formatted versions are more complicated, so that input and output can be precisely controlled.

FORMAT DESCRIPTION

Each formatted **read** or **print** statement has associated with it a labelled **format** specification. The label must be a number, the format identifier, that appears just following the word **read** or **print** and is repeated in columns 1 to 5 of the line, which contains the **format** specification, for example,

        print *3,'she bought ',n,' eggs'*

  3   **format** *('1',a11,i2,a5)*

The label 3 must be different from any other label in columns 1 to 5 in the program. If *n* has the value 12 then this is the output:

she bought 12 eggs

In the format specification, the '1' is the **carriage control character** and specifies that the line is to be output on the top of a new page. Carriage control characters are used to control the feeding of lines on a printer. Other carriage control characters will be given in this chapter. There are three format items, *a11, i2* and *a5*. The format item *a11* specifies that *'she bought '* is to be output in 11 positions, then *i2* specifies that 12 is to be output in the next 2 positions and finally *a5* specifies that *' eggs'* is output in the next five positions. Besides *a* format items, for alphabetic information, and *i* format items, for integers, there are others including *e* format items for numbers with exponents. Each data item in a formatted **read** or **print** must have a format item in the corresponding **format** specification. The data items are expressions in the Fortran language, that is, constants, literals, variables, or arithmetic expressions.

Basically, the format items describe the location of the data item on the input or output line, the size of the field that is to be allotted to it, and the form that it is to take if alternate forms are possible. Alternate forms are possible for **real** numbers; as you already know, on input we can use either the exponent form, or the form with a decimal point and no exponent. As a standard parctice we will place the format specification immediately after the **read** or **print** statement that makes reference to it although, in fact, it may be placed anywhere in the program.

OUTPUTTING REAL NUMBERS

The *f* format item lets you avoid outputting exponents with **real** numbers. As well, it allows control over the number of digits output to the right of the decimal point. For example,

> **print** *8, 4/ 3.0, 2/ 3.0*
> 8   **format** *(' ', f10.4, f6.3)*

will output

bbbb1.3333b0.667

We have used *b* to represent a blank. Notice that the 8 is the label and is not a data value. We have used the ' ' (blank) carriage control character, which simply means that a new line is to be output, just like what happens with the format-free **print** statement. The first number after the *f* in each format item gives the total width of the field in which the data is to appear. The second number, after the period, is the number of digits to be output to the right of the decimal point. The fractional parts are rounded off. Note that the numbers are right-justified in their fields and that the decimal point takes up one character position. If a minus sign occurs it also takes a position.

Outputting **real** numbers in this way requires more thought on your part because you must be sure to leave enough room to the left of the decimal point. In the format-free form with the exponent there is always a decimal point and a fixed number of digits to the right.

As an example of the use of the f format item, suppose the dimensions of a box in centimeters are expressed to the nearest hundredth of a centimeter and input as

           10.31   4.25   6.35

and you want the volume to the nearest hundredth of a cubic centimeter. Here is the program for doing this.

```
        program box
        real length,width,height,volume
        print *,'Enter length, width, and height'
        read *,length,width,height
        volume = length*width*height
        print 1,volume
1       format(' ',f14.2)
        stop
        end
```

Here is a sample display:

Enter length, width, and height
10.31 4.25 6.35
bbbbbbbb278.24

We have one format item $f14.2$, as there is only one output data item. The carriage control blank is not shown as a **b**.

The output of **real** numbers can also be controlled in the exponent form. The format-free **print** instruction always outputs the same number of digits to the right of the decimal point; compilers sometimes output nine. This represents about the maximum number of digits that are meaningful or **significant**. Since numbers are stored in memory locations that have a fixed size, only a limited precision is possible in representing them. You might, however, want to output fewer than nine digits to the right of the decimal. Also, you might want to allow fewer total output positions for the entire number. With a format item $e12.3$ you would be allowing a total of 12 character positions for the output and 3 digits to the right of the decimal in the fractional part. For example,

print *7, − 12.3665e1*

7   **format** *(' ',e13.4)*

would produce an output

bbb−.1237e+03

Notice that the number being output is rounded off. The minimum field width must be 7 plus the number of digits to the right of the decimal; this allows for a space, the sign, the decimal point itself, and the four spaces for the exponent. The number is right-justified in its field. Again the carriage control blank is not shown.

OUTPUTTING CHARACTER STRINGS

In the example with the volume of the box we did not include our usual labelling of the results with *volume* =. This was because we have not yet said how to describe the format for a character string. We do this by the format item *aw* where *w* is the width of the field to be allotted to the string. So for our box volume program, if we had used the output statement

print *13,'volume is',volume,' cubic cm'*

13   **format** *(' ',a9,f7.2,a9)*

the output would have been

volume is 278.24 cubic cm

Here we have reduced the size of the field used for outputting the numerical value and allowed character string fields of just the right size to hold the strings that are output. This permits much greater flexibility for making attractive output. When the width *w* given in *aw* is the same as the number of characters in the string to be output we may write it as an *a* without an integer. If *w* is larger than the number of characters in the literal or character variable to be output, the characters are right justified in the field and padded on the left with blanks.

OUTPUTTING INTEGERS

Using the formatted **print** statement requires the specification of the field width for all numbers, whether **integer** or **real**. The format item for **integer**s is *iw* where *w* is the number of character positions allotted to the number. The integer will be right-justified in this field. For example,

```
        print 1,235,26,5261
1       format (' ',i4,i3,i6)
```

will produce the output

b235b26bb5261

CARRIAGE CONTROL CHARACTERS

In Fortran each formatted **print** statement has a carriage control character as first format item in its **format** specification. We have seen that the format item ' ' (blank) causes output to proceed to the next line (just as in the format-free **print** statement) and that '1' causes a new page to be started. The other allowed carriage control characters are '0' (zero) for double spacing between lines and '+' for overprinting. On the display screen overprinting merely wipes out the first line displayed when the second is overlaid. On a printer overprinting can be useful. For example,

```
        print 2,'is O a greek letter '
2       format ('0',a19)
        print 3,' / '
3       format ('+',a4)
```

This causes a line to be skipped before *'is O a greek letter '* is printed. Then, on top of this is printed '/ ' which produces:

is ϕ a greek letter

The '/ ' on top of the 'O' makes a character like the Greek letter phi. Sometimes overprinting using the '+' is used to underline words in a title; first the title is output and then it is overprinted with underscores (_).

Carriage control characters are used in every formatted **print** statement to specify where the line is to be output. They are not used in formatted **read** statements, because reading always proceeds to the next input line.

READING NUMBERS

There is considerable flexibility in the input of **integer** or **real** numbers provided by the format-free **read** statement since the numbers need not occupy any specific fields on the line; **real** numbers can be presented in either the exponent form or simply with a decimal point. There are reasons why you might want to use the formatted **read** statement for numbers. One of these is to insert a decimal point into an integer. This can be done by using an *fw.d* format item. The number of columns allotted to the integer is *w*. It is input right-justified in this field. It would be read into a **real** variable as if there were a decimal point input so as to give *d* of its digits to the right of the point. As an example, suppose that measurements are given in centimeters and we want, on reading, to store the values in meters. We could use

> **read** *4, width*
>
> 4   **format** *(f5.2)*

If the integer 416 was right-justified in the first five columns of the line, it would be read as a real number whose value was 4.16 into the **real** variable *width*.

READING CHARACTER STRINGS

One awkward feature of using the format-free **read** statement is that character strings must be surrounded by quotes. Alphabetic data can be entered without quotes if they are entered consistently in definite fields of the line. They are read using an *aw* format item where *w* indicates the field width. For instance, if names are left-justified in the first 30 columns, addresses in the next 42 columns and an integer code number right-justified in the next 7 columns, the following input statement would be appropriate:

> **read** *4, name, adress, code*
>
> 4   **format** *(a30, a42, i7)*

SKIPPING POSITIONS

Some format items do not correspond to any data items but have the effect of either skipping columns on input or leaving blank positions on output. This is accomplished by writing a format item *nx* where *n* is the number of positions to be skipped. For example, the statement

> **print** *3, 'cost', 'value', 'sales'*
>
> 3   **format** *(' ', 4x, a4, 6x, a5, 5x, a5)*

would give a output line suitable for heading columns. It would be

> bbbb**cost**bbbbbb**value**bbbbb**sales**

In this way you can space headings without having to include all the blanks in the literal itself. Notice that the *x* format items do not cause a data item to be read or output. The carriage control blank (not shown) can also be written as *1x* instead of ' '. Also since the alphabetic items are the same size as the format specification we could had this format specification.

3   **format** *(1x,4x,a,6x,a,5x,a)*

In order to help us enter formatted input data in the right columns a prompt is often given with labels over the correct columns, showing where the data entry is to begin. For example, this sequence might be used:

> **print** *5,'Name','Address','Code999'*
> 5   **format** *(1x,a,26x,a,35x,a)*
> **read** *10,name,adress,code*
> 10   **format** *(1x,a30,a42,i7)*

Because the first position of the prompt output line must be blank we leave a blank in the input data in the first column. This means the name you enter can line up with the *Name* prompt. Notice how the output format uses *a* and *nx* to get the literals on the left of the fields. The code must be entered right justified in its field so we included some 9s after the prompt *Code* to help.

The *x* format item for skipping spaces can not be used to plot a graph of a function if the number of blanks desired before an asterisk is proportional to the height of the curve. This is because *n* must be a constant. We can however use a substring of *n* blanks with the *a* format item. For example, this program will plot a graph of *sin(x)* for *x* between *0* and *pi* at intervals of *pi/ 20*.

```
         program plot
c        Plots sin(x) between 0 and pi
         integer n,i
         real pi,delta,scale
         character *30 blanks
         blanks = '
         parameter (pi = 3.14159)
         delta = pi/ 20
         scale = 30
         do 10 i = 0,20
             n = sin(i * delta) * scale
             print 5,blanks(1: n),'*'
5            format (' ',a,a1)
10           continue
         print *,'Graph of sin(x) between 0 and pi'
         stop
         end
```

Here the scale is chosen so that 30 character positions represent the value 1 which is the maximum value of *sin(x)*.

READING AND OUTPUTTING CHARACTER ARRAYS

Sometimes an entire line is to be read as a unit. If *line* is declared as **character** **80* then a line can be read by:

        read *1,line*
1   **format** *(a80)*

There is a more convenient way to read the line when the program is to inspect various columns. This is done by declaring *line* to be an array of 80 **character*1** elements by the declaration

        character **1 line(80)*

and using the *naw* format item the line can be read by

        read *6,line*
6   **format** *(80a1)*

Here *n* is 80 and *w* is 1 meaning to read 80 single characters into *line*. The first column of the line goes into *line(1)*, the second into *line(2)*, and so on. The input line is automatically padded with blanks if it is not the full 80 characters. Now the program can inspect any column of the line. In this example, column 1 of a Fortran program is inspected:

        if *(line(1).***eq.** *'c')***then**
           print *7,'comment line: ',line*
7   **format** *(' ',a14,80a1)*
        end if

The *n* in *naw* must be the same as the size of the array, in this case 80. The *naw* format item will be used in a later chapter to show how the computer can process text.

CHAPTER 10 SUMMARY

In this chapter we have introduced the formatted **read** and **print** statements. These use format items to give details about how to perform the input-output. The formatted **print** statement has the form:

        print label, variables separated by commas
label   **format**(control, format items separated by commas)

The **label** is a number, repeated in the **print** and **format** parts, that is different from other labels in the program. In the **format** part it must appear in columns 1 to 5. As a normal practice we place the **format** that belongs with a **print** or **read** statement immediately after it although this is not necessary. The **control** is a carriage control character and must be one of the following:

' ' (blank)	— means start a new line.
'1' (one)	— means start a new page.
'0' (zero)	— means double space.
'+' (plus)	— means overprint the last printed line.

List-directed **print** statements always leave a blank at the beginning of the line. Formatted **read** statements are similar to formatted **print** statements but do not include a carriage control character:

> **read** label, variables separated by commas
>
> label   **format**(format items separated by commas)

Variables listed in **read** and **print** statements can be entire arrays. If the array is of one dimension and is indexed starting at 1 it can be read or output by its name without index. If the array has one dimension and is of character type, then the entire array can be read using the *naw* format item. The following format items are available.

Format Item	Example	Explanation
nx	*3x*	Skips the next *n* columns.
iw	*i5*	Outputs or reads an integer in a field of *w* columns.
fw.d	*f6.2*	Outputs or reads a **real** quantity
ew.d	*e12.5*	Outputs or reads a **real** quantity with an exponent using a field of width *w* and *d* digits to the right of the decimal point.
aw	*a5*	Outputs or reads *w* characters.
naw	*80a1*	Outputs or reads *n* sets of *w* characters from or to an array of *n* **character** *w* elements.

Real quantities are rounded before being output.

Numbers read or output by the *i, f,* and *e* format items are right-justified in their fields. The variable or literal that corresponds to *aw* should be *w* characters long. Padding with blanks may be necessary on input. If an end of line occurs on input, blanks are automatically added as required. On output if there are too few characters they are right justified and padded on the left with blanks.

Each variable in a formatted **read** or **print** must correspond to an *i, f, e,* or *a* format item. The *x* format item can precede or be intermixed with *i, f, e,* and *a* items, but must **not** be last in a list of format items.

Here are examples illustrating the use of formatted **read** and **print** statements.

	print *1, 24, 5*	
1	**format** *(' ',i2,3x,i2)*	(outputs **24bbbb5**)
	print *2, 61.248e+00*	
2	**format** *(' ',f7.2)*	(outputs **bb61.25**)
	read *3, line*	
3	**format** *(80a1)*	(reads 80 characters)

The carriage control blank is not shown.

CHAPTER 10 EXERCISES

1. What do the following statements output? Assume *j* is **integer**, *y* is **real**, and *c* is **character** **15.*

	j = 29
	y = 5.427
	c = 'Try formatting'
	print *1,j,y,c*
1	**format** *(' ',1x,i3,f6.2,2x,a14)*
	print *2,c,y*
2	**format** *('0',a14,f6.1)*
	print *3,'___ _____'*
3	**format** *('+',a14)*

2. What do the following statements output? Assume *credit* is an **integer** variable.

	credit = 2154
	print *1,'October credit: ',credit*
1	**format** *(' ',a16,i5)*
	credit = credit − 10000
	print *2,'as updated: ',credit*
2	**format** *(' ',a12,5x,i5)*
	print *3,'you win ',100000000*
3	**format** *('0',a8,i10)*
	print *4,10000*
4	**format** *('0',6x,i6)*
	print *5,credit*
5	**format** *(' ',6x,i6)*

print *6,'____'*
6   **format** *(' ',6x,a6)*
print *7,'total',2154*
7   **format** *('0',a5,1x,i6)*

3. The first five columns of a particular data line contain five digits. Give a formatted **read** statement that reads those five digits into **integer** variables *a, b, c, d,* and *e.*

4. The layout of stock ordering entries for P&A Groceries is:

columns	contents
1-5	stock number
6-12	supplier's name
13-14	month first ordered
15-16	year first ordered
17-27	item name

Give a **read** statement that reads these data into appropriate variables, for example, the stock number and the product name into variables declared by

> **integer** *stock*
> **character** **11 item*

5. Write a program that outputs a calendar. The program should read the day of the week for January 1 and the year. The program can determine whether it is a leap year via the **if...then...else** statement:

> **if** *(mod(year,4)*.**eq.** *0)***then**
>   *feb = 29*
> **else**
>   *feb = 28*
> **end if**

As used here the built-in function *mod* will return a value of zero for years that can be exactly divided by 4. If your program outputs the calendar for the entire year, it will produce 12 pages of output, if it uses one page for each month. You should use less space by making your program read the number of a month and output the calendar only for that one month or by putting several months on one page. Can you get the entire year's calendar on one page?

6. You are to write a program for the First Gibraltar Bank to output monthly statements for checking accounts. Here is a sample monthly statement, the amounts are in cents.

First Gibraltar Bank

Ms. Marie Beyer
2116 Oak Blvd.
Clintonville

for period ended	*account no.*	*date fwd.*	*balance fwd.*
Dec 14,1984	*8881-605223*	*Nov 16*	*114142*

Checks	*Deposits*	*Date*	*Balance*
2000		*Nov 21*	*112142*
1500		*Nov 22*	*110642*
1685		*Nov 25*	*108957*
	84146	*Nov 28*	*193103*
15449		*Dec 08*	*177654*
6012		*Dec 14*	*171642*
			(Final Balance)

Deposits	*1*	*84146*
Checks	*5*	*26646*

This statement was output as a result of reading the following input:

Dec 14,1984
Ms. Marie Beyer
2116 Oak Blvd.
Clintonville
8881-605223
Nov 16 114142
Nov 21   2000
Nov 22   1500
Nov 25   1685
Nov 28   84146cr
Dec 08   15449
Dec 14   6012
xxx 00   0

Your program should read data, such as the above, and output a monthly statement.

7.   Compute values for and plot a graph for x between 0 and 5 of the function

$$y = 100(1 - e^{-x})$$

Chapter 11

SUBPROGRAMS

In this chapter we will be introducing the idea of subprograms. The purpose of having subsidiary programs or subprograms is so that a larger program can be divided into parts. In this way we "divide and conquer" a complicated problem. Sometimes a part of the solution of one problem can be used in different problems, and making it into a subprogram creates a module or building block which can be used in many programs.

DEFINITION OF A SUBPROGRAM

The process of sorting a list alphabetically is a very common one; if we had a subprogram for doing this we might use it frequently. The subprogram must take in certain information, in particular the name of the list of items say *list* and the number of items *n* in the list. It must then give out information, namely the sorted list. We say that the subprogram has two ingoing parameters, *list* and *n*, and one outgoing parameter *list*, the list sorted in alphabetic order. To define a subprogram that will do this we must give it a name, say *sort*, and begin the **subprogram definition** in this way:

subroutine *sort(list, n)*

This gives the keyword **subroutine** followed by the name of the subroutine. In parentheses is a list of the subprogram **parameters**. Some of these are ingoing to the subprogram; some are outgoing from the subprogram. In this case *list* is both an ingoing and an outgoing parameter. Each subprogram must contain declarations for all its parameters. The declarations **must** give the parameter types.

The declaration for the variable *list* must show the length of each element, we choose 30 characters as before; the number of elements in the array *list* may be declared as *n*. We thus have declarations

integer *n*
character *30 list(50)*

As well as these declarations for the parameters of the subprogram we will also declare some variables that are used in the subprogram but are not used outside the subprogram. We will declare integer variables *i* and *last,* the logical variable *sorted*, and character variable *temp*. These are called **local variables**.

Here is the complete definition for the *sort* subprogram:

```
          subroutine sort(list,n)
c         Sorts a list of names
c         Declarations for parameters
          integer n
          character *30 list(n)
c         Declaration for local variables
          integer i,last
          logical sorted
          character *30 temp
c         Swap elements of list until sorted
          sorted = .false.
          last = n
10        if (sorted.or.last.lt.2)go to 35
              sorted = .true.
              do 25 i = 1,last − 1
                  if (list(i).gt.list(i + 1))then
                      sorted = .false.
                      temp = list(i)
                      list(i) = list(i + 1)
                      list(i + 1) = temp
                  end if
25                continue
              last = last − 1
              go to 10
35            continue
          return
          end
```

Subprograms are placed after the main program's **end**. Notice that the keyword **return** precedes the **end** of the subroutine.

USING SUBPROGRAMS

We have just constructed a subprogram for sorting a list alphabetically. Now we must learn how to use this subprogram. You will notice that the reading of the list to be sorted and the output of it after it is sorted are not included in the subprogram. We could now write a main program that will use the *sort* subprogram and handle the input and output. We will read, sort, and output a list of names as we did before.

```
          program order
c         Uses the subprogram sort
          character *30 name(50)
          integer number,i
c         Read number then list of names
          print *,'Enter number of names to be sorted'
          read *,number
          print *,'Enter names one to a line'
          do 5 i = 1,number
              read 3, name(i)
3             format (1x,a20)
5             continue
          call sort(name,number)
c         Output sorted list of names
          print *,'Here is sorted list'
          do 10 i = 1,number
              print 8,name(i)
8             format (' ',a20)
10            continue
          stop
          end
```

(include complete sort subprogram here)

Here is a sample display:

Enter number of names to be sorted
3
Enter names one to a line
Scott, G.D.
Collins, A.
Wentzell, B.
Here is sorted list
Collins, A.
Scott, G.D.
Wentzell, B.

You can see how convenient it is to have a subprogram. The single statement

        call *sort(name,number)*

causes the list *name* to be sorted. In the **call** statement the names inside the parentheses are called **arguments**. The variables *name* and *number* are the arguments to be used in this particular call to the *sort* subroutine.

ARGUMENTS AND PARAMETERS

We have introduced two words in connection with subprograms, the words arguments and parameters. The parameters are the identifiers used in the definition of a subprogram for information that is to be fed into a subprogram or to be given out. Arguments are the expressions (often variables) in the **calling program** that are to be put into correspondence with the subprogram parameters. And there must be a one-to-one correspondence between the number and type of the arguments and the parameters. Sometimes we refer to the parameters as **dummy arguments**.

No space reservations are made for the parameters because the space needed is already reserved in the calling program for the arguments. All references to parameters in a subprogram actually refer to the corresponding argument. This is done by means of **pointers** to the locations that hold the arguments. These pointers are set automatically each time the subprogram is called. When the subprogram is executing, changes to the value of a parameter cause the corresponding argument to be altered. In our example, the argument *name* is in correspondence with the parameter *list* and the argument *number* with the parameter *n*. When the statement

        list(i) = list(i + 1)

of the subprogram is executed, it is equivalent to the statement

        name(i) = name(i + 1)

being executed.

Here is a diagram to show the association between parameters and arguments, and the variables local to the subroutine *sort*.

name $<$ ----- *list*
number $<$ ----- *n*
                    i
                    last
                    sorted
                    temp

Because the parameters of a subprogram are associated with arguments at the time the subprogram is called, it means that a subprogram may be used in the same program with a different set of arguments in another **call** statement. Notice that *i, last, sorted, temp,* the local variables, are ordinary variables in the subprogram and do not refer to any variables in the calling program. These local variables cannot be referenced outside the subprogram. Each time the subprogram is called, these variables must be given values before being used, because their values from any previous calls may be discarded.

It is important in the description of a subroutine to indicate which of its parameters are modified or assigned values by the subroutine. Unless such notification is given, values of parameters should not be altered by the subroutine. In our example, *n* is not altered. The local variable *last* is assigned the value of *n* and *last* is altered.

CONSTANTS AS ARGUMENTS

We will do another simple example to show how constants can be used as arguments. Suppose we write a subprogram that will add the elements of an integer array, *array*, of *n* elements and call the total *sum.* Let us call the subprogram *total.*

```
        subroutine total(array,n,sum)
c       Add the n elements of array
        integer n,sum
        integer array(n)
        integer i
        sum = 0
        do 5 i = 1,n
            sum = sum + array(i)
5           continue
        return
        end
```

Here, as before, the number of elements of *array* is given as *n*. This kind of declaration is possible only in subprograms. Notice that the *n* must be declared as integer before *array* can be declared as having a dimension *n*.

Now let us write a calling program for this. This program finds the gross total for a number of outstanding bills.

```
        program bills
c       Uses subprogram total
        integer bill(5),i,gross
        print *,'Enter 5 integers'
        do 10 i = 1,5
            read *,bill(i)
10          continue
        call total(bill,5,gross)
        print *,'gross = ',gross
        stop
        end
```

(include definition of total subprogram here)

If these data items are placed one to a line

25 36 21 7 2

the output will be

gross= 91

In this example, notice that the argument *bill* is in correspondence with the parameter *array*. References in the subroutine to *array(1)* will point at *bill(1)*. It is essential that the number of elements of the array *bill* be the same as the number of elements of *array*. Since the parameter *n* is given the value 5 the array *bill* must have 5 elements.

When a constant is used as an argument an error will occur if any attempt is made inside the subprogram to modify the value of the corresponding parameter. This means that constants can be used as arguments only with care.

Notice that the same variable identifier *i* is used in the main program and also as a local variable in the subprogram *total*. These are treated as absolutely separate variables. These is no need to worry about accidental coincidences between names of variables. Inside the subprogram, the local one is used exclusively. Outside the subprogram, the one local to the subprogram is not visible. We will show later how it is possible for programs and subprograms to share variables in common.

FUNCTIONS

There are really two kinds of subprograms. The ones we have described so far are called **subroutine subprograms** or subroutines for short. We will now describe a quite different kind of subprogram called a **function subprogram** or **function** for short.

Function subprograms may have many parameters but give as a result a single value. To understand this we will look at a function that we have already been using, the square root function *sqrt*. To use the function we write:

> *sqrt* (number whose square root is wanted)

There is one parameter provided to this function and the function itself provides the result, namely the required square root.

To program a function subprogram ourselves we do exactly what we did for a subroutine subprogram, with two exceptions. Ahead of the name of the function we write **function** preceded by the type (**integer** or **real**) of the value of the function that is returned as a result. Then before the **return** and **end** that terminate the body of the subprogram, we write an assignment statement whose left-hand side is the name of the function and whose right-hand side is an expression whose value is what is to be returned as a result. For example, if we were preparing a function subprogram for the function *sqrt*, it would be of the form

> **real function** *sqrt(number)*
> **real** *number*
> (declarations of variables other than parameter)
> (statements of function subprogram)
> *sqrt* =value to be returned
> **return**
> **end**

This would be the function subprogram definition and would be included after the **end** of the main program. The function *sqrt* is a built-in function; it is already stored in the computer with the Fortran compiler. So there is no need to include its definition.

Another function that is built into the Fortran 77 compiler is one to determine the length of a string of characters. When it is used in the form *len(string)* it returns a value whose type is **integer**. It has just one argument. Unfortunately the function *len* gives us the length of the variable in which the string is stored rather than the actual length of the string. The function *len* is not useful since if *string* is declared as a character string variable of length *n* then the value given by *len* will always be *n*, no matter what is stored in *string*. We would like a function which will tell us the

actual length of the string stored in the variable. We will program a function which we will call *length*. Here is the function subprogram definition:

> **integer function** *length(string,n)*
> (declarations)
> (statements of function subprogram)
> *length* =expression giving value to be returned
> **return**
> **end**

We can program a function to find the actual length of a string provided
one character, such as a blank, is not allowed in the string; we cannot do
it for any string in general. The string for this particular subprogram we
will store as an array of *n* elements each holding one character. The first
non-blank character of the string must be in *string(1)*. Here is a complete
definition for the function subprogram called *length*.

```
        integer function length(string,n)
c       Finds length of string ending with a blank
        integer n
        character *1 string(n)
        integer i
        i = 1
c       Scan string until blank reached
5       if (string(i).eq.' ')go to 10
            i = i + 1
            go to 5
10          continue
        length = i - 1
        return
        end
```

Here is a program that uses the function *length*, so it must include a
declaration specifying *length* to have an **integer** value.

```
        program size
c       Read words and determine their lengths
        integer length
        character *1 word(30)
        print *,'Enter words one to line, end with +'
        read 10,word
10      format (1x,30a1)
15      if (word(1).eq. '+')go to 40
            print 20,length(word,30)
20          format (' ',i2)
            read 30,word
```

```
30              format (30a1)
                go to 15
40              continue
         stop
         end
```

(include *length* subprogram here)

Here is a sample display:

Enter words one to line, end with +
elephant
8
diagram
7
vector
6
+

We could also store a string in a character variable of length 30 and examine the characters of the string one at a time using the substring facility. The subprogram *lenth* uses this:

```
         integer function lenth(string,n)
c        Finds length of string up to first blank
         integer n
         character *n string
         integer i
         i = 1
c        Scan string until blank reached
5        if (string(i: i).eq.' ')go to 10
             i = i + 1
             go to 5
10           continue
         lenth = i - 1
         return
         end
```

The substring *string(i: i)* is the *i*th character of string.

A function should never change the values of any of its parameters; the single value returned by a function is assigned to its name. If you want a subprogram to return more than a single value you should use a subroutine.

The built-in function *index* is useful in finding the actual length of a string; the value of

> *index(string,substring)*

is the position of the first occurrence of the substring in the string. If the substring does not occur in the string the value of *index* is zero. For example,

> *index('million','ill')*

is 2. Here is another length function called *long* that can be used when the *string* is a character variable of length *n*.

```
         integer function long(string,n)
c        Finds length of string up to first blank using index
         integer n
         character *n string
         long = index(string,' ') - 1
         return
         end
```

You will notice that there is only one statement in the body of this function subprogram. We could just use the expression

> *index(' ',string) - 1*

in a program whenever we want the actual length of a string.

EXAMPLES OF SUBROUTINES AND FUNCTIONS

Of the two kinds of subprograms in Fortran: subroutines and functions, subroutines allow you to invent new Fortran statements, while functions allow you to invent new operations. We will give examples of these two. Suppose we wish to determine the larger of two integers.

```
         program max1
         integer data1,data2,maxi
         print *,'Enter two integers'
         read *,data1,data2
         call larger(data1,data2,maxi)
         print *,'the larger is',maxi
         stop
         end


         subroutine larger(first,second,result)
c        Finds the larger of 2 numbers
         integer first,second,result
         if (first.gt.second)then
             result = first
         else
```

```
        result = second
    end if
    return
    end
```

When the *larger* subroutine is called, via the statement

call *larger(data1, data2, maxi)*

the parameter *first* is in correspondence with *data1*, *second* with *data2*, and *result* with *maxi*. The *larger* subroutine is entered and *result* is set to the larger of *first* and *second*. What actually happens is that maxi is set to the larger of *data1* and *data2*. When the *larger* subroutine reaches its **return** statement, execution returns to the statement just beyond the **call** statement, which is the **print** statement. Given the data values 5 and 31, the program will output

the larger is 31

Conceptually, our subroutine provides us with a new Fortran statement which we can use whenever we want to find the larger of two numbers. This has been a very simple example; if you were writing such a simple program as this one you would not bother to use a subprogram.

We could have found the larger number by writing a function rather than a subroutine. A function named *bigger* is used in the following.

```
    program max2
    integer bigger
    integer data1,data2,maxi
    print *,'Enter two integers'
    read *,data1,data2
    maxi = bigger(data1,data2)
    print *,'the larger is',maxi
    stop
    end

    integer function bigger(first,second)
c   Returns the bigger of 2 numbers
    integer first,second
    if (first.gt.second)then
        bigger = first
    else
        bigger = second
    end if
    return
    end
```

With input data 5 and 31 this will output the same as before:

the larger is 31

The *bigger* subprogram is a function because it has a type, namely **integer**, in its definition. This type must also be declared in the main program. The name *bigger* appears in the first **integer** declaration. Since *bigger* is a function, it must explicitly return a value. This is done by giving *bigger* a value as is done in either

$$bigger = first \quad \text{or} \quad bigger = second$$

The *bigger* function is entered as a result of the fact that its name appears in the assignment statement:

$$maxi = bigger(data1, data2)$$

When the *bigger* function is entered, the parameter *first* is in correspondence with *data1* and *second* with *data2*. Then *bigger* is given the value of the larger of *first* and *second*. The statement,

return

both terminates the *bigger* function and returns the value of *bigger* so it can be assigned to *maxi*. Conceptually, our function provides us with a new arithmetic operation which we can use in arithmetic expressions. We could without changing the answer output have replaced the assignment to *maxi* and the immediately following **print** statement by the statement

print *, 'the larger is ', bigger(data1, data2)*

Our example subprograms *larger* and *bigger* illustrate the following differences between subroutines and functions. The definition of a function must include the type of the function both in the main program and in the first line of the function definition, a subroutine does not have any type.

The returned value for a function must match the type of the function. A subroutine is entered when it is invoked via the **call** statement. A function is entered when its name appears in an expression, such as the right-hand side of an assignment statement.

SUBPROGRAMS AND NESTING

Once a subroutine has been defined, it can be used, via the **call** statement, just like any other Fortran statement. It is even possible to use **call** statements inside subprograms. We will give simple examples to illustrate this. The following job outputs the largest of three values.

```
        program best
c       Outputs the largest of its data items
        integer data1,data2,data3,maxi
        print *,'Enter three integers'
        read *,data1,data2,data3
        call largst(data1,data2,data3,maxi)
        print *,'the largest is',maxi
        stop
        end


        subroutine larger(first,second,result)
c       Finds the larger of 2 numbers
        (exactly as previous version of larger subroutine)
        return
        end


        subroutine largst(first,second,third,result)
c       Finds the largest of 3 numbers
        integer first,second,third,result
        integer greatr
        call larger(first,second,greatr)
        call larger(greatr,third,result)
        return
        end
```

With input data 5 31 27 this will output

the largest is 31

The subroutine named *largst* determines which of its first three parameters is largest and assigns the largest value to its fourth parameter, named *result.* It accomplishes this by first using *larger* to assign the larger of the first two parameters to the variable *greatr,* and by using *larger* again to assign the larger of *greatr* and the third parameter to *result.*

The subroutines *larger* and *largst* both have parameters named *first* and *second.* This causes no trouble because the parameters of *larger* are hidden from *largst* and vice versa. As a rule it is good programming practice to avoid duplicate names, as they may confuse people reading a program. However, in some cases, such as this example, it seems natural to repeat names in separate subprograms. Since duplicate names in separate subprograms are kept separate in Fortran, this causes no difficulty.

We will now show an example of nesting calls to our *bigger* function. We will use it in the following program to output the largest of three numbers.

```
      program tops
c     Outputs the largest of 3 data items
      integer bigger
      integer data1,data2,data3
      print *,'Enter three integers'
      read *,data1,data2,data3
      print *,'Largest is',bigger(bigger(data1,data2),data3)
      stop
      end


      integer function bigger(first,second)
c     Returns the bigger of 2 numbers
      (definition as before)
      return
      end
```

The input data is the same as before namely

> 5   31   27.

This program finds the larger of the first two data items using the *bigger* function, and uses the *bigger* function again to compare that value to the third data value. In the **print** statement, the first argument to the *bigger* function is actually another call to the *bigger* function. This causes no trouble, because the inner call to *bigger* first returns 31, which is the larger of 5 and 31. Then the outer call to *bigger* compares 31 to 27 and returns the value. Using a call to *bigger* inside a call to *bigger* is actually no more complicated than, say,

> *((5 + 31) + 27)*

This expression means add 5 and 31 and add 27 to the result. By comparison,

> *bigger(bigger(5,31),27)*

means find the larger of 5 and 31 and then find the larger of this and 27.

In Fortran it is illegal for a subprogram to contain a call to itself. A program that does this is said to be a **recursive** program. Recursive programs are not legal in Fortran. Note that the *bigger* subprogram does not call itself. Some implementations of Fortran 77 may permit recursive programs.

MATHEMATICAL FUNCTIONS

We have been using the built-in mathematical functions *sqrt, sin, cos, exp, alog,* and so on. It is possible to create some of our own. There is no built-in function for calculating the cube root of a number although we could do it by using *alog* and *exp.* The cube root of *number,* a real variable, is given by:

$$exp(alog(number)/ 3)$$

We can produce a function for the cube root which we will call *cubert* using Newton's method of iteration. As an initial guess x_0 we use the number divided by 3 then successive approximations are obtained from the formula

$$x_{j+1} = (2x_j + number/x_j^2)/3$$

Here is the function subprogram

```
        real function cubert(number)
c       Compute the cube root of number
        real number,next,prev
c       Initialize the values of prev and next
        prev = 0
        next = number/ 3
10      if (abs(next − prev).lt. 1e − 3) go to 20
            prev = next
            next = (2*prev + number/ prev**2)/ 3
            go to 10
20          continue
        cubert = next
        return
        end
```

Newton's method for obtaining the square root of a number by successive approximation uses as a starting approximation the number divided by 2 and the recursion formula

$$x_{j+1} = (x_j + number/x_j)/2$$

MATHEMATICAL SUBROUTINES

There are many subroutine programs that are not built into the Fortran compiler but are available from libraries of subroutines. We will show how you might design some subroutines of your own to handle matrices. We will program three subroutines called *inmat, mltmat,* and *outmat* which will read in a matrix, multiply two matrices, and output a matrix.

The program *inmat* reads a matrix called *matrix,* with *n* rows and *m* columns of real values, a row at a time. We say it is an $n \times m$ matrix.

```
        subroutine inmat(matrix,n,m)
c       Reads in matrix row at a time
        real matrix(n,m)
        integer i,j
        do 20 i = 1,n
            do 10 j = 1,m
                read *,matrix(i,j)
10          continue
20      continue
        return
        end
```

A shorter version of *inmat* can be programmed using implied **do** loops.

```
        subroutine inmat(matrix,m,n)
c       Reads in matrix row at a time
        real matrix(m,n)
        integer i,j
        read *,((matrix(i,j),j = 1,m),i = 1,n)
        return
        end
```

The subroutine *outmat* is similar

```
        subroutine outmat(matrix,n,m)
c       Outputs matrix one element to a line, row at a time
        real matrix(n,m)
        integer i,j
        do 20 i = 1,n
            print *,'This is row number',i
            do 10 j = 1,m
                print *,matrix(i,j)
10          continue
20      continue
        return
        end
```

If two matrices, A of dimension $n \times k$ and B dimensions $k \times m$, are multiplied they produce a matrix C of dimensions $n \times m$. The element $C(i,j)$ or C_{ij} is given by

$$C_{ij} = \sum_{p=1}^{k} A_{ip} B_{pj}$$

Here is the *mltmat* subroutine:

```
          subroutine mltmat(A,B,C,n,k,m)
c         Multiplies matrix A by matrix B to give matrix C
          integer n,k,m
          real A(n,k),B(k,m),C(n,m)
          integer i,j,p
          real sum
          do 30 i = 1,n
              do 20 j = 1,m
                  sum = 0
                  do 10 p = 1,k
                      sum = sum + A(i,p)*B(p,j)
10                continue
                  C(i,j) = sum
20            continue
30        continue
          return
          end
```

Here is a main program which uses these three subroutines to read in a matrix *mat1* of dimensions 4×6 and *mat2* of dimensions 6×3 to produce the product matrix *prod* of dimensions 4×3 and output it.

```
          program mult
          real mat1(4,6),mat2(6,3),prod(4,3)
          print *,'Enter first matrix, row at a time, one element to a line'
          call inmat(mat1,4,6)
          print *,'Enter second matrix row at a time, one element to a line'
          call inmat(mat2,6,3)
          call mltmat(mat1,mat2,prod,4,6,3)
          print *,'Here is the product matrix, row at a time'
          call outmat(prod,4,3)
          stop
          end
```
          (Copy subroutines *inmat,outmat,mltmat* here.)

RANDOM NUMBERS

Many high-level languages like Fortran have built into them functions for producing random numbers uniformly distributed between 0 and 1. The numbers are not really random; they are pseudo-random numbers. You begin with the first number, the seed, then each time the function is called it produces the next number in the pseudo-random sequence. The algorithm for generating the sequence is often

$$n_{i+1} = (a*n_i + c)\,mod\,m$$

where the numbers, a, c, and m are chosen to produce a reasonably long sequence before the squence starts to repeat. If the sequence produces a number that is the same as any previously produced number, it will cycle. We will choose these values

$$a = 25173$$
$$c = 13849$$
$$m = 2^{16} = 65536$$

The numbers produced by these values will be integers between 0 and 100000. We will have to divide by 100000 to produce numbers between 0 and 1. Here is a function called *randu* that will produce uniformly distributed random numbers

```
real function randu(seed)
integer seed
seed = mod((25173*seed + 13849), 65536)
randu = seed/65536.
return
end
```

We must start the pseudo-random sequence of numbers by setting the value of the seed. A different seed will produce a different sequence. The seed should be an odd integer between 0 and 65536.

Here is a program which uses the function *randu* to simulate the roll of a dice. The result will be an integer between 1 and 6 where each result is equally probable. It will roll 20 times. Try it with different seeds.

```
       program dice
       integer seed,roll,i
       print *,'Enter seed between 0 and 65536'
       read *,seed
       do 10 i = 1,20
            roll = randu(seed)*6 + 1
            print *,'You rolled a',roll
10          continue
       stop
       end
       (Include definition of function randu here)
```

Note that by multiplying the random number between 0 and 1 by 6, adding 1, and assigning it to an integer variable will produce integer values between 1 and 6.

VARIABLES IN COMMON

So far we have indicated that with subprograms there is a one-to-one correspondence between the arguments given in the calling statement and the parameters, or dummy arguments, given in the definition of the subprogram. Arguments and parameters in correspondence must be of the same type. Arrays that are in correspondence must have the same type and dimensions although the dimensions may be passed in as a parameter. Corresponding strings must be of the same length although the length may be passed in as a parameter. Variables in the calling program other than the arguments are not accessible to the subprogram. Variables in the subprogram other than the parameters are not accessible to the calling program. Communication between program and subprogram is only through the argument-parameter list.

There is another way for programs to communicate which is not strictly approved in structured programming; it is done through special areas of storage called **common**. When variables are placed in the **common** storage they may be made accessible to two, or more, programs. To accomplish this we must include, as well as the type declarations, a definition of variables to be held in **common**. We will give the area in **common** a name; we say that it is labelled. The form of the **common** definition that must appear in each program that shares the variables is

common/ name/ list of variables

When two subprograms share variables in **common** the definition of them must appear in the main program as well as in each subprogram that uses the variables. Corresponding lists are usually identical lists of variables but you can use different names in the different programs that share the variables in common as long as there is a strict one-to-one correspondence similar to the parameter-argument correspondence. You can have as many different labelled blocks of **common** as needed.

We will now show an example in which a program calls two different subprograms. One block of **common** named *grades* is shared by all three; a second block called *width* is shared by the main program and the subroutine called *range*. The subroutines have no parameters because all communication is through the **common** blocks. Each subroutine has a single local integer variable with the identifier *i*. In giving the declarations for a subprogram the sequence to be followed is

    declaration of parameters
    declaration of function names called by the subprogram
    declaration of blocks in **common**
    declaration of local variables

The purpose of the example program with its subprograms is to read a list of students' names and marks, and output those which fall within a certain letter grade. In the example we are outputting all students that got a D grade mark.

```
        program place
c       List students with particular marks
        common/ grades/ pupil,mark,size
        character *25 pupil(40)
        integer mark(40),size
        common/ width/ maxi,mini
        integer maxi,mini
        character *1 letter
c       Read letter grade and its numeric range
        print *,'Enter letter grade and range'
        read *,letter,mini,maxi
c       Read names, marks and determine class size
        call input
        print *,'Students with letter grade',letter
c       Output names of students with the grade
        call range
        stop
        end


        subroutine input
c       Input students' names and marks
        common/ grades/ pupil,mark,size
        character *25 pupil(40)
        integer mark(40),size
        integer i
        i = 1
        print *,'pupil','          ', 'mark'
        read *,pupil(i),mark(i)
5       if (pupil(i).eq. 'zzz')go to 6
            i = i + 1
            read *,pupil(i),mark(i)
            go to 5
6           continue
        size = i - 1
        return
        end
```

```
         subroutine range
c        Output names having marks in given range
         common/ grades/ pupil,mark,size
         character *25 pupil(40)
         integer mark(40),size
         common/ width/ maxi,mini
         integer maxi,mini
         integer i
         do 10 i = 1,size
              if (mark(i).ge.mini.and.mark(i).le.maxi)then
                   print *,pupil(i),mark(i)
              end if
10            continue
         return
         end
```

Here is a sample display:

Enter letter grade and range
'D' 50 59

pupil	mark
'Alexander, Stephen'	*84*
'Bliss, Michael'	*52*
...	
'zzz'	*0*

Student with letter grade D
Bliss, Michael   **52**

...

In this example the division of the program into subprograms seems somewhat artificial but modular programming, namely dividing larger programs into parts, can simplify the work. Communication through **common** blocks is used in modular programming when the number of variables shared becomes too large to be cited in a parameter list in a calling statement. It is probably best to avoid the use of common variables.

CHAPTER 11 SUMMARY

In this chapter we have introduced subprograms. Subprograms allow us to build up programs out of modules. The reasons for using subprograms in programs include the following:

1. Dividing the program into parts which can be written by different people.

2.   Dividing a program into parts which can be written over a period of time.

3.   Making a large program easier to understand by building it up out of conceptually simple parts.

4.   Factoring out common parts of a program so they need not be written many times within a program.

5.   Factoring out commonly-used logic so that it can be used in a number of different programs.

6.   Separating parts of a program so they can be individually tested.

There are two kinds of subprograms in Fortran: subroutines and functions. Essentially, a subroutine provides a new kind of Fortran statement and a function provides a new kind of operation. The following important terms were discussed in this chapter.

Subprogram definition — means giving the meaning of a subprogram to the computer. Subprogram definitions come just after the **end** of the main program. Subroutine subprograms can be defined using the following form:

> **subroutine** name(parameters)
> declarations for parameters
> declarations for variables for this subprogram
>
> ...
>
> **return**
> **end**

Function subprograms can be defined using the following form:

> type **function** name(parameters)
> declarations for parameters
> declarations for variables for this subprogram
>
> ...
>
> name = expression
> **return**
> **end**

If a subroutine has no parameters, the parameters and their enclosing parentheses are omitted. Often there are no parameters when the subroutine shares variables in **common** with other subprograms or the main program. Functions must have at least one parameter and must be declared as **integer** or **real** in each calling program.

Subprogram name — follows the rules for variable identifiers. Names for subprograms are limited to 6 characters.

Calling a subprogram (invoking a subprogram) — causing a subprogram to be executed. A subroutine subprogram is called by a statement of the form

>   **call** subroutine name (arguments)

If the subroutine has no parameters, then the arguments with their enclosing parentheses are omitted. A function subprogram is called by using its name, followed by a parenthesized list of arguments, in an expression. It must have at least one argument. The types of corresponding arguments and parameters must agree.

Returning from a subprogram — terminating the execution of a subprogram and passing control back to the calling place. When the end of a subroutine is reached, there is a return to the statement just beyond the calling statement. A function subprogram must return a value by assigning a value to its name. This assignment statement followed by **return** terminates the function and causes the returned value assigned to the name to be used in the expression containing the function call. The **return** need not be just before the **end**.

Arguments — A call to a subprogram can pass it arguments. For example, in the statement

>   **call** *sort(name,number)*

the arguments are *name* and *number*. If an argument is a constant an error will result if any attempt is made within the subprogram to alter the value of the corresponding parameter.

Parameters (sometimes called dummy arguments) — Inside a subprogram, the arguments for each call are referred to via parameters. All parameters must be declared in a subprogram. There must be a one-to-one correspondence between the arguments and the parameters.

common — blocks of variables may be shared between two subprograms or between the main program and a subprogram by putting a definition of the form

>   **common**/ name/ list of variables
>   declarations of variables

in each of the sharing programs and the main program. The name is the same and the list of variables is usually the same. The use of common blocks should be avoided as much as possible so that program modules are more independent of each other.

CHAPTER 11 EXERCISES

1.   What does the following program output?

```
program abslut
integer mag
integer i
do 10 i = 1,10
    print *,mag(i − 6)
10      continue
stop
end


integer function mag(value)
integer value
if (value.ge. 0)then
    mag = value
else
    mag = − value
end if
return
end
```

Compare the results with those obtained by using the built-in function *abs*.

2.   What does the following program output?

```
program wether
real temp(31),rain(31)
integer day,time
read *,time
do 5 day = 1,time
    read *,temp(day),rain(day)
5       continue
print *,'average temperature:'
call avrage(temp,time)
print *,'average rainfall:'
call avrage(rain,time)
stop
end


subroutine avrage(array,count)
integer count
real array(count)
integer i
```

```
        real sum
        sum = 0.
        do 8 i = 1,count
            sum = sum + array(i)
8           continue
        print *,sum / count
        stop
        end
```

Here is sample input data:

```
    4
    45.0    0.
    47.2    0.
    48.0    .3
    47.5    2.1
```

3. Design a function like *length* given in this chapter to find the length of the first word on a line assuming that it may or may not have blanks in front of it. Also try the built-in function *len*.

4. Read words placed one to a line and join them into lines of not more than 80 characters for output. Arrange that there is one blank between each word. You may use the function *length* developed in the previous problem if you like.

5. Eliminate the first word from a line of text and output the remaining text.

6. Write a subroutine that sorts an array of names into alphabetical order by a different method than the ones shown in this book. For example, your subroutine could be used in the following program.

```
        program system
        character *20 worker(50)
        integer i
        do 5 i = 1,50
            read *,worker(i)
5           continue
        call sort(worker,50)
        do 10 i = 1,50
            print *,worker(i)
10          continue
        stop
        end
```

```
subroutine sort(name,count)
integer count
character *20 name(50)
(you can write this part)
return
end
```

Data is a list of 50 employees' names, each in quotes, one to a line.

7. Design a subroutine for determining the roots of a quadratic equation of the form $ax^2 + bx + c = 0$.

8. Without having any arguments or parameters, but by making use of a **common** block, design a subroutine to eliminate punctuation marks from a line of text of length 80 characters.

9. Write a function subprogram called *sroot* using Newton's method of successive approximation and compare the values obtained with those obtained using the built-in function *sqrt*.

10. Write a subroutine called *stats* that will accept an array of real numbers x of length n and produce their mean and variance. The mean and variance are given by

    $$\text{mean} = \left[\sum_{i=1}^{n} x_i \right] / n$$

    $$\text{variance} = \left[\sum_{i=1}^{n} (x_i - mean)^2 \right] / n$$

    The subroutine would be invoked by a statement of the type:

    call *stats(x,n,mean,var)*

    Is there a better expression for the variance?

11. Write a subroutine that finds the median of an array of integers. The median is defined as the value that half of the integers are less than. You may want to call another subroutine to sort the array of integers and then find the one half way down in the list.

12. Write a program to simulate the result of rolling two dice 200 times. Keep a histogram (or frequency distribution) of the results in an array called *result* which has eleven entries corresponding to the results 2 to 12. Compute the fraction of rolls in each category. How do these results compare with the theoretical values of the probabilities of the different results?

13. A particle moves randomly back and forth along a line. In a given time interval there is an equal probability of it moving 1 unit to the left or to the right. Simulate this one-dimensional random walk for 100 time units and find the final distance from the starting point. Repeat the simulation a number of times. Call the *stats* program of exercise 10 to find the mean and variance of the results of the simulation experiment.

14. The area under the curve $y = f(x)$ between $x = a$ and $x = b$ can be found be evaluating the function at a number of points chosen at random in the interval, taking their mean and multiplying it by *(b-a)*. Write a program to use this method of evaluating the area under $y=3x^2-2x+1$ between $x=0$ and $x=1$. This is not a particularly efficient method of integrating numerically.

15. Random numbers x from an exponential distribution with a given mean can be generated from uniformly distributed random numbers u using the transforation

$$x = -\text{ mean } *alog(u)$$

Write a function to produce exponentially distributed random numbers with a given mean.

16. Random numbers from a standard normal distribution can be obtained by generating twelve uniform random numbers, adding them, and subtracting 6 from the sum. Write a function program that produces such random numbers. This method depends on the central limit theorem.

17. Write a program that will deal cards for a game such as blackjack. We will only be dealing about 10 cards for each game. Generate the card to be dealt next using *randu* to pick a suit then a value from 1 to 13. Keep track of whether or not a card has been dealt by keeping a (13×4) two-dimensional array. Set the elements of the array initially to zero then as cards are dealt change the element corresponding to the dealt card to a 1.

18. A random number from a uniform distribution between 0 and 1 is obtained by using a function such as *randu*. This is sometimes called a rectangular distribution. A random number from a triangular distribution, where the probability of the number between 0 and 1 grows linearly as you go from 0 to 1, can be obtained by generating two numbers from a rectangular distribution and chosing the smaller of the two. Write a function subprogram called *trian* which uses *randu* to generate random numbers from a triangular distribution.

19. Write a program that uses the *randu* function developed in this chapter to generate integers uniformly distributed between 1 and 10. Generate 100 such numbers and see how they are actually distributed.

20. Write a program that uses the *randu* function to generate a number between 1 and 99 then lets you see if you can guess the number it has generated. Have it give clues after each guess you make such as "Much too high" or "Very close but still too small".

21. Write a subroutine to find the largest element in a matrix and by interchanging rows and columns of the matrix bring the element to the upper left-hand corner. Have the subroutine use two other subroutines to switch rows and columns.

Chapter 12

SCIENTIFIC CALCULATIONS

Computers were originally developed with scientific and engineering calculations in mind. This is because many scientific and engineering calculations are so long that it is not practical to do them by hand, even with the help of a calculator. Fortran as a language was developed to do scientific calculations; it has in Fortran 77 been extended so that we can handle character string variables. You will see that the ability to handle character variables is very helpful when it comes to plotting graphs of scientific data. We have been giving scientific and engineering examples throughout this book as examples of the programming constructs. In this chapter we will gather a few considerations about scientific calculations that have not yet been summarized.

Often the scientific laws describing a physical situation are known in the form of equations, but these equations must be solved for the situation of interest. We may be designing a bridge or aircraft or an air-conditioning system for a building. A computer can be used to calculate the details of the particular situation.

Another important use of computers in science is to find equations that fit the data produced in experiments. These equations then serve to reduce the amount of data that must be preserved. Science as a word means knowledge. The object of scientific work is to gather information about the world and to systematize it so that it can be retrieved and used in the future. There is such a large amount of research activity now in science that we are facing an **information explosion**. We have talked about retrieving information from a **data bank** and computers will undoubtedly help us in this increasingly difficult and tedious job. But the problem of **data reduction** is of equal importance.

In this chapter we will try to give some of the flavor of scientific calculations. We will give only an overview of this important use of computers. In the next chapter we will present more details and applications of scientific calculations.

EVALUATING FORMULAS

To solve certain scientific problems we must substitute values into formulas and calculate results. For example, we could be asked to calculate the distance traveled by a falling object after it is dropped from an airplane. A formula that gives the distance d in meters traveled in time t seconds, neglecting air resistance, is

$$d = 4.9\, t^2$$

here the constant 4.9 is one-half the acceleration due to gravity. Here is a program to compute the distance at the end of each second of the first 10 seconds after the drop:

```
        program fall
c       Output table of distance fallen versus time
        real meters,time
        integer i
        time = 0.0
c       Label time— distance table
        print *,'time              distance'
        do 10 i=1,10
            time = time + 1.0
            meters = 4.9*time**2
            print 5,time,meters
5           format (' ',e15.9,e15.9)
10          continue
        stop
        end
```

The output for this program is

time	distance
.100000000e+01	.489999962e+01
.200000000e+01	.195999985e+02
.300000000e+01	.440999985e+02
.400000000e+01	.783999939e+02
.500000000e+01	.122499992e+03
.600000000e+01	.176399994e+03
.700000000e+01	.240099976e+03
.800000000e+01	.313599976e+03
.900000000e+01	.396899963e+03
.100000000e+02	.489999969e+03

This example outputs a table of values of *meters* for different times. Preparation of tables is an interesting and historic scientific use of computers. Scientific calculations are usually done using **real** variables. In the output the distances and times are output with nine digits in the significant digits part. Not all these digits are really **significant**; the constant in the formula is only expressed with two digits. We must realize then that only about two digits of the distance traveled are significant.

The calculations are carried out in the computer keeping 9 digits, but this does not imply that they are meaningful. Even if the constant in the formula were entered to 9-digit **precision**, we would not necessarily have 9 significant digits in the answer. Because computers represent **real** numbers only to a limited precision, there are always what are called numerical errors. These are not mistakes you make but are inherent in the way that **real** numbers are represented in the computer. When two **real** numbers are multiplied, the product is rounded off to the same precision as the original numbers; no more digits in the product would be significant. As calculations proceed, the rounding process can erode the significance even of some of the digits that are maintained. We usually quote numerical errors by saying that a value is, for example,

$$19.25 \pm 0.05$$

This means that the value could be as high as 19.30 or as low as 19.20. If the error were greater, say 0.5 instead of 0.05, then the values could range between 19.75 and 18.75. In this case the fourth digit in the value is certainly not significant, and you would say instead that the value was

$$19.2 \pm 0.5$$

Or we might round it off instead of truncating the insignificant digit, and write

$$19.3 \pm 0.5$$

The estimation of errors is an important job that is done by **numerical analysts**. If you are doing numerical calculations, you should be aware of the fact that answers are not exact but have errors.

GRAPHING A FUNCTION

Frequently a better understanding of a scientific formula can be had if you draw a graph of the function. In the first example of this chapter we evaluated a function at regular intervals. It is possible to use these values to plot a graph on the display screen. We could, for instance, plot a distance-time graph for the falling object. We will show one way to plot a graph on the screen, but there are lots of other ways.

When you draw a graph of x versus y you usually make the x-axis horizontal and have the y-axis vertical. The values of x, which is the independent variable, increase uniformly; the corresponding values of y

are obtained by substituting x into the function $y = f(x)$.   When we plot a graph on the screen the lines of output are uniformly spaced, so we will use the distance between lines to represent the uniform interval between the xs. This means that the x-axis will be vertical and the y-axis hor- izontal. Here is a graph for $y = x^2 - x - 2$ plotted between the values $x = -2$ and $x = 3$:

```
GRAPH OF Y VERSUS X
MINIMUM OF Y        -.224000000e+01
MAXIMUM OF Y         .400000000e+01
-.20000e+01                             I                                    *
-.18000e+01                             I                              *
-.16000e+01                             I                          *
-.14000e+01                             I                     *
-.12000e+01                             I        *
-.10000e+01                          *
-.80000e+00                   *         I
-.60000e+00                *            I
-.40000e+00             *               I
-.20000e+00          *                  I
 .00000e+00        *                    I
 .20000e+00      *                      I
 .40000e+00     *                       I
 .60000e+00     *                       I
 .80000e+00      *                      I
 .10000e+01        *                    I
 .12000e+01          *                  I
 .14000e+01           *                 I
 .16000e+01              *              I
 .18000e+01                 *           I
 .20000e+01                             *
 .22000e+01                             I    *
 .24000e+01                             I         *
 .26000e+01                             I             *
 .28000e+01                             I                  *
 .30000e+01                             I                              *
```

We represent the y-value corresponding to the x of a particular output line by outputting an asterisk in the column that approximates its value. We use 51 columns to output the range of ys. If the lowest y- value that we must represent is *ymin* and the highest is *ymax*, then the 51 columns must represent a range of

$$yrange = ymax - ymin$$

To find the column for a value y we compute an integer variable *yprint* from

$$yprint = 50 * (y - ymin) / yrange + 1.5$$

The value 1.5 is added to round to the nearest integer and put *ymin* in the first position. We are assuming *yrange* is not zero so that we can divide by it.

We use an array of single characters called *line* to hold each line of the graph to be output. First, all the characters of *line* are set to be blanks. Next, we put an *x*-axis on our graph if it is in the proper range. To do this we place a capital *I* into the line of blanks at the position where a zero value of *y* would be placed. Here is the program segment for putting in the capital *I* for the *x*-axis.

```
xaxis = 50*(0 - ymin)/ yrange + 1.5
if (xaxis.gt. 1.and.xaxis.le. 51) then
     line(xaxis) = 'I'
end if
```

Before outputting the line we place an asterisk in position *yprint*. After outputting the line we must replace the asterisk by a blank. If the asterisk was on the *x*-axis, we must again mark the *x*-axis using a capital I. Here is the program segment for doing this.

```
     line(yprint) = '*'
     print 20,x(i),line
20   format(' ',e12.5,51a1)
     if (yprint.eq.xaxis) then
          line(yprint) = 'I'
     else
          line(yprint) = ' '
     end if
```

We do not output a *y*-axis, but we list the *x*-values corresponding to each line opposite the line.

A SUBROUTINE FOR PLOTTING GRAPHS

Here is the complete subroutine for plotting a graph from n pairs of **real** values of x and y stored in arrays of those names. The values of x are uniformly spaced. The actual names of the variables to be plotted will be given as arguments *xname* and *yname*, which are character variables. The calling statement would be of the form *call graph(x,y,n,xname,yname)*

We will call a subroutine to find *ymax* and *ymin*. It will be called *minmax*.

```
          subroutine graph(x,y,n,xname,yname)
c         Plot a graph
          integer n
          real x(n),y(n)
          character *8 xname,yname
          character *1 line(51)
          real ymin,ymax,yrange
          integer column,xaxis,yprint, i
c         Find range of y to be plotted
          call minmax(y,n,ymin,ymax)
          yrange = ymax − ymin
c         Clear line to blanks
          do 10 column=1,51
              line(column) = ' '
10            continue
c         Place x-axis mark in line
          xaxis = 50*(0 − ymin)/ yrange + 1.5
          if (xaxis.ge. 1.and.xaxis.le. 51) then
              line(xaxis) ='I'
          end if
c         Label the graph
          print *,'GRAPH OF ',yname,'VERSUS',xname
          print *,'MINIMUM OF ',yname,ymin
          print *,'MAXIMUM OF ',yname,ymax
c         Prepare and output lines of graph
          do 30 i=1,n
              yprint = 50*(y(i) − ymin)/ yrange + 1.5
              line(yprint) ='*'
              print 20,x(i),line
20            format(' ',e12.5,51a1)
              if (yprint.eq.xaxis) then
                  line(yprint) ='I'
              else
                  line(yprint) =' '
              end if
30            continue
          return
          end
```

```
        subroutine minmax(number,n,min,max)
c       Find smallest and largest values in array
        integer n
        real number(n),min,max
        integer i
        min = number(1)
        max = number(1)
        do 10 i = 2,n
            if (number(i).lt. min) then
                min = number(i)
            end if
            if (number(i).gt. max) then
                max = number(i)
            end if
10          continue
        return
        end
```

USING THE GRAPH SUBROUTINE

We will now give the program that was used to plot the function of x,

$$y = x^2 - x - 2$$

between the values $x = -2$ to $x = 3$. We plot it at intervals of x that are 0.2 wide. There are 26 points in all. Here is the program:

```
        program plot
c       Plot the function y = x*x - x - 2
        real x(26),y(26)
        integer i
c       Compute values for x and y arrays
        do 10 i=1,26
            x(i)=-2.0 + (i - 1)*0.2
            y(i)=x(i)*x(i) - x(i) - 2.0
10          continue
        call graph (x,y,26,'X    ','Y    ')
        stop
        end
```

(include here the graph and minmax subroutines)

The output for this program was shown earlier in this chapter. You will notice that as the graph crosses the x-axis the capital *I* is replaced by an asterisk. It crosses twice, at

$$x = -1.0$$
$$x = +2.0$$

We say that $x = -1$ and $x = 2$ are the roots of the equation

$$x^2 - x - 2 = 0$$

The function $(x^2 - x - 2)$ becomes zero at these values of x. This graphical method is one way of finding the roots of an equation. We will look later in this chapter at another way of finding roots that is numerical rather than graphical.

FITTING A CURVE TO A SET OF POINTS

In the last sections we have seen how to compute a set of points of corresponding x and y values from a formula and then to plot a graph of these points. In some scientific experiments we measure the value of a variable y as we change some other variable x in a systematic way. The results are displayed by plotting x and y. If there is a theory that relates the values of x to y in a formula or equation, then we can see how well the results fit the theoretical formula.

One way would be to compute the values of y for each x from the formula. The measured values could be called y(experimental) and the calculated ones y(theoretical). The differences between corresponding values

$$y\text{(experimental)} - y\text{(theoretical)}$$

are called **deviations** of experimental from theoretical values.

We have spoken so far as if it were possible to compute the proper theoretical value that corresponds to each experimental value.   This is the case if the formula has no other variable in it.   Frequently there are other variables in the formula that can change.   For example, here is the formula for v, the velocity of an object at time t, given that its initial velocity is *vinit* and its acceleration is a.

$$v = vinit + a * t$$

If we measured the velocity of an object that has a uniform acceleration we could plot a graph between v and t:

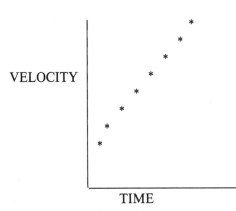

VELOCITY

TIME

Theoretically, the graph should be a straight line, but the experimental points are scattered. It is possible to draw a line by eye that is placed so that the deviations of points from the line are small. Since some deviations, v(experimental) $-$ v(theoretical), are positive and some negative their sum might be small even though individual deviations were large. To get a good fit we minimize the sum of the squares of the deviations rather than the sum of the deviations. The squares of the deviations are always positive. We choose as the best straight line the one that makes the sum of the squares of the deviations the least. This is called **least squares fitting** of a curve (here a straight line) to experimental points. This process can be done very efficiently by a computer. Most computer installations provide standard subroutines for least squares fitting, so that scientists do not have to write their own.

Sometimes no theoretical curve is known. We can still fit our data to an equation. We choose an equation that has a form resembling our data. If there is no theory we say it is an **empirical** fit, meaning that it is an equation based on the observations.

SOLVING POLYNOMIAL EQUATIONS

The graph that we plotted as an example was of the function

$$y = x^2 - x - 2$$

This is a **polynomial** function of x. The places where the graph crosses the x-axis are the roots of the equation

$$x^2 - x - 2 = 0$$

This is a second-degree equation since the highest power of the unknown x is the second power. It is a **quadratic equation**. There are general formulas for the roots of a quadratic equation. For the equation

$$ax^2 + bx + c = 0$$

the two roots x1 and x2 are given by the formulas

$$x1 = (-b + \sqrt{b^2 - 4ac})/(2a) \quad \text{and}$$

$$x2 = (-b - \sqrt{b^2 - 4ac})/(2a)$$

If the quantity $(b^2 - 4ac)$ inside the square root sign is positive, all is straightforward. If it is negative, then the formula requires us to find the square root of a negative number, and we say the roots are **complex**. This means, in graphical terms, that the curve does not cross, or touch, the x-axis anywhere. It is either completely above or completely below the x-axis. There is no use looking for values of x where the function is zero.

Here is a subroutine for finding the roots of a quadratic equation. In the subroutine the formulas for finding the roots do not provide values that are accurate under various circumstances. For example, if *root1* is nearly zero because b and *sqroot* are very close in value, a better approximation to it can be obtained by working out *root2* and using the relationship

$$root1 = c/(a*root2)$$

to compute *root1*. This relationship holds in general so it can always be used. Can you see why it is true?

```
       subroutine roots(a,b,c)
  c    Find root of a*x*x + b*x + c
       real a,b,c,test,sqroot,root1,root2
       test=b*b − 4*a*c
       if (test.ge. 0.0) then
           sqroot=sqrt(test)
           root1=(−b + sqroot)/(2*a)
           root2=(−b − sqroot)/(2*a)
           print *,'roots are',root1,root2
       else
           print *,'roots are complex'
       end if
       return
       end
```

For equations that are polynomials in x of degrees higher than two, the method for finding the roots is not as easy. For an equation of degree three, there is a complicated formula for the three roots. For larger degrees there are no formulas and we must look for the roots by a **numerical method**.

The secret of any search is first to be sure that what you are looking for is in the right area, then to keep narrowing down the search area. One method of searching for roots corresponds to the binary search often used in searching sorted lists like phone books. First we find two values of x for which the function has different signs. Then we can be sure that, if it is continuous, the graph will cross the x-axis at least once in the interval between these points. The next step is to halve the interval and look at the middle. If there is only one root in the interval, then in the middle the function will either be zero, in which case it is the root, or it will have the same sign as one of the two end points. Remember they have opposite signs. We discard the half of the interval that is bounded by the middle point and the end with the same sign and repeat the process. After several steps we will have a good **approximation** to the location of the root. We can continue the process until we are satisfied that the error, or uncertainty, in our root location is small enough. There is no point in trying to locate it more accurately than the precision with which the numbers are stored. A numerical analyst could determine the accuracy of the calculated answer.

SOLVING LINEAR EQUATIONS

Computers are used to solve sets of linear equations. If we have two unknowns, we must have two equations to get a solution. We can solve the set of equations

$$x - y = 10$$
$$x + y = 6$$

to get the result $x = 8, y = -2$. To solve the equations we first eliminate one of the unknowns. From the first equation we get

$$x = y + 10$$

Substituting into the second eliminates x. It gives

$$(y + 10) + y = 6 \text{ or } 2y = -4 \text{ or } y = -2$$

Then substituting back gives

$$x = -2 + 10 \text{ or } x = 8$$

This process of elimination can be carried out a step at a time for more equations in more unknowns. Each step lowers the number of unknowns by one and the number of equations by one. A computer program can be written to perform this job, and can be used to solve a set of linear equations. What we must provide is the coefficients of the unknowns and the right-hand sides of the set of equations. A common method is called the **Gauss elimination method**.

AREAS UNDER CURVES

Another numerical method that is relatively easy to under-stand is the calculation of the area under a curve by the trapezoidal method. This is **numerical integration** or **quadrature**. Suppose we have a curve of $y = f(x)$ and we want to find the area between the curve and the x-axis and between lines at $x = x1$ and $x = xn$. (Area "under" the curve will be negative if the curve is below the x-axis.)

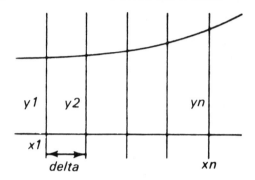

We will divide the distance between $x1$ and xn into intervals of size *delta*. In the drawing we have shown four intervals. The area of the first section, thinking of it as a trapezoid, is

$$(y1 + y2) * delta/ 2$$

The total area under the curve is approximated by the sum of all the trapezoids. The total area of the trapezoids is

$$(y1 + y2) * delta/ 2 + (y2 + y3) * delta/ 2 + ... (y(n-1) + yn) * delta/ 2$$

If we factor out *delta* the formula becomes

$$((y1 + yn)/ 2 + y2 + y3 + ... + y(n-1)) * delta$$

This is half the sum of $y1$ and yn plus the sum of the other ys multiplied by the width of the trapezoids. As *delta* is made smaller, the sum of the areas of the trapezoids comes closer and closer to the area under the curve. It is a better and better approximation. There is, however, a limit to the accuracy that can be obtained, due to the precision of the **real** numbers. Here is a program segment to compute the area if the ys are stored in an array:

```
          sum = (y(1) + y(n))/ 2.0
          final = n − 1
          do 10 i = 2,final
              sum = sum + y(i)
  10          continue
          area = sum*delta
```

CHAPTER 12 SUMMARY

This chapter has summarized some of the uses of computers in scientific calculations. Generally, these calculations are done using **real** numbers. The scientist needs to know the accuracy of the final answers. The answers may be inaccurate because of:

Measurement errors — the original data was collected by measuring physical quantities, such as length or speed. These measurements can never be perfect and an estimate of the measurement error should be made.

Roundoff errors by the computer — a given computer stores **real** numbers with a particular precision, typically 9 decimal digits of accuracy. Calculations using **real** numbers will be no more accurate than the number of digits of precision provided by the computer. They could even be less accurate due to the cumulative effect of roundoff. (Note: sometimes the programmer can choose between single-precision **real**, giving typically 7 digits of accuracy and double-precision **real**, giving typically 16 digits accuracy.)

Truncation errors in repeated calculations — some calculations, such as searching for the roots of a polynomial equation, produce approximations that are successively closer to the exact answer. When the repeated calculation stops, we have a truncation error, which is the difference between the final approximation and the exact answer (ignoring errors due to measurement and roundoff).

The number of digits of accuracy in a particular answer is called its number of **significant figures**. The scientist needs to know that the computer produces a particular answer with enough significant figures for his purposes.

This chapter presented the following typical scientific and mathematical uses of computers.

Evaluating formulas — a computer can produce tables of numbers, for example tables of navigational figures used on sailing boats.

Graphing functions — a computer can plot a particular function; sometimes a special **graphics package** permits devices attached to the computer to draw continuous lines as well as displaying characters.

Fitting a curve to a set of points — data points from an experiment can be read by a program and used to determine an equation (a curve) that describes the data.

Solving polynomial equations — a polynomial equation such as

$$x^3 + 9x^2 + 6x - 23 = 0$$

can be solved by a program that reads the coefficients (1, 9, 6, and −23).

Solving linear equations — a set of equations such as

$$2x + 9y = 7$$
$$10x - 4y = 2$$

can be solved by a program that reads the coefficients of the unknowns (2, 9, 10, and −4) and the right-hand sides of the equations (7 and 2).

Areas under curves — a program can find the area under a given curve by using the heights of the curve at many points. (Note that heights are negative when the curve is below x-axis, so that areas below the axis are negative, those above positive). Essentially, the program slices the area into narrow strips and adds up the areas of the strips. This process is called numerical integration or quadrature.

CHAPTER 12 EXERCISES

1. One jet plane is flying 1083.7 kilometers per hour; another jet plane, chasing it from behind, is flying 1297.9 kilometers per hour. What is the relative speed of the second plane, that is, how fast is it catching up to the first plane? The speed of the first plane is known to an accuracy of 5 km/hr and the speed of the second is known to an accuracy of 0.5 km/hr. How accurately can we calculate the relative speed? How many significant figures are there in the first plane's speed, the second plane's speed, and the relative speed?

2. Use the graphing subroutine given in this chapter to plot the function $sin(x)$ for x varying from 0 to 3 in steps of one-tenth.

3. Use the graphing subroutine given in this chapter to plot the function $x*sin(x)$ for x varying from 0 to 12 in steps of 0.25.

4. A moon rocket has an instrument that measures the rocket's acceleration every second and transmits the measurement to an on-board microcomputer. A program in the microcomputer estimates the speed of the rocket, assuming a speed of zero at launch time. Essentially, this program determines the area under the curve of acceleration plotted against time. Using the trapezoidal method the speed at time tn will be approximately

$$((a1 + an)/2 + a2 + a3 + .. + a(n-1)) * delta$$

In this case, *delta* is 1 second and each acceleration is measured in kilometers per second per second. The formula to give the speed in kilometers per second n seconds after blast-off is

$$(a1 + an)/2 + a2 + a3 + ... + a(n-1)$$

Write a program that reads in the accelerations and outputs the speeds after each second. If you are clever you can avoid recalculating the entire series for each acceleration reading, and you can avoid using an array.

5. A polynomial such as $y = ax^3 + bx^2 + cx + d$ can be evaluated more efficiently by writing it as $y = (((a*x + b)*x + c)*x + d)$. Write a subroutine called *poly* to evaluate polynomials of degree *n* by this method. Assume that the coefficients of the various powers of *x* are stored as an array. Test your subroutine by tabulating values for $y = x^2 - x - 2$ using it.

6. In evaluating formulas care must be taken to avoid illegal calculations such as taking the square root of a negative number or dividing by zero. Tabulate values for the formula

    $$y = (x^2 - 6x + 2)/(x - 3)$$

    for values of *x* going in steps of 1 from $x = -10$ to $+10$ where *y* has a defined value.

Chapter 13

NUMERICAL METHODS

In the last chapter we outlined some of the important types of calculations used in scientific and engineering computing. In this chapter we will look at some of the methods which have been devised for doing these numerical calculations. In any calculations, for example those for evaluating functions such as the trigonometic functions sin and cos, or finding the area under a curve, the calculation can be carried out to varying degrees of accuracy. Usually the more calculating you do, the more accurate the answer you get. But some methods are better than others; for the same amount of work you get greater accuracy. We will, for instance, be looking at a way of finding areas under curves that is usually superior to the trapeziodal rule described in the last chapter. As well we will show a general method of solving linear equations and a method for least squares fitting of a straight line to a set of experimental points. But first we will look at an efficient way of evaluating a polynomial.

EVALUATION OF A POLYNOMIAL

In doing numerical calculations we should be concerned with getting the best calculation we can for the least cost in terms of computer time. This is one of the concerns of people who design what are called **numerical methods**. They are not just concerned about getting an answer but about whether the cost of getting the answer can be decreased.

As an example of how different methods giving apparently the same result can have different costs, we will look at the calculation of the value of a polynomial. We will look at a third-degree polynomial and then generalize the result later for a polynomial of degree n. A third-degree polynomial has the form

$$y(x) = a3\ x^3 + a2\ x^2 + a1\ x + a0$$

One way of evaluating this in Fortran is to write

$$y = a3{*}x{**}3 + a2{*}x{**}2 + a1{*}x{**}1 + a0$$

When the exponent of an exponentiation operation is a positive integer the result is obtained by repeated multiplications so that $x**2$ is the same as $x*x$. So our polynomial evaluation is the same as

$$y = a3*x*x*x + a2*x*x + a1*x + a0$$

In this evaluation there are 6 multiplications (count the asterisks) and 3 additions (count the plus signs). For a fourth-degree polynomial there would be 10 multiplications and 4 additions. For an nth-degree polynomial there would be $n + (n-1) + (n-2) + ... + 1 = n(n+1)/2$ multiplications and n additions.

Now we will look at a different method of evaluating the third-degree polynomial. It is

$$y = ((((a3)*x+a2)*x+a1)*x+a0)$$

Here there are 3 multiplications and 3 additions. (Just count the asterisks and plus signs.) For an nth-degree polynomial there would be n multiplications and n additions. This method is called Horner's rule and is certainly much more efficient, particularly for polynomials of higher degree.

We will now write a function subprogram that will evaluate a polynomial of degree n by this method given that the coefficients of the powers of x namely the as are stored in a one-dimensional array. In a Fortran array, unless we specify otherwise, the index of the variables goes from 1 to the length of the array. We want our array to be from $a(0)$ to $a(n)$ so we write its dimension as $a(0: n)$. Here is a program segment which would work for the third-degree polynomial

```
        poly = a(3)
        do 10 i = 2,0, -1
            poly = poly*x + a(i)
10          continue
```

If we extend this now to work for an nth degree polynomial we would write

```
        poly = a(n)
        do 10 i = n-1,0, -1
            poly = poly*x + a(i)
10          continue
```

The complete function subprogram would be

```
        real function poly(a,n,x)
c       Evaluate polynomial of degree n
        integer n
        real a(0: n)
```

```
        integer i
        poly = a(n)
        do 10 i = n − 1,0, − 1
            poly = poly*x + a(i)
10          continue
        return
        end
```

ROUNDOFF ERRORS

When a real number is represented in a computer by a finite string of bits an error is usually introduced. This error is called a **roundoff error**. The last bit in the string may be inexact. In decimal notation if the fraction .132762 is to be represented by a string of decimal digits of length 4 then the four digits will be either .1327 or .1328. The string may simply be chopped off after the 4th digit, which is called rounding by chopping, or 5 may be added to the 5th digit and the sum then chopped to 4 digits. This latter form of roundoff is probably somewhat better and is the method that you usually are thinking of if you ask that a number be rounded off.

As numbers are combined in the arithmetic operations of addition, subtraction, multiplication, and division, the roundoff error may increase. We say that a further error is generated. As operations continue, the **generated error** may grow and is said to be a **propagated error**.

In adding, or subtracting two numbers, the error in the sum, or difference, is equal to the sum of the errors in the two numbers. Suppose for instance that the number .132762 is represented as the 4-digit string .1328. The error in this representation due to rounding off is .000038. If the number .521689 is represented as 0.5217 the error is .000011. The sum of the numbers will be .6545 as compared with the result of adding the two 6-digit representations which gives .654451. The error in the sum is .000049 which is the sum of .000038 and .000011.

In multiplication the relative (or percentage) error introduced in the product is equal to the sum of the relative (or percentage) errors of the two factors. In division the relative error of the quotient is the difference between the relative errors of the dividend and divisor. In any event all arithmetic operations serve to propagate errors due to rounding.

We found that Horner's rule was more efficient for evaluating polynomials than the straightforward method because there were fewer multiplications. Now we can see that it is also more accurate since the propagation of roundoff error is less when there are fewer arithmetic operations. This is why we can say that it is a better method; it is more accurate and costs less.

LOSS OF SIGNIFICANT FIGURES

We have seen that arithmetic operations result in errors and these cause the rounding errors due to the finite representations of real numbers in a computer to grow larger. The number of digits in our final result that are significant gradually decreases as errors are propagated.

There are more drastic ways of losing significant figures. One place where this occurs is in the situation where two nearly equal numbers are subtracted. When .3572 is subtracted from .3581 the answer is 0.0009 which is normalized to .9???e-03. only the 9 is significant. We had 4 significant figures in each of the original numbers and now we have only 1 significant figure in the difference. One way to cope with this loss of accuracy is to avoid calculations of this sort. Often by regrouping or resequencing operations the offending subtraction can be eliminated. If it is not possible then it may be necessary to work to greater precision, say double precision, during the part of a calculation where this can occur.

To declare a variable as a double-precision variable we use a declaration of the form

double precision name of variable

Double-precision constants are written with a *d* instead of an *e* in front of their exponents. Formatted output in the exponent form uses *d* instead of *e* in the format specification. Many built-in functions exist that require double-precision arguments and yield double-precision results. These are self explanatory; many are the usual names preceded by a *d*. The list includes *dsqrt, dabs, dmod, dsin, dcos, dtan, datan, dexp, dlog,* and *dlog10.* (Note that *a* of *alog* is dropped.) A special function *dprod* has two real (single-precision) arguments and returns their double-precision product.

EVALUATION OF INFINITE SERIES

Many mathematical functions can be represented by an infinite series of terms to be added. For example,

$$\exp(x) = 1 + (x/1!) + (x^2/2!) + (x^3/3!) + ...$$

$$\sin(x) = (x/1!) - (x^3/3!) + (x^5/5!) - ...$$

$$\cos(x) = 1 - (x^2/2!) + (x^4/4!) - \ldots$$

$$\log(1+x) = (x/1) - (x^2/2) + (x^3/3) - \ldots$$

The series for *sin* and *cos* are for angles x in radians. The series for *log(1 + x)* is valid only for values of x whose magnitudes are less than 1.

If we evaluated the infinite series for say *sin(x)* for a value of $x = pi/4$ we would get terms that alternately are positive and negative and decrease in magnitude as successive terms are calculated. Here is a program that outputs the value of the sum of the sine series up to a given term as well as the value of the latest term added for eight terms. We say we have truncated the series after eight terms and thereby incur a **truncation error**.

```
         program series
c        Compute the series for sin(x) term by term
         real pi,x,sqx,sine,term
         integer i
         pi=3.141592
         x=pi/4.
         sqx=x*x
         print *,'sin(x)        ','term'
         term=x
         sine=term
         do 20 i=2,16,2
              print 15,sine,term
15            format(' ',e16.7,e16.7)
              term= -1*(term*sqx)/ ((i)*(i + 1))
              sine=sine+term
20            continue
         print 25,'value of sin(pi/ 4) is',1./ sqrt(2.)
25            format(' ',a24,e16.7)
         stop
         end
```

the output for this program is

sin(x)	term
.7853979e+00	.7853979e+00
.7046525e+00	−.8074545e−01
.7071429e+00	.2490391e−02
.7071063e+00	−.3657614e−04
.7071066e+00	.3133610e−06
.7071066e+00	−.1757243e−08
.7071066e+00	.6948431e−11
.7071066e+00	−.2041019e−13
value of sin(pi/4) is	**.7071068e+00**

You can see that the terms become progressively smaller right from the start. This is because x is less than 1. The ratio of the one term to the next term is $x^2/(i(i+1))$. This ratio becomes smaller as i becomes larger. The terms are decreasing faster and faster. Terms after the 5th do not make any difference. This series for *sin(x)* can be used even when x is greater than 1. Here is the output if we run the previous program again with the statement *x=pi/ 2.* instead of *x=pi/ 4.* and output the value of *sin(pi/ 2)* which is 1.

sin(x)	term
.1570796e+01	.1570796e+01
.9248323e+00	−.6459636e+00
.1004524e+01	.7969253e−01
.9998431e+00	−.4681746e−02
.1000003e+01	.1604408e−03
.9999999e+00	−.3598833e−05
.9999999e+00	.5692154e−07
.9999999e+00	−.6688010e−09
value of sin(pi/2) is	**.1000000e+01**

This time the terms do not decrease as rapidly; but they are not affecting the result after the 6th term. The accuracy obtained from the evaluation of a fixed number of terms depends on the value of the argument *x.*

If the series is stopped after 3 terms the value of sine differs from the true value of sin(pi/ 2) which is .1000000e+01 by .0004524e+01 which is 4/10 of 1 percent. We say that this error is partly due to truncating the series. If truncation occurs after 4 terms the error is .0001569e+01 which is 1/10 of 1 percent. The more terms we calculate, the smaller is the truncation error. By taking sufficient terms we can make the truncation error as small as we want.

One way of deciding how many terms of a series are enough is to stop when the absolute value of the most recent term is less than a certain amount. The amount we usually choose is such that it will not change the value of the sum in a noticeable way. It is useless to evaluate more terms because they do not matter.

Even when we have evaluated enough terms so that the contribution of the last term is insignificant, there still remain errors due to round off. In our example, the roundoff error would be present even in the first term of the series; as each term is added another roundoff occurs. These errors may tend to cancel each other; sometimes the number is rounded up, sometimes down. It is possible that all errors are in the same direction so that the total possible error introduced in this way grows larger with the number of terms. We must expect the worst. The roundoff error in the sine of pi/4 seems to be .0000002, that in sine of pi/2 seems to be .0000001. In each case the last figure output is dubious.

One way of avoiding the accumulation of roundoff errors is to work in double precision. In double precision each number is represented by a string of bits that is twice as long as in single precision. The roundoff error will then accumulate in the least significant bits of the double precision number. When the result is finally reduced to single precision, a single roundoff occurs. Try reprogramming the example using double precision.

A relationship between the functions sine and cosine may be used to improve the accuracy of the result for a given number of terms in the series. This relationship is

$$sin(x) = cos((pi/ 2.)-x)$$

This means that for angles greater than *pi/ 4* but less than *pi/ 2* we can compute the sine by using the series for cosine with *((pi / 2.)− x)*. This will be equal to or less than *pi / 4* and comparable accuracy can be obtained using the same number of terms in the series.

When a fixed number of terms has been decided on, say six, the evaluation of the series becomes the evaluation of a polynomial. We can take advantage of the efficiencies of Horner's method. In the series for sine and cosine not every power of x is present so the polynomial is really like one in x^2 rather than x. For example, the series for sine to 5 terms can be written as

$$sin(x) = ((((x^2/9!)-(1/7!))x^2 + (1/5!))x^2 + 1)x$$

The coefficients $(1/9!)$, $(1/7!)$, and $(1/5!)$ can all be evaluated once and for all and stored as constants in the program.

All values of angles greater than *pi/ 2* must be reduced to be related to either the *sin* or *cos* series for x less than or equal to *pi/ 4*.

ROOT FINDING

In the last chapter we looked at one method for finding the value of x where a polynomial in x has a zero value. This same method applies to any function of one variable, say $f(x)$. If there are two values, say $x1$ and $x2$, of x at which $f(x)$ has opposite signs then, provided the function is continuous, there must be at least one point in between these values where the function has a zero value. We described a search technique that halved the interval between the given values of x and determined in which half the zero of the function lay. This process can then be repeated in a manner similar to a binary search used in searching files.

This interval-halving method can be improved upon and numerous other methods for finding zeros or roots of a function of one variable have been devised. The purpose of these methods is to provide a faster way of homing in on a root once it has been located between two values of x.

A technique called the **secant method** uses, instead of the midpoint, the point at which a line drawn between the point $(x1,f(x1))$ and the point $(x2,f(x2))$ cuts the x-axis. This will be at a point x given by solving the equation

$$f(x2)/(x2 - x) = f(x1)/x - x1)$$

or
$$x = (f(x1)x2 + f(x2)x1)/(f(x2) + f(x1))$$

You can see this from the diagram.

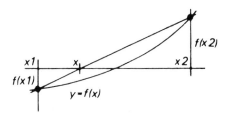

This process is repeated using the point x as a replacement for either x1 or x2. The choice depends on which gives a value to the function opposite to the value at x. As the iteration proceeds the interval is always being narrowed down.

Both the interval-halving method and the secant method will converge on the root. The rate of the convergence depends on the particular function whose zero is being sought. The rate of convergence can sometimes be improved at the cost of the guarantee of convergence.

In the secant method, instead of using one of the end points all the time, two intermediate points can be used. Of course, there may not be a zero between these points but the search interval is much smaller.

A method called the **Newton-Raphson method** is useful for simple functions, like polynomials, whose slopes can be computed using calculus. The iteration formula for approximating the root is

$$x(n + 1) = xn - f(xn)/ s(xn)$$

where $x(n + 1)$ is the approximation to the root at the $(n + 1)$th iteration, xn is the nth approximation, $f(xn)$ is the value of the function at xn, and $s(xn)$ is the value of the slope of the function at xn.

In terms of calculus if, for example,

$$f(x) = 3x^2 + 2x + 1 \quad \text{then}$$
$$s(x) = 6x + 2$$

The function $s(x)$ is the derivative of $f(x)$.

The Newton-Raphson method has very rapid convergence, but convergence is not always guaranteed.

SUBROUTINE FOR ROOT FINDING

We will give a program for a subroutine which uses the interval-halving method. It is perhaps slow, but safe. For the function evaluations it will call on a function *func*. The parameter *eps* stands for the Greek letter epsilon. In mathematics, we use epsilon to stand for the small difference between an approximation and a true value. We will use as a stopping condition the fact that two successive approximations to the root differ from each other by less than *eps*. When you use the subroutine *solve* you must decide what accuracy you want. Of course there is no use asking for greater accuracy than is permitted by the finite representation of the numbers.

```
          subroutine solve(left,right,root,eps)
   c      Find root of func(x) = 0 by interval halving
          real left,right,root,eps
          real func
          real x1,x2
          x1=left
          x2=right
          root=(x1+x2)/ 2.
   5      if (x2 - x1.le.eps) go to 10
              if (func(x1)*func(root).gt. 0) then
                  x1=root
```

```
            else
                x2=root
            end if
            root = (x1+x2)/ 2.
            go to 5
10          continue
        return
        end
```

To use this subroutine in a program we must call the function whose root is sought by the name *func* and be sure to declare its type in the main program. We will use it to find the zero of

$$f(x) = x^2 - x - 2$$

that is between $x = 0$ and $x = 3$ to an accuracy of .00005e00.

```
        program findrt
c       Find one root of f(x)=x*x - x - 2
        real func,answer
        call solve(0.,3.,answer,5e- 5)
        print 10,'root between 0 and 3 is',answer
10      format(' ',a,e13.7)
        stop
        end


        real function func(x)
        real x
        func=(x - 1.)*x - 2.
        return
        end
```
(include definition of solve here)

The output for this program is

root between 0 and 3 is   .2000015e+01

Notice that the polynomial is being evaluated by Horner's method. We do not need to use this kind of method of root finding for a quadratic but it illustrates the method in a case where we can compute the correct answer which is

.2000000e+01

It is possible to refer to a function or subroutine in a subroutine or function subprogram by including as one of the parameters, the dummy argument for the function or subroutine. For example, in *solve* we could include *func* as another parameter. Then the use of *solve* in the main program would have, as the corresponding argument, the name of the actual function to be used.

NUMERICAL INTEGRATION

In calculus, we find that the area under a curve can be calculated by evaluating the definite integral of the function that represents the curve between the two limiting values of the independent variable. Not every function can be integrated analytically but a numerical approximation can be obtained for any continuous function. In the last chapter we presented the trapezoidal rule for calculating areas under curves; the function is evaluated at uniformly spaced intervals between the limiting values and the function values are used to find the area. The accuracy of the result improves as smaller intervals are chosen and more function evaluations made.

For the same number of function evaluations it is possible to have an integration formula that combines the values to give a better approximation to the area.

One formula which is often better than the trapezoidal formula is called **Simpson's rule**. The trapezoidal formula assumes that each little slice of the area has the shape of a trapezoid; Simpson's rule assumes that the curved boundary of two adjacent slices has the shape of a parabola (a second-degree polynomial). It uses the area under such a parabola that can be found using calculus to give a way of finding the area under the curve. The area must be divided into an even number of slices. The area of any pair of slices is the slice width *delta*, multiplied by one-third of the sum of the values of the function at the outsides together with four times the value in the middle. If the complete area is divided into 2 pairs of slices then the area is

$$delta*(f(x1)+4*f(x2)+2*f(x3)+4*f(x4)+f(x5))/\ 3.$$

You can see how to extend this for more pairs of slices.

We will write a program to compare the accuracy of the result obtained with the same number of function evaluations (slices) using the trapezoidal rule and Simpson's rule. We will calculate the area for a simple curve so that a calculus result can give the exact area for comparison. We will compute the area under the curve

$$f(x)\ =\ sin(x)$$

between the values of $x = 0$ and *pi*. From calculus we know the answer should be 2.0000000. We will use 6 slices so that *delta* will be *pi/ 6*.

```
        program simptr
c       Compare Simpson's and trapeziodal rule
        real pi,delta,x,trap,simp,odd,even,middle,f(7)
        pi=3.141592
        delta=pi/6.
c       Evaluate sin(x) at 7 values of x
        x=0.
        do 5 i=1,7
            f(i)=sin(x)
            x=x+delta
5           continue
c       Compute area by trapezoidal rule
        middle=f(2)+f(3)+f(4)+f(5)+f(6)
        trap=delta*(f(1)+2*middle+f(7))/2.
c       Compute area by Simpson's rule
        even=f(2)+f(4)+f(6)
        odd=f(3)+f(5)
        simp=delta*(f(1)+4*even+2*odd+f(7))/3.
c       Output results for comparison
        print 10,'trapezoidal method gives',trap
        print 10,' Simpson''s  method gives',simp
10      format(' ',a,e16.7)
        stop
        end
```

Here is the output

trapezoidal method gives   .1954097e+01
Simpson's method gives   .2000863e+01

You can see that the error in the trapezoidal method is .04590, that in Simpson's rule is .00086. This shows that Simpson's rule is a superior one here, the error is smaller.

LINEAR EQUATIONS USING ARRAYS

We have looked at the problem of solving two linear equations in two unknowns. We do not use computers to solve such simple systems. But computers are useful when we have many equations in many unknowns. In handling these problems we store the coefficients of the unknowns in an array. If we had four equations in four unknowns the equations might be written as

$$a(1,1)x1 + a(1,2)x2 + a(1,3)x3 + a(1,4)x4 = b1$$

$$a(2,1)x1 + a(2,2)x2 + a(2,3)x3 + a(2,4)x4 = b2$$

$$a(3,1)x1 + a(3,2)x2 + a(3,3)x3 + a(3,4)x4 = b3$$

$$a(4,1)x1 + a(4,2)x2 + a(4,3)x3 + a(4,4)x4 = b4$$

where *a* is a two-dimensional array of the coefficients. We can write the *b*s, the right-hand sides of these equations, as part of the *a* array by letting $b1=a(1,5)$, $b2=a(2,5)$, and so on. To solve the equations we must reduce these equations in turn to three equations in three unknowns, two equations in two unknowns, and then one equation in one unknown. This method eliminates all the unknowns except one. Then by substituting back you can find the value of all the unknowns. If the array of coefficients was of the form

```
a(1,1) a(1,2) a(1,3) a(1,4) a(1,5)
0      a(2,2) a(2,3) a(2,4) a(2,5)
0      0      a(3,3) a(3,4) a(3,5)
0      0      0      a(4,4) a(4,5)
```

then we could see from the last line that $x4 = a(4,5)/a(4,4)$. Then using this we could substitute back into the equation represented by the second last line namely

$$a(3,3)x3 + a(3,4)x4 = a(3,5)$$

and solve for *x3*, and so on to get *x2* and *x1*.

What we have to do is move from the original array of coefficients to the one with all the zeros in the lower left corner. We do this by dividing each element of the first row by $a(1,1)$ and storing it back in the same location. This makes the new value of $a(1,1)$ a 1. Next multiply this row by $a(2,1)$ and subtract it from each element of row two, storing the result back in the same location. The new value of $a(2,1)$ will be zero. The process will eventually result in an array with zeros in the lower left.

Certain problems of loss of precision can arise if the element that is currently to be reduced to 1 is small. This element, referred to as the pivot element, should be as large as possible. Various ways of rearranging the array can help prevent difficulties but trouble is always possible.

LEAST SQUARES APPROXIMATION

Very often in scientific experiments, measurements of a quantity *y* are made at various values of an independent variable *x*. It may be known from theory that the relationship between *y* and *x* is a linear one, for example

$$y = ax + b$$

If the various corresponding values of *x* and *y* were plotted on a graph these would be a number of points, say *n*. A straight line drawn through any two of these points would not pass exactly through the others. We want to choose the values of the constants *a* and *b* so that they define a straight line in such a way that the sum of the squares of deviations of the actual points from the straight line is a minimum, that is, the sum of squares is least. For the *i*th point, say at *(xi,yi)*, the deviation squared is

$$(yi - (a*xi + b))^2$$

For a function to have a minimum value implies, in calculus, that the derivatives with respect to the variables are zero. We can differentiate a sum of squares of this type partially with respect to *a* and *b*, the values that can be varied, and set the derivatives equal to zero. This gives two equations. One is the sum of *n* terms of the form

$$yi - (a*xi + b)$$

set equal to zero. The value of *i* goes from 1 to *n*. The other is the sum of *n* terms of the form

$$(yi - (a*xi + b))*xi$$

set equal to zero. These two equations can be written as two equations in two unknowns, *a* and *b*. These are

$$c1*a + c2*b = c3$$

$$c4*a + c5*b = c6$$

where *c1* is the sum of values *xi* with *i* going from 1 to *n*. The coefficient *c2* is *n* and *c3* is the sum of values *yi* with *i* going from 1 to *n*. The coefficient *c4* is the sum of *xi*xi* from 1 to *n*, *c5* the sum of *xi* from 1 to *n*, and *c6* the sum of *xi*yi* from 1 to *n*. The solution to the two equations can easily be found once they are formed.

This same technique can be used for points that in theory lie on a higher degree curve than a straight line but the calculation is more complex.

MATHEMATICAL SOFTWARE

We have been describing a few of the simpler numerical methods used in scientific calculations. Over the years these methods have been changed and made more reliable, more efficient and more accurate. Nowadays we usually rely on a packaged program for carrying out this type of calculation. We call the program packages mathematical software, to distinguish them from the programs that operate the system or compile programs. These latter are called systems software and compilers respectively.

Packages in Fortran exist for almost every standard numerical calculation. All that you must do is to find out how to call them in your program, and what their limitations are. Every piece of software should be documented so that you do not need to read it to be able to use it. You must know what each input parameter of the subprogram is and what range of values is permitted. You must know also how the output is stored so that you can use it.

Frequently software packages are stored in the secondary memory of the computer and may be included in your program by using special **include** statements.

One of the great things about science is that we build on the work of others and using subprograms prepared by others is good scientific practice. Of course these must be of the highest standards.

CHAPTER 13 SUMMARY

In this chapter we have been examining numerical methods for evaluating polynomials and infinite series, calculating areas under curves, solving systems of linear equations and obtaining least squares approximations. We were concerned particularly with certain properties of the methods.

Efficiency of a method — the amount of work, as measured in number of basic arithmetic operations required to obtain a certain numerical result. Horner's rule for polynomial evaluation is more efficient than the straightforward method. It is more efficient because it requires fewer multiplications.

Horner's rule — a method for computing the value of a polynomial that is efficient. The polynomial

$$y = 5x^2 + 2x + 3$$

is evaluated by the Fortran statement which represents Horner's rule

$$y = (5^*x + 2)^*x + 3$$

rather than either

$$y = 5^*x^*x + 2^*x + 3$$

or the equivalent

$$y = 5^*x^{**}2 + 2^*x + 3$$

Roundoff error — error in real numbers introduced basically because a computer represents the numbers by a finite string of bits. When real numbers are added or subtracted the roundoff error of the sum or difference is the sum of the roundoff errors of the two individual numbers. In multiplications relative errors add.

Generated error — roundoff errors produced due to arithmetic operations. The fewer the arithmetic operations the smaller the roundoff error generated.

Propagated error — generated errors that grow as calculations proceed.

Significant digits — digits in the representation of a real number that are not in error. Numbers are often quoted with a final decimal digit that may be in error by as much as unity. Digits that are not significant should not be quoted in an answer.

Loss of significant digits — This may occur as the result of subtraction of nearly equal numbers.

Infinite series — many mathematical functions such as sin, cos, exp, and log can be written as a sum of an infinite series of terms. These series may be used to evaluate the functions. Because the terms in the series eventually decrease in magnitude a good approximation can be obtained by stopping the addition after a certain number of terms.

Rate of convergence — the ratio of the magnitude of two adjacent terms of an infinite series. For $sin(x)$ the ratio is $x^2/(i(i + 1))$. If x is less than 1 then this ratio is always less than one. If x is greater than 1 the terms might initially get larger but eventually get smaller. A series is non-convergent if the term ratio never becomes less than 1.

Double precision — keeping twice the normal number of bits to represent a number in the computer. Calculations carried out to double precision maintain a larger number of significant figures.

Interval-halving method — for finding a root of an equation $f(x)=0$ by a method similar to binary search. The method is guaranteed to converge on a root since the root is always kept between the end points of the interval and the interval is constantly decreasing.

Secant method — a method that sometimes has better convergence properties than interval halving for finding a root of an equation.

Newton-Raphson — a method for finding a zero of a function whose derivative can be computed. Convergence is rapid but not guaranteed.

Stopping criterion — the size of error that is to be tolerated in a result due to truncating such as in evaluating an infinite series term by term or iterating to find a root.

Numerical integration — approximation of the value of the definite integral representing the area under a curve between limits.

Simpson's rule — for numerical integration assumes each pair of slices of area under a curve is bounded by a parabola. The trapezoidal method assumes each slice is bounded by a straight line. Simpson's rule often gives greater accuracy for the same number of slices (function evaluations).

Array of coefficients — for linear equations. This is manipulated so as to be transformed into an array that is triangular, that is, has zero elements on the lower left of the diagonal. This is accomplished by operations such as multiplying a row by a constant and subtracting one row from another. Neither of these operations alters the values of the unknowns.

Back substitution — evaluating the unknowns once the transformed set of linear equations can be represented by a triangular array.

Least squares approximation — finding an equation to represent experimental information so that the sum of the squares of the deviations is a minimum. We investigated the case of fitting a straight line to a set of experimental points.

Mathematical software — prefabricated subprograms embodying good numerical methods for getting standard results. The software should be documented to alert the user to the accuracy to be expected, the cost of the result, and any limitations.

CHAPTER 13 EXERCISES

1. Write a function subprogram that will give the sine of an angle whose value in radians is between 0 and *pi/ 2*. Use the series for sine for angles between 0 and *pi/ 4* and for cosine between *pi/ 4* and *pi/ 2*. Use the same number of terms in each series. Test your program and compare the results with those obtained by using the built-in function *sin*. Try varying the number of terms.

2. Compute the value of *exp(1.)* using the series. Find the values as each term is added up to a maximum of 8 terms.

3. Use the built-in function for *exp(x)* to tabulate values of this function for x going from $-10.$ to $+10.$ Sketch the graph of the function for this range. You might think of using the program for graph plotting on the screen.

4. Use the interval-halving subroutine to find a root of the equation

    $$2x - tan(x) = 0$$

    given that there is at least one between 0 and *pi* radians.

5. Use Newton's method of finding roots to find a root of the polynomial

    $$x^4 + 6x^2 - 1 = 0$$

6. Use Simpson's rule to find the area under the curve

    $$y = x^2 - 2x - 1$$

    from $x = 0$ to 3. Test whether the number of slices matters.

7. Write a subroutine that keeps doubling the number of slices in an area calculation using Simpson's rule until two successive results for the area under a curve agree to within an accuracy *eps*. Make sure you do not reevaluate the function at places already computed.

8. Compare Simpson's rule and the trapezoidal rule for finding areas under a curve for $y = exp(x)$ between $x = 0$ and $x = 1.$ Do you know the answer from calculus?

9. Write a subroutine that will solve a set of n equations in n unknowns. Do not include any form of pivoting. Would you expect this to be a good piece of mathematical software?

10. Write a subroutine that will solve two linear equations in two unknowns. Do you encounter any problems about loss of accuracy with such a small system of equations? What happens when there is no solution, for example, if equations represent parallel lines?

11. Write a subroutine that accepts two arrays x and y of n values that represent n points and outputs the equation of the straight line that gives the sum of the squares of the deviations of the points from the straight line a minimum value.

12. The curve described by the equation

    $$y = (1/2\pi)^{1/2} e^{-x^2/2}$$

is called the normal or Gaussian distribution curve. It is used in statistics. The area under this curve for $-\infty < x < \infty$ is 1. Write a program to compute the area under this curve for $-3 < x < 3$ and see how close an approximation you get. What is the area for $-1 < x < 1$. Try drawing a graph of the curve using the graph program.

Chapter 14

PROCESSING TEXT

In the handling of alphabetic information so far you learned how to compare strings, either for the purpose of recognizing particular strings or for putting various strings in order. Now that arrays and formatted input and output have been introduced you can do many more things with character strings.

WORD RECOGNITION

When you first learn how to read you must learn to recognize words. To do this you must recognize what a word is. You learn the basic characters, the letters, then you learn that a word is a string of characters with a blank in front and a blank after it and no blanks in between. We are now going to write a program that will input a line of text and split it up into words. To simplify the job, we will begin our problem without any punctuation marks in the text. The method of dealing with problem solving by simplification is very helpful. Solve a simpler problem before you try a harder one. We will learn to cope with punctuation marks later. Our solution tree for this problem is:

Read a line of text and output a word at a time

Read line of text   Split off and output each word

Reading a line is straightforward. "Split off and output each word" must be refined further:

> **do** for each character of text
>   **if**(character is not a blank) **then**
>   Add character to word
>   **else if**(there is a word) **then**

Output word and prepare for next word
end if
end of **do** loop

We must choose a way of storing our character strings that will allow us to have access to one character at a time. The way that this is done in Fortran is to store each string in an array of locations each of which has the space to hold one character. For instance, for holding *text* we choose an array of 80 elements, each to hold one character. It would be declared as

character *1 text(80)*

To read the contents of a data line into this array we can use the formatted input statement

```
         read 5,text
5        format (80a1)
```

This will cause column 1 of the line to be read into *text(1)*, column 2 to go to *text(2)*, and so on. If we use a second array to hold a word of maximum length 20 characters declared by **character** *1 word(20)* we can move characters one at a time from the *text* array to the *word* array by an assignment statement such as *word(letter) = text(column)*. The index *letter* will keep track of the proper character position in *word*, the index *column* the proper character position in *text*.

```
         program words
c        Read text and output a word at a time
         character *1 text(80),word(20)
         integer column,letter,fill
c        Read a line of text
         print *,'Enter line of text'
         read 5,text
5        format (80a1)
c        Initialize loop, set word to receive first letter
         letter = 1
c        Split off and output each word
         do 10 column = 1,80
             if (text(column).ne.' ')then
c                Add character to word
                 word(letter) = text(column)
                 letter = letter + 1
             else
c                See if there is a word
                 if (letter.ne.1)then
```

```
c                    Output word and prepare for next word
c                    Fill out word with blanks
          do 7 fill = letter,20
              word(fill) = ' '
7              continue
          print 8,word
8         format (' ',20a1)
          letter = 1
       end if
     end if
10   continue
  stop
  end
```

Here is a sample display:

Enter line of text
See the computer read
See
the
computer
read

Again, we see how the English entries in the solution tree become comments in the program. We have added two more comments concerning loop initialization and filling out *word* with blanks. Since the array *word* is used over and over again, it either must all be set to blanks after each use or the remaining parts set to blank when the correct characters are in place.

WORDS WITH PUCTUATION

We want now to modify the previous program to do the same thing when there are punctuation marks present, that is, find the words in a text and output them one by one. We usually try to build on the previous work so that we do not need to do everything from scratch. If we could reduce the text with the punctuation marks to one without such marks, we could then use the old program. The solution tree would be:

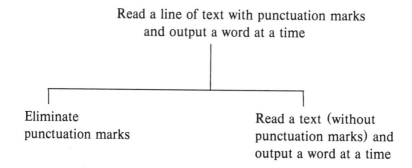

Read a line of text with punctuation marks
and output a word at a time

Eliminate
punctuation marks

Read a text (without
punctuation marks) and
output a word at a time

Our problem is to eliminate punctuation marks from the text. This is accomplished in this program segment:

> **do** for each character of punctuated text
>   **if**(character is not punctuation mark)**then**
>   Move character to new text
>   **end if**
>   End of **do** loop

A complete program for removing punctuation marks will be:

```
        program comma
c       Eliminate punctuation marks from text
        character *1 text1(80),text2(80)
        integer i1,i2,fill
        i2 = 1
        print *,'Enter line of text with punctuation'
        read 1,text1
1       format(80a1)
        do 10 i1 = 1,80
c          If character of text1 not a punctuation mark,
c             move it to text2
           if (text1(i1).ne. ','.and.text1(i1).ne. '.'.and.
     +         text1(i1).ne. '?'.and.text1(i1).ne. ':'.and.
     +         text1(i1).ne. ';'.and.text1(i1).ne. ')'.and.
     +         text1(i1).ne. '(')then
              text2(i2) = text1(i1)
              i2 = i2 + 1
           end if
10         continue
c       Fill text2 with blanks
        do 20 fill = i2,80
           text2(fill) = ' '
20         continue
```

```
            print *,' '
            print 30,text2
  30        format(' ',80a1)
            stop
            end
```

Here is a sample display:

Enter line of text with punctuation
This text has commas, parentheses (two of them), and a period.
This text has commas parentheses two of them and a period

This program for eliminating punctuation marks could now be combined with the program for reading text without punctuation marks, word by word, to produce a program for reading a text with punctuation marks word by word.

NAME RECOGNITION

You often want to sort names alphabetically, and this is a problem if the names are written out in full with the surname last. For a name like *Yiu Kwok Tham* the sorting must be on *Tham*. We are not certain in general how many names precede the surname. Some people have one, some two, some even three or four. We would like to write a program that takes a full name and rewrites it with the surname first then initials like

Tham, Y. K.

Since in a sorting process blanks have a lower value than any character, it is important that the position and number of the blanks be consistent from one person's name to another, so we will have one blank after the comma and one after each period.

This book is set by a computer using a **text editor** so that the words in any line are both left and right justified; there is one non-blank character in the leftmost and one in the rightmost position of each line of text. This is accomplished by inserting extra blanks between words so that some have two or three blanks instead of one. It is a job that used to require a skilled linotype operator. We will speak more of **text editors** a little later, but now we are working on reading a person's name and bringing it to a standard form. We want the standard form so that a list of names can be sequenced alphabetically. As we read the full name initially we should not count on there being only one blank between names.

The full name is a string of characters which is a series of words separated we will assume by one or more blanks. The last of the series is the surname. We now have two different ways of handling this problem. One is to start at the end of the string and read the surname backwards until a blank is reached; after finding the surname, the process of extracting the initials from the first names can proceed using a loop. Another method would be to read the character position of the beginning of each name into an array location, keeping count of the number of names in the full name. Then the name in the form of surname followed by initials can be assembled. We will use this method.

We will use the one-dimensional array variable *text* for the name as input, the one-dimensional array *name* to store the name in the form with initials following the surname. We will assume that *text* contains a surname and one to seven first names. The character position in *text* of the start of each word will be recorded in an integer array *start*. The words are counted in the integer variable *wordno*. The last name must be followed by blanks.

Here is the program:

```
            program srname
c           Change form of name to surname followed by initials
            character *1 text(80),name(80),lastch
            integer start(8),wordno,column,i,init,fill
c           Full name is read into 'text' and then put in standard
c           form in 'name'.
c           Beginning of each word is recorded in 'start'
c           Last inspected character of text is 'lastch'
            print *,'Enter full name'
            read 1,text
1           format (80a1)
            lastch = ' '
            wordno = 0
            column = 1
5           if (column.gt. 80)go to 15
                if (text(column).ne.' '.and. lastch.eq.' ')then
c                   Record position of start of this word
                    wordno = wordno + 1
                    start(wordno) = column
                end if
                lastch = text(column)
                column = column + 1
            go to 5
```

```
15          continue
c       Move surname into beginning of name
            column = start(wordno)
            i = 1
17          if (text(column).eq.' ')go to 18
                name(i)=text(column)
                i = i + 1
                column = column + 1
                go to 17
18          continue
            name(i) = ','
            i = i + 1
c       Add initials to surname
            init = 1
21          if (init.ge.wordno)go to 25
                name(i) = ' '
                name(i + 1) = text(start(init))
                name(i + 2) = '.'
                i = i + 3
                init = init + 1
                go to 21
25          continue
c       Fill out name with blanks
            do 30 fill = i,80
                name(fill) = ' '
30          continue
            print 40,name
40          format (' ',80a1)
            stop
            end
```

Here is a sample display:

Enter full name
James Nairn Patterson Hume
Hume, J. N. P.

WORD STATISTICS

We have learned to read words of a text, eliminate punctuation marks, and rearrange words and parts of words as we did with the surname and initials. Another important use of a computer in dealing with words involves keeping statistics about the lengths of words. Different authors have different patterns of use of words and this shows up in the frequency with which they use words of different lengths. Some authors use a lot of long words; others rarely do.

In this section we will read a text and from it prepare a frequency distribution of word lengths. To add a little extra interest to this problem, we will display the results in graphic form. For instance, we will have a display like this for output:

Length of word	Frequency
1	***
2	******
3	********
4	*****

This display, called a histogram, represents the result of analyzing the frequency of different word lengths in a text. It shows that there were 3 one-letter words, 6 two-letter words, 8 three-letter words, and 5 four-letter words.

We will use what we have learned so far about reading words, but instead of forming the words we will just count the number of letters, then after each word add 1 to the value stored in an array location corresponding to the letter count. We will use the array *freq* to store the letter counts; *freq(4)* will store the number of four-letter words. We will assume a maximum of 20 letters in a word and that there are no punctuation marks. We will also assume that the total number of words is small enough that there are no more than 30 words of any given length. Here is our program:

```
          program stats
   c      Determine freqiencies of word lengths
          character *1 text(80),stars(30)
          integer freq(20),i,count,j,column
   c      Initialize frequency array
          do 2 i = 1,20
              freq(i) = 0
   2          continue
          print *,'Enter lines of text, + at end'
          read 5,text
   5      format (80a1)
   6      if (text(1).eq. '+')go to 13
              count = 0
              do 10 column = 1,80
                  if (text(column).ne. ' ')then
   c                  Count letters in word
```

```
                        count = count + 1
                else
                    if (count.ne. 0)then
c                           Add word length to frequency
                            freq(count) = freq(count) + 1
                            count = 0
                    end if
                end if
10              continue
            read 12,text
12          format (80a1)
            go to 6
13          continue
        print *,' '
c       Output labels on display
        print 15,'Length of word','Frequency'
15      format (' ',a,6x,a)
c       Output display of asterisks
        do 40 i = 1,20
c           Put stars into array, padded with blanks
            do 20 j = 1,30
                if (j.le.freq(i))then
                    stars(j) = '*'
                else
                    stars(j) = ' '
                end if
20          continue
            print 30,i,stars
30          format (' ',i7,13x,30a1)
40          continue
        stop
        end
```

Here is a sample display:

Enter lines of text, + at end
roses are red
violets are blue
honey is sweet
and so are you
+

Length of word	Frequency
1	
2	**
3	******
4	*
5	***
6	
7	*
...	
20	

You can see how similar the program is to the one for reading names. We could make parts of these various programs into subprograms for use in other programs.

READING FORTRAN

We have been reading English text and performing operations on it, or as the result of it. All these operations, we see, are absolutely mechanical but give the impression that the computer is capable of doing things we think of as "intelligent work". One of the fields of artificial intelligence that has been explored is the translation from one language to another. The translation of one natural language into another, such as English to French, has had only qualified success. It works, but not well when the text is ambiguous or difficult. The translations are not good literature, to say the least.

But computers are being used for language translation every day, for the translation of programming languages into machine languages. The reason this is possible is that programming languages are well defined and quite limited.

Your Fortran programs are translated by the compiler program into machine language programs before execution. We want to look a little at how this can be done. The different parts of the program are placed on separate lines for input. Except for blanks, starting in column 7 there is a keyword with one exception, and that is if the statement is an assignment statement. These keywords are limited to a very small list; they include **read, print, stop, go to, continue, do, if, end**. We can thus decide whether or not a statement is an assignment statement by reading the first word after column 6. If it is not one of the keywords it is an assignment statement. You can at least see how the keywords can be used in the translation process.

CHAPTER 14 SUMMARY

In this chapter we have shown how the computer can, in a sense, understand English. The computer can recognize words by scanning for their beginnings and endings. Typically, words in English are surrounded by blanks or special characters; programs can be written which separate out words by searching for these characters. Due to the great speed of computers, they sometimes have the appearance of being intelligent, in spite of the fact that their basic mode of operation is very simplistic, such as seeing if a given character is a blank. Fortran compilers have been developed to read text which looks somewhat like English; the text which they have been designed to read is Fortran programs.

CHAPTER 14 EXERCISES

1. A **palindrome** is a word or phrase which is spelled the same backwards and forwards. The following are examples of word palindromes: "I", "mom", "deed" and "level". Blanks and punctuation are ignored in phrase palindromes, for example, "Madam, in Eden I'm Adam" and "A man, a plan, a canal, Panama". Write a program which reads a string and determines if it is a palindrome.

2. You are to write a program which will help in reviewing a script to determine its suitability for television screening. Your program is to give a list of the frequency of use of the following unacceptable words:

   'phooey' 'shucks' 'jeepers' 'golly'

   Make up a few lines of script to test out your program.

3. You are employed by an English teacher who insists that "and" should not be preceded by a comma. Hence, "Crosby, Stills, Nash and Young" is acceptable, but "Merril, Fynch, and Lynn" is not. Write a program which reads lines of text, searches for unacceptable commas, removes them, and makes stern remarks such as the English teacher would make about errors. (We are somewhat inconsistent in this book.)

4. Write a program which reads text and then outputs it so that its left and right margins are vertical. First the program is to read the number of characters to output per line. Whenever enough words for one line have been collected, blanks are inserted between words to expand the line to the desired width. Then the expanded line is output.

5.   Write a program that reads a Fortran program and outputs the first word of each line appearing after column 6. Note that there may be blanks in front of the word. Assume that a blank follows the first word. In a Fortran program it is not necessary to have a blank after a keyword or variable identifier.

Chapter 15

SEARCHING
AND SORTING

When a large amount of information is stored in a computer, it must be organized so that you are able to get at the information to make use of it. This problem of **data retrieval** is at the heart of all business operations. Records are kept of employees, customers, suppliers, inventory, in-process goods, and so on. These records are usually grouped in some way into what are called **files**. We might have, for example, a file of employee records, a file of customer records, an inventory file, and so on. Each file must be kept up to date.

A file that we all have access to is printed in the telephone book. It consists of a series of **records** of names, addresses, and telephone numbers. We say that there are three **fields** in each of these records: the name field, the address field, and the phone-number field. The file is in the alphabetic order of one of the three fields, the name field. We say that the name field is the **key** to the ordering of the file. The file is in alphabetic order on this field because that is how it can be most useful to us for data retrieval. We know someone's name and we want their phone number. We might also want their address and that too is available. The telephone company also has the same set of records, ordered using the phone-number field as the key.

In this chapter we will be investigating how a computer can search for information in a file and how records can be sorted.

LINEAR SEARCH

One way to look for data in a file is to start at the beginning and examine each record until you find the one you are looking for. This is the method people use who do not have large files. But for more than about 12 records it is not a good filing system. It will serve as an example to introduce us to the idea of searching mechanically and give us a bad method to compare our better methods to. The file which consists of names and telephone numbers is not ordered by either name or number.

We will keep the file in two one-dimensional arrays, one called *name* and one called *phone*. The element *phone(i)* will be the correct telephone number for *name(i)*. We will read this file, then read a list of names of people whose phone numbers are wanted. The file of names and phone numbers is entered without quotes.

```
       program phones
c      Looks up phone numbers
       character *20 name(25),friend
       character *8 phone(25)
       integer i,size
c      Read file of names and numbers
       i = 1
       print *,'Enter name and number, end with zzz'
       print 5,'Name','Phone'
5      format (1x,a,16x,a)
       read 10,name(i),phone(i)
10     format (1x,a20,a8)
15     if (name(i).eq.'zzz')go to 25
          i = i + 1
          read 20,name(i),phone(i)
20        format (1x,a20,a8)
       go to 15
25     continue
       size = i - 1
       print *,'Enter names to be looked up, end with zzz'
       read 30,friend
30     format (1x,a20)
35     if (friend.eq.'zzz')go to 65
c         Look up friend's number
          i = 1
37        if (friend.eq.name(i).or.i.gt.size)go to 38
             i = i + 1
          go to 37
38           continue
          if (friend.eq.name(i))then
             print 40,friend,phone(i)
40           format (' ',a20,a8)
          else
             print 50,friend,'unlisted'
50           format (' ',a20,a8)
```

```
              end if
              read 60,friend
60            format (1x,a20)
              go to 35
65            continue
          stop
          end
```

Here is a sample display:

Enter name and number, end with zzz

Name	Phone
Perrault,R.	*483-4865*
Borodin,A.	*782-8928*
Cook,S.	*763-3900*
Enright,W.H.	*266-1234*
zzz	*999-9999*

Enter names to be looked up, end with zzz

Borodin,A.

Borodin,A.	**782-8928**
Davies,R.	
Davies,R.	**unlisted**

We have stored the phone number as a character string because of the dash between the first three and the last four digits.

TIME TAKEN FOR SEARCH

In the last section we developed a program for a linear search. The searching process consists of comparing the friend's name, *friend*, with each name in the file of names *name(1), name(2), name(3),* and so on until either the name is found or the end of the file is reached. For a small file, a linear search like this one may be fast enough, but it can be time-consuming if there is a lengthy file.

If there are *n* records in the file and the name is actually in the file, then on the average there will be *n/2* comparisons. The largest number of comparisons would be *n* if the name were last in the file, the least number would be 1 if the name were first. A file of 1000 names would require 500 comparisons on the average. This gets to look rather formidable. It is for this reason that we do something to cut down on the effort. What we do is to sort the file into alphabetic order and then use a method of searching called **binary searching**. We will look at sorting later, but first we will see how much faster binary searching can be.

BINARY SEARCH

The telephone book is sorted alphabetically and the technique most of us use for looking up numbers is similar to the technique known as binary searching. We start by opening the book near where we think we will find the name we are looking for. We look at the page that is open and compare any name on it with the name being sought. If the listed name is alphabetically greater we know we must look only between the page we are at and the beginning of the book. We have eliminated the second part of the book from the search. This process is repeated in the part that might contain the name until the search is down to one page.

In binary searching, instead of looking where we think we might find the name, we begin by looking at the name in the middle of the file and discard the half in which it cannot lie. This process cuts the possible number of names to be searched in half at each comparison. When we have only one name left, if that is not the one we are looking for, it is not in the file.

A file of 16 names would require a maximum of 4 comparisons: one to cut the list to 8, another to 4, another to 2, and another to 1. Of course, we might find it earlier, but this is the **most** work we have to do. It is the maximum number of comparisons. With a linear search of 16 records we might have to make 16 comparisons, although 8 is the average. If we have a file of 1024 records, the binary search takes a maximum of 10 comparisons. This can be calculated by seeing how many times you must divide by 2 to get down to 1 record . Put mathematically, 1024 is equal to 2^{10}:

$$2*2*2*2*2*2*2*2*2*2$$

Just one more comparison, making 11 altogether, will let you search a list of 2048 entries. Then 4096 can be done with 12 comparisons. You can see how much more efficient binary searching can be when the file is a long one.

A SUBROUTINE FOR BINARY SEARCH

We will now design a program for doing a binary search and write it so that it can be called as a subroutine. When we write

call *search(file,key,size,where)*

we are asking for the value of *where* for which *file(where)* = *key*. The variable *file* is an array of *size* items declared as *character*. If the *key* is not in the file, *where* will be set to *size + 1*.

We will develop the algorithm for the binary search in two stages as an illustration of step-by-step refinement. We will write out our solution in a mixture of English and Fortran.

```
10        if(there is only one entry left in the file)go to 20
              Find middle of file
              if(middle value matches or comes after key)then
                  Discard last half of remainder of file
              else
                  Discard first half of remainder of file
              end if
              go to 10
20            continue
          if(remaining entry matches key)then
              Set where to point to it
          else
              Set where to size + 1
          end if
```

It will be important to know the *first* and *last* of the remainder of the file at any time in order to establish the *middle* and to discard the appropriate half. Also when *first* and *last* are the same then there is only one entry left in the file. We initially set *first* to 1 and *last* to *size*. Then to find the middle we use

$$middle = (last + first)/ 2.0$$

It will not matter that this division is truncated as the process of finding the middle is approximate when the number of entries in the file is an even number. Refining the expression, "Discard last half of remainder of file," becomes

$$last = middle$$

and, "Discard first half of remainder of file," becomes

$$first = middle + 1$$

The subroutine can now be written:

```
          subroutine search(file,key,size,where)
c         Locate key using binary search
          integer size,where
          character *20 file(size),key
          integer first,last,middle
c         Initialize the search loop
          first = 1
          last = size
10        if (first.eq.last)go to 20
```

```
                 middle = (first+last)/ 2.0
                 if (file (middle).ge. key)then
c                        Discard last half
                         last = middle
                 else
c                        Discard first half
                         first = middle + 1
                 end if
                 go to 10
20               continue
                 if (file (first).eq. key)then
                     where = first
                 else
                     where = size + 1
                 end if
                 return
                 end
```

A program that uses this subroutine can now be written.

We will use it to find the telephone numbers, and so replace the five lines of our phone-number look-up program following the comment *Look up friend's number* by this single statement:

call *search (name,friend,size,i)*

We are assuming now that the file of names is sorted alphabetically. The subroutine *search* would be included right after the main program.

You will notice that the binary search program has more instructions than the linear search that it is replacing. Each step is more complicated, but the whole process is much faster for a large file because fewer steps are executed.

SEARCHING BY ADDRESS CALCULATION

We have seen that the efficiency of the searching process is very much improved by having a file sorted. The next method of searching uses data organized in a way so there is "a place for everything, and everything in its place".

Suppose you had a file of *n* records numbered from 1 to *n*. If you knew the number of the record, you would immediately know the location. The number would be the index of the array that holds the file entries. Each entry would have a location where it belonged. The trouble usually is to find the location of a record when what you know is some other piece of information such as a person's name.

Files are sometimes arranged so that they are organized on serial numbers that can be calculated from some other information in the record. For example, we could take a person's name and, by transforming it in a certain definite way, change it into a serial number. This transformation often seems bizarre and meaningless, and we say the name is **hash-coded** into a number. When the number has been determined the location is then definite and you can go to it without any problem.

Usually with hash coding it happens that several records have the same hash code. This means that, instead of the code providing the address of the exact record you want, what you get is the address of a location capable of containing several different records. We call such a location a **bucket** or **bin**. We then must look at the records in the bin to find the exact one we are interested in. Since the number is small they need not be sorted. A linear search is reasonable when the file is small.

If fixed-size bins are used to store the file, it is important to get a hash coding algorithm that will divide the original file so that roughly the same number of records is in each bin.

As an example of a hash-coding algorithm, suppose that we had 1000 bins and wanted to divide a file of 10,000 records into the bins. The file might already have associated with each record an identifying number. For example, it might be a Social Insurance number or a student number. These numbers might range from 1 to 1,000,000. One way to divide the records into bins would be to choose the last three digits of the identifying number as the hash code. Another hash code might be formed by choosing the third, fifth, and seventh digit. The purpose is to try to get a technique that gives about the same number of records in each bin. More complicated hashing algorithms may be necessary.

SORTING

We have already developed a sorting program as an example of step-by-step refinement. The first method we used is called a **bubble sort**. Each pair of neighboring elements in a file is compared and exchanged, to put the element with the larger key in the array location with the higher index. On each exchange pass, the element with the largest key gets moved into the last position. The next pass can then exclude the last position because the element in it is already in order. As well, we showed how the straight bubble sort could be improved by detecting at any stage if the list happened to be sorted. Then we showed the Shell sort which is more efficient for a larger file.

We have shown that the binary search technique is much more efficient for a large file than a linear search. In the same way, although a bubble sort is a reasonable method for a small file, it is not efficient for a larger file. The Shell sort is good for a larger file but is not efficient for a really large file. What we usually do to sort a large file is to divide it into a number of smaller files. Each small file is sorted by a technique such as the Shell sort, then the sorted smaller files are merged together into larger files.

We will look at an example in which two sorted files are merged into a single larger sorted file.

MERGING SORTED FILES

We will develop a subroutine called *merge* to merge *file1*, which has *size1* records, with *file2*, which has *size2* records. The records in *file1* and *file2* are already in order. We will invoke this subroutine with the statement

        call *merge(file1,size1,file2,size2,file3)*

Here is the *merge* subroutine:

```
            subroutine merge(file1,size1,file2,size2,file3)
c           Merge two sorted files
            character *20 file1(size1),file2(size2),file3(size1 + size2)
            integer size1,size2
            integer i1,i2,i3
            i1 = 1
            i2 = 1
            i3 = 1
c           Merge until all of one file is used
10          if(i1.gt.size1.or.i2.gt.size2)go to 20
                if(file1(i1).lt.file2(i2))then
                      file3(i3)=file1(i1)
                      i1=i1+1
                else
                      file3(i3)=file2(i2)
                      i2=i2+1
                end if
                i3=i3+1
                go to 10
```

```
20          continue
c           Add remaining items to end of new file
30          if (i1.gt. size1) go to 40
                file3 (i3) = file1 (i1)
                i1 = i1 + 1
                i3 = i3 + 1
                go to 30
40          continue
50          if (i2.gt. size2) go to 60
                file3 (i3) = file2 (i2)
                i2 = i2 + 1
                i3 = i3 + 1
                go to 50
60          continue
            return
            end
```

EFFICIENCY OF SORTING METHODS

The number of comparisons required to merge the two previously sorted files in our example is *size1* + *size2*. To sort a file of length *n* by the bubble sort we can count the maximum number of comparisons that are needed. It is

$$(n - 1) + (n - 2) + (n - 3) + ... + 1$$

This series can be summed and the result is

$n(n - 1)/2$ which is
$n^2/2 - n/2$

When *n* is large, the number of comparisons is about $n^2/2$, since this is very large compared to $n/2$. We say the execution time of the algorithm varies as n^2; sorting 100 items takes 100 times the number of comparisons that sorting 10 items does. We will now make calculations to see why sorting by merging is useful for long files. To sort a file of *n* items, by first using a bubble sort on two files $n/2$ in length then merging, requires $n^2/4 - n/2$ for the bubble sort and *n* for the merge. This makes a combination total of

$n^2/4 + n/2$ comparisons.

Using a bubble sort on the whole file gives a result of

$n^2/2 - n/2$ comparisons.

When *n* = *100*, the bubble sort merge method requires 2,550 comparisons, the straight bubble sort requires 4,950 comparisons. Other methods that are more efficient than the bubble sort may be used.

CHAPTER 15 SUMMARY

This chapter has presented methods of searching and sorting that are used in computer programs. These methods manipulate files of records. Each record consists of one or more fields.

A search is based on a key, such as a person's name, that appears as one field in a record of a file. A linear search locates the desired record by starting at the first record and inspecting one record after another until the given key is found. A linear search is slow and should not be used for large files; a faster search method, such as binary search, should be used for large files.

A binary search requires that the file be ordered according to the key field of the records. An unordered file can be ordered using one of the sorting methods given in this chapter. The binary search inspects the middle record to determine which half of the file contains the desired record. Then the middle record of the correct half is inspected, to determine which quarter of the file contains the desired record, and so on, until the record is located.

If the key is a number that is identical to the index of the desired record then no searching is required, because the key gives the location of the record. Sometimes the key can be manipulated to create a hash code that locates a small set of records, in a location called a bucket, that includes the desired record.

A file of records can be ordered using the bubble sort. This method repeatedly passes through the file, interchanging adjacent out-of-order records until all records are in order. The bubble sort is slow and should not be used for large files; a Shell sort is more efficient but a faster sorting method, such as sorting by merging, should be used for large files.

A file can be sorted by merging in the following manner. First the file is divided into two sub-files and each of the sub-files is sorted by some method, such as the bubble sort or the Shell sort. Then, starting with the first records of the two sub-files, the ordered file is created by passing through the sub-files and successively picking the appropriate (smaller key or alphabetically first key) record. If the sub-files are large, they should be sorted by a fast method, such as a merge, instead of by a Shell sort.

CHAPTER 15 EXERCISES

1. The students for a particular high-school class have their names recorded, for example:

   'Abbot, Harold'

   These entries are arranged alphabetically. The names of newly-entered students for the same class are to be entered and inserted into the ordered list. Write a program which maintains the list in alphabetic order.

2. Write a program that maintains a lost and found service. First the program reads entries giving found objects and the finders' names and phone numbers. For example, this entry

   'Siamesse cat' 'Miss Mabel Davis' '714-3261'

   means Miss Mabel Davis, having phone number 714-3261, found a Siamese cat. These entries are to be read and ordered alphabetically and then a similar entry are to be processed. If a lost object matches a found object, then the program should output the name of the object as well as the finder, the loser and their telephone numbers. Process each loser entry as it is read, using a binary search.

3. Write a program to sort a mailing list of names and addresses and eliminate any possible duplicates. Assume that the names are always given in a standard form.

Chapter 16

FILES AND RECORDS

So far we have spoken about files of records and discussed the process of searching for particular records. This process was made more efficient by having the files sorted. We then looked at ways of sorting files of records. All sorting methods involve moving records around in the computer memory. In our sorting examples, we did not really deal with the situation of sorting records that consisted of more than the one field, namely the key field of the ordering. In our examples, then, moving the record meant only moving this one field. In most data processing applications, records contain a number of fields, so in this chapter will show how such records are handled in Fortran.

When large quantities of data have to be processed, it is impossible to store files of records completely within the main memory of the computer. It is usual to keep large files in secondary storage in disk storage. We must then be able to read records from such a file and write records into it. We will be looking at the statements in Fortran that permit us to manipulate files in secondary storage.

RECORDS IN FORTRAN

Some programming languages like Cobol, Pascal, Turing, and PL/1 provide special constructs for handling records. These allow the programmer to collect several variables into a record and use a name for the entire the record. For example, a *client* record could have name, address and phone number fields as this diagram shows.

client

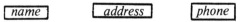

This is the kind of record that might be found in a telephone book. You have noticed that arrays, which can also be thought of as collections of variables, are different from records because all elements in an array are of the same type.   But in records each field can be of a different type.

Since Fortran does not provide a special way of designating records, we must declare each field of the record as an ordinary variable. Our *client* record can be created this way:

```
c       Set up a client's record
        character*20 name
        character*30 adress
        character*8 phone
```

In other languages the record could be assigned as a unit to another record that has the same types of fields.   But in Fortran, the record must be assigned field by field.   Similarly, if the record is to be read or output this must be done a field at a time.

ARRAYS OF RECORDS

There can be arrays of records, just like there can be arrays of simple types such as integers.   To set up an array of records using Fortran we declare each field to be an array and then consider record number *i* to be the collection of fields with index *i*.   An array of 100 records such as those used in a telephone book could be declared by:

```
character*20 name(100)
character*30 address(100)
character*8 phone(100)
```

Now the collection *name(i), address(i), phone(i)* makes up record number *i*.

We can use our array of records to group records for sorting purposes. A subroutine for sorting these records will be given.   The records are to be sorted on the key *phone*.   The array of records will be in **common** with the main program.   The only parameter is *size* which gives the actual number of records in the array.   The sorting will be done by swapping records, so a temporary record is set up to hold a record during a swap.

```
        subroutine sort(size)
c       Sort records by phone number
        integer size
        common/ table/ name,adress,phone
        character *20 name(100)
        character *30 adress(100)
        character *8 phone(100)
c       Set up a temporary record
        character *20 tname
```

```
          character *30 tadres
          character *8 tphone
          integer i,j,big,last
          i = 1
10        if (i.ge. size) go to 40
              last = size − i + 1
c             Put biggest phone number of 1 to last into last
              big = last
              j = 1
20            if (j.ge. last) go to 30
                  if (phone (j).gt.phone (big)) then
                      big = j
                  end if
                  j = j + 1
                  go to 20
30            continue
c             Swap record(last) and record with biggest
c                phone number in 1 to last
              tname = name (last)
              tadres = adress (last)
              tphone = phone (last)
              name (last) = name (big)
              adress (last) = adress (big)
              phone (last) = phone (big)
              name (big) = tname
              adress (big) = tadres
              phone (big) = tphone
              i = i + 1
              go to 10
40            continue
          return
          end
```

In many applications the natural way to think of the data is in terms of records. Sometimes each record corresponds to a input line of data or to a output line, but it can also correspond to a larger or smaller collection of information. We will give a program that reads each record of a small telephone directory from keyboard, uses our *sort* subroutine to put the records in order by phone number, and then outputs the result. As you can see, each record is read and output a field at a time, in this case by formatted **read** and **print** statements.

```
        program direct
c       Read a small phone directory and output it in
c       order by phone number
        common/ table/ name,adress,phone
        character *20 name(100)
        character *30 adress(100)
        character *8 phone(100)
        integer i,size
        print *,'Enter number of records'
        read *,size
c       Read entries into array of records
        print 5,'Name','Address','Phone'
5       format (' ',a,16x,a,23x,a)
        do 20 i = 1,size
            read 10,name(i),adress(i),phone(i)
10          format (1x,a20,a30,a8)
20          continue
        print *,' '
c       Sort records by phone number
        call sort(size)
c       Output sorted array of records
        print 25,'Phone','Name','Address'
25      format (' ',a,5x,a,16x,a)
        do 40 i = 1,size
            print 30,phone(i),name(i),adress(i)
30          format (' ',a8,2x,a20,a30)
40          continue
        stop
        end
```

(include here the sort subroutine)

Here is a sample display:

Enter number of records
5

Name	Address	Number
Johnston,R.L.	53 Jonston Cres.	491-6405
Keast,P.	77 Kredle Haven Dr.	439-7216
Lipson,J.D.	15 Weedwood Road.	787-8515
Mathon,R.A.	666 Regina Ave.	962-8885
Crawford,C.R.	39 Treatherson Ave.	922-7999

Phone	Name	Address
439-7216	Keast,P.	77 Kredle Haven Dr.
491-6405	Johnston,R.L.	53 Jonston Cres.
787-8515	Lipson,J.D.	15 Weedwood Road.
922-7999	Crawford,C.R.	39 Treatherson Ave.
962-8885	Mathon,R.A.	666 Regina Ave.

FILES IN SECONDARY MEMORY

In our discussion of files so far, we have had the files stored in the main memory. In most real file applications, the files are too large to be contained in main memory. The part of the file being processed must be brought into main memory, but the complete file is stored in secondary memory. The secondary memory is the disk.

A file in secondary storage is called a **data set**. One record at a time may be transferred from the data set to the main memory, or from the main memory to the data set. If the record that is transferred must be the **next** record in the sequence of records in the data set we say that the file is read sequentially from the secondary memory to the main memory or written sequentially from the main memory to secondary memory. This type of file is called a **sequential file**. It is not possible at any moment to get access to an arbitrary record in the file; the next record in sequence is the only one that is available.

Files in which any record can be read or written at any time are called **random access files**. Before a sequential file in secondary storage can be accessed, we must write a statement of the form

> **open** (file number,**file**='file name'*)*

The file number is an unsigned non-zero integer constant. File number zero is reserved for the display screen. We write the file number as * for the screen as output and the keyboard as input. If the file is a new one we include the specification **status='new'** in the parentheses. For sequential files the **open** statement should position the file reader at the first record of the file. On Vax computers it is necessary to give the statement

> **rewind** file number

after the **open** to position the reader at the first record. To write the next, or first, record onto a file in secondary storage, we use a statement of the form

> **write**(file number,format identification)list of variables separated by commas

The list of variables makes up the record to be written. Each of these must be an array element or a simple, non-array variable.

The types of the fields of a record are called its **template**. For example, in the telephone book example the template consists of *character*20, character*30*, and *character*8*. All the records written on a file should have the same template.

After the final record of a file is written the file should be closed off, or ended, by the statement

close (file number)

If it is desired, in the same program the file can then be reopened and read. Otherwise the file can be left to be read by a different program, possibly days or months later.

When we want to read a sequential file from secondary storage we must first open it and then use a statement of the form

read (file number, format identification) list of variables separated by commas

The next, or first, record on the file is read into the list of variables. The types of the variables must be the same as the template of the records on the file. Care must be taken not to try to read beyond the end of the file. This can be avoided by checking for a special dummy record that is typically the last record written before the file is ended by the **close** statement.

Once a sequential file has been opened it can be written or read but not both. But the file can be opened again to start reading or writing from the beginning. Once writing of a file is started, any previous contents of the file are lost and the file must be ended by a **close** statement after the final record is written.

FILE MAINTENANCE

As an example of reading and writing sequential files we will program a simple file-maintenance operation. We will assume that there exists a file of customer records called *custom* to which we will assign the file number 3, and we want to update this file by adding new customers. The information about the new customers is entered from the keyboard. Each entry corresponds to a **transaction** that must be **posted** in the file to produce an up-to-date customer file, which we will call *newcus* and to which we will assign the file number 4. This is an example of **file maintenance**. The original file is ordered alphabetically by customer name and the transactions must be arranged alphabetically. The last record of each file has a *name* with a value *zzz*. This program will be very similar to the merge-sort program we showed earlier, except that the records of the two files being merged are not in an array.

```
        program update
c       Add new customers to customer file
        character *20 name,tname
        character *30 adress,tadres
        character *8 phone,tphone
        open (3,file = 'custom ')
        rewind 3
        open (4,file = 'newcus',status='new')
c       Read first customer record from file
        read (3,10)name,adress,phone
        print *,'Enter transactions in alphabetic order '
        print 5,'Name','Address','Phone '
5       format (1x,a,16x,a,23x,a)
c       Read first transaction from keyboard
        read (*,10)tname,tadres,tphone
10      format (1x,a20,a30,a8)
c       Post transactions to customer file
15      if (name.eq.'zzz'.and.tname.eq.'zzz') go to 25
            if (name.lt.tname) then
                write (4,10)name,adress,phone
                read (3,10)name,adress,phone
            else
                write (4,10)tname,tadres,tphone
                read (*,10)tname,tadres,tphone
            end if
            go to 15
25          continue
c       Add dummy record to end of file
        write (4,10)name,adress,phone
        close (4)
        close (3)
        stop
        end
        (transactions one per line, end with )
        zzz              null              null
```

RANDOM ACCESS FILES

So far we have been looking at files which had to be read or written in sequence. Files where records can be read or written in any order whatever are called **random** or **direct access files**. Records are addressed by their serial number in the file; the first record is number 1, the second number

2, and so on. All records must be of exactly the same length so that they will fit into the space without disturbing their neighbors.

A random access file is opened with a statement of the form

open(file number,**file**='file name',**access**='direct',**recl**=number of characters)

To write records to the file we use statements of the form

write(file number,format identification,**rec**=record number)list of variables

To read records we use a statement of the form

read(file number,format identification,**rec**=record number)list of variables

When using a direct access file you must never access a record which is not there. It is a good idea to place dummy data in all records. Then entries can be made into the file at random, overwriting the dummy data. Some records will remain as dummy records. Inquiries can then be made against the file with no fear that a **read** error will occur, because there is no record there. The inquiries must test to see if the data retrieved is a dummy record or a genuine one.

A file is assumed to be an old one, already in existence, unless you specify in the **open** statement after the name that **status**=**new**. A direct access file may be an unformatted file if the **open** statement contains the specification **form**=**unformatted**. This speeds up the inquiries to a direct access file. Direct access files can only be prepared or read by a Fortran program. Formatted files, used for sequential access, can be prepared using the editor of the operating system.

Here is a program that reads a sequential file of formatted employee records and stores them in a random access file in unformatted form so that they can be accessed directly. The employee number will be the record number. Not every employee number is in use at any given time. The numbers range from 1 to 999. The sequential records consist of four fields, employee number, name, address, and annual salary. The sequential file is called *employ*. We will call the random access file *people*.

```
         program change
c        Sets up direct access file people
c        from sequential file employ
         integer number
         character *20 name
         character *30 adress
         real salary
         open (3,file = 'employ ')
         rewind 3
         open (4,file ='people',status='new',access='direct',
```

```
      +   form='unformatted',recl=60)
c         Set all records of people file to dummy
          name = 'zzz'
          adress = 'zzz'
          salary = 9999.99
          do 10 number = 1,999
              write (4,rec=number)name,adress,salary
10            continue
c         Read records from employ file to people file
          read (3,20)number,name,adress,salary
20        format (1x,13,ix,a20,a30,f10.2)
30        if (name.eq.'zzz')go to 40
              write (4,rec=number)name,adress,salary
              read (3,20)number,name,adress,salary
              go to 30
40            continue
          close (3)
          close (4)
          stop
          end
```

At this stage the *people* random access file has been created and we can make changes to it or inquiries against it interactively. After we enter the employee number we will be prompted to indicate the type of transaction and will enter *c* for change and *i* for inquiry. We will enter an employee number of -1 when we are finished with the transactions.

Here is the program:

```
          program inform
c         Used to change the file or make an inquiry
          character *1 reply
          integer number
          character *20 name
          character *30 adress
          real salary
          open (2,file='people',access='direct',form='unformatted',recl=60)
          print *,'Enter employee number'
          read *,number
c         Determine if end of transactions
5         if (number.eq.-1) go to 30
              print *,'Enter i for inquiry or c for change'
              read (*,3) reply
3             format (1x,a1)
```

```
                    if (reply.eq. 'i') then
                        read (2,rec = number)name,adress,salary
                        write (8,20)name,adress,salary
                    else if (reply.eq. 'c') then
                        write (*,10)'Name','Address','Salary9.99'
10                      format (1x,a,16x,a,23x,a)
                        read (*,20)name,adress,salary
20                      format (1x,a20,a30,f10.2)
                        write (2,rec =number)name,adress,salary
                    end if
                    print *,'Enter employee number'
                    read *,number
                    go to 5
30                  continue
                close (2)
                stop
                end
```

Notice that when a change is required we enter the new values for *name*, *adress*, and *salary* in a formatted way. The prompt provides us with a guide to where in the line the information is to go. In particular since the salary must be lined up on the right side of the field we added 9.99 to the word salary.

Here is a sample output:

Enter employee number
727
Enter i for inquiry or c for change
c
Name   **Address**   **Salary 9.99**
Janet Yeo   *12 Islington Ave.*   *45000.00*
Enter employee number
215
Enter i for inquiry or c for change
i
Jim Clarke   15 Markham St.   35000.00
Enter employee number
− 1

CHAPTER 16 SUMMARY

In this chapter we showed how records are used in Fortran and how they can be written to or read from files in secondary memory. The following important terms were discussed in this chapter.

Record — a collection of fields of information. For example a record might be composed of a name field, an address field, and telephone number field.

Template — the list of types of variables in a record.

Data set — a file of information residing on secondary storage, typically on a disk or tape.

Sequential files — files that are always accessed (read or written) in order, from first record, to second record, to third record, and so on.

open — the statement of Fortran that initializes a file so it can be written or read. A sequential file should be started at its first record. To be sure follow the **open** statement by a **rewind** file number statement. The **open** statement has the form:

> **open** (*file number*,**'file**='*file name'*,[**status**='**new'**])

Read from a sequential file — the next or first record is read from a file using the statement

> **read**(file number,format specification) variables separated by commas
> The record is read into the variables. The record's template must match the types of the variables. The file number is a constant integer, such as 3, that refers to a file.

Write to a sequential file — the next or first record is written to a file using the statement

> **write**(file number,format specification) variables separated by commas

close(file number) — the statement of Fortran that must be used to close off a file after the final record is written.

File maintenance — means to keep a file up-to-date. This involves reading transactions and adding, deleting, or modifying file records. An existing file can be modified or extended by creating a new file.

open — a random access file with a statement of the form

> **open**(file number,**file**='file name',**access**='direct',**recl**=no. of char.)

Include the specification **form='unformatted'** if records are to be unformatted. Include the specification **status='new'** if the file is a new one.

Read from a random access file — the record number required using:

   read(file number,format specification,**rec**=record number)list of variables

Write to a random access file — the record number required using:

   write(file number,format specification,**rec**=record number) list of variables

CHAPTER 16 EXERCISES

The exercises for this chapter are based on a data processing system to be used by Apex Plumbing Supplies. For each customer the record is:

   Name
   Address
   Balance
   Credit limit

These records are to be entered on the keyboard and transferred to a disk file by the following program:

```
        program create
c       Create a master file
        character *20 name
        character *20 adress
        integer balnce
        integer credit
        character *20 prev
        open (4,file ='master',status='new')
        name ='AAA'
        write (*,3)'Name','Address','Balance999','Credit limit'
3       format (1x,a,16x,a,13x,a,4x,a)
5       if (name.eq. 'zzz') go to 15
            prev=name
            read (*,10)name,adress,balnce,credit
10          format (1x,a20,a20,i10,i16)
c           Make sure that records are in order
            if (name.gt.prev) then
                write (4,10)name,adress,balnce,credit
            else
                print *,'record out of order:',name
            end if
            go to 5
15          continue
        print *,'master file created'
        close (4)
```

stop
end

Here is a sample display:

Name	Address	Balance999	Credit limit
Abbot Plumbing	*94 N.Elm*	*3116*	*50000*
Durable Fixit	*247 Forest Hill*	*0*	*10000*
Erico Plumbing	*54 Gormley*	*9614*	*5000*
...			
zzz	*zzz*	*0*	*0*

The exercises for this chapter require you to write programs for various parts of the data processing system for Apex.

1. The program given above creates a master file for Apex Plumbing Supplies. Modify the program so that it sorts the records before creating the file. You can assume that there are at most 50 accounts.

2. Write a program that takes an existing master file for Apex and creates a new master file by deleting or adding new customer records. For example, the transaction records for your program might be

Davis Repair	4361 Main	2511	10000
Erico Plumbing	delete	0	0
zzz		0	0

   You can assume that these transactions are in alphabetic order. If the address field of the record specifies *delete*, the account is to be deleted from the file.

3. Write a program that reads the Apex master file and outputs the list of customers whose balances exceed their credit limits.

4. Write a program that reads the Apex master file and outputs a bill for each customer whose balance is greater than zero. For example, for the file record

Davis Repair	4361 Main	2511	10000

   your program should output

       to: Davis Repair
       4361 Main
   Dear sir or madam:
       Please remit $25.11 for plumbing supplies.
                   thank you,
                   John Apex, Pres.
                   Apex Plumbing Supplies
                   416 College St.

You can output the decimal point in this bill by dividing by 100.0 and using the f8.2 format item.

5.   Write a program that updates the master file using billing and payment transactions. A billing transaction is a record of the form

    name   (columns 2-21)
    amount   (columns 42-50)

For each billing transaction, the balance of the account is to be increased by the specified amount. A payment transaction is a record of the form

    name   (columns 2-21)
    amount   (columns 42-50)
    cr   (columns 51-52)

For each payment transaction, the balance of the account is to be decreased by the specified amount. The billing and payment transactions are not in order, so they should be sorted before creating the new master file.

6.   Write a program that prepares a random access file from the sequential file. To do this assign a customer number to each customer and use it to access the records. Write a program that updates the file interactively accepting billing and payment transactions in any order.

Chapter 17

ASSEMBLY LANGUAGE AND MACHINE LANGUAGE

In this book we have presented programming in terms of the Fortran 77 language. Fortran is a **high-level language**; it provides us with a convenient means for directing a computer to do work. The computer cannot execute Fortran programs directly; it can only execute programs in machine language, a **low-level language**. Before a Fortran program can be executed by a computer, the program must be **translated** or **compiled** to machine language. In this chapter we will explain how a computer carries out instructions. We will present features of machine languages and their associated assembly languages.

MACHINE INSTRUCTIONS

In Chapter 2 we gave a brief introduction to machine language. We explained that the instructions a computer can execute are much more basic than Fortran statements. These **machine instructions** use a special location, called the **accumulator**, when doing arithmetic or making assignments. For example, the assignment of j to i, written as the Fortran statement

$i = j$

could be translated to the instructions

load j	(copy j into the accumulator)
store i	(copy the accumulator into i)

As another example, the Fortran statement

$i = j + k$

could be translated into the three instructions

load	*j*	(copy j into the accumulator)
add	*k*	(add k to the accumulator)

> *store*   *i*   (copy the accumulator into *i*)

Different   kinds   of   computers   have   different   machine languages. Some computers have many accumulators and some have few. Some computers have many instructions and some have few. We will introduce common features of machine languages by inventing a very simple computer. We will call our computer VS, for **very simple** computer.

The machine instructions for the VS computer are designed to be convenient for representing programs written in a very small subset of Fortran 77.   The   VS   computer has   never   been   built; it is just a hypothetical machine that we will use to illustrate points about computer languages.

The instructions for the VS computer have the form

> operator operand

for example,

> *store i*

The **operator** of an instruction tells the computer what to do; the **operand** tells the computer what to do it to.

After the computer executes one instruction, it continues to the next, unless the executed instruction directs the computer to jump to another instruction or to skip an instruction. We can translate the Fortran statements

> **if** *(i*.le.*k)***then**
> > *k = i + j*
>
> **end if**
> *i = j*

into the VS computer instructions

	load	*k*	(copy *k* into the accumulator)
	skiple	*i*	(**if** *i*.**le.** accumulator, skip next instruction)
	jump	*m*	(jump to instruction labelled *m*)
	load	*i*	(copy *i* into the accumulator)
	add	*j*	(add *j* to the accumulator)
	store	*k*	(copy the accumulator into *k*)
m:	*load*	*j*	(copy *j* into the accumulator)
	store	*i*	(copy the accumulator into *i*)

In this example, *m* is the label of an instruction; instructions are labelled so they can be jumped to. The following statements, which are not used in the way we presented in this book, are equivalent to the example we just gave:

> **if** (*i*.**gt**.*k*)**go to** *5*
> $k = i + j$
> 5 $i = j$

go tos were purposely restricted in this book because careless use of them leads to unreadable programs. One of the reasons that low-level languages are inconvenient to use is that they do not directly provide looping constructs, such as the counted **do** loop, and selection constructs, such as the **if...then...else** statement. The programmer must build up these constructs using instructions like jumps and skips. In a sense the presence of **go to**s in the conditional loop is an indication of the need for a different language construct in Fortran. Such a construct is called **do while** in PL/1.

INSTRUCTIONS FOR A VERY SIMPLE COMPUTER

The VS computer has an instruction to output the accumulator:

> *putint*

This instruction needs no operand because the accumulator's value is always output. There is an instruction to output messages:

> *putstr* operand

The operand represents a string to be output. There is an instruction that directs the machine to stop executing a program:

> *halt*

The *halt* instruction has no operand. Altogether the VS computer has nine instructions; most real computers have many more instructions, typically around 100. This table lists the VS instructions.

	Operator	Operand	Action by Computer
1	*load*	variable	Assign variable to accumulator.
2	*store*	variable	Assign accumulator to variable.
3	*add*	variable	Add variable to accumulator.
4	*sub*	variable	Subtract variable from accumulator.
5	*jump*	label	Jump to labelled instruction.
6	*skiple*	variable	If variable **.le.** accumulator then skip next instruction.
7	*putint*	(none)	Output the integer in the accumulator.
8	*putstr*	string	Output the string.
9	*halt*	(none)	Halt, the program is finished.

We have purposely kept the VS computer simple by leaving out instructions that might normally be part of the instruction set of a computer.

We have left out a whole set of skip instructions, such as *skipgt* (skip when greater than). We left out instructions for doing **real** arithmetic and for reading data. We left out instructions for manipulating character strings, indexing arrays, and calling and returning from subroutines. These additional instructions are important in an actual computer; if you like, you can design a super VS computer that includes them.

TRANSLATION OF A FORTRAN PROGRAM

If we use some care in picking our example, we can translate an entire Fortran program into VS instructions. This example Fortran program requires only the types of instructions available on the VS computer:

	High-Level Language		*Low-Level Language*	
	integer *i*			
	print *, 'powers of 2'*		*putstr*	*title*
	i=1		*load*	*one*
			store i	
5	**if** *(i.gt. 8)* **go to** 6	*l1:*	*load*	*eight*
			skiple	*i*
			jump	*12*
	print *,i*		*load*	*i*
			putint	
	i=1+1		*load*	*i*
			add	*i*
			store	*i*
	go to 5		*jump*	*l1*
6	**continue**			
	stop	*12:*	*halt*	
	end			

The first VS instruction in this example has as its operand *title; title* gives the location of the string *'powers of 2'*. Similarly, *one* and *eight* give the locations of the values 1 and 8.

MNEMONIC NAMES AND MACHINE LANGUAGE

Up to this point we have written VS instructions using names such as *load, store, i,* and *j.* These names are not present in the machine language that a computer executes; they are replaced by numbers. We will now show how these names can be translated into appropriate numbers.

As you may recall from Chapter 2, the main memory of the computer consists of a sequence of **words**. The words of memory are numbered; the number that corresponds to a particular word is called the **location** or **address** of the word. Words can be used to represent variables. For example, the variables *i, j,* and *k* could be represented by the words with locations 59, 60, and 61. Here we show these three words after *i, j,* and *k* have been assigned the values 9, 0, and 14.

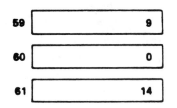

There is no special significance to 59, 60, and 61. We could just as well represent *i, j,* and *k* by locations 42, 3, and 87; the important thing is to remember which location corresponds to which variable.

If *i, j,* and *k* correspond to location 59, 60, and 61, we can write the instructions

load	*j*
add	*k*
store	*i*

as

load	*60*	(copy contents of word 60 into accumulator)
add	*61*	(add contents of word 61 to accumulator)
store	*59*	(copy accumulator into word 59)

The VS instruction operators, *load, store,* and so on, are numbered. *load* is operator number 1, *store* is 2, *add* is 3, and so on. The names *load, store,* and *add* as used in the VS instructions are **mnemonic names**; a mnemonic name is an easy-to-remember name. We can choose the names of the operands so that they too are easy to remember.

Using the numbers of the operators we can write

load	*60*
add	*61*
store	*59*

as

1	*60*
3	*61*
2	*59*

Instructions that consist only of numbers are in **machine language**. Instructions that contain mnemonic names, such as *load* and *i*, are in **assembly language**.

Assembly Language		Machine Language	
load	*j*	*1*	*60*
add	*k*	*3*	*61*
store	*i*	*2*	*59*

As you can see, there is a simple translation from assembly language to machine language. Writing programs in machine language is even more inconvenient than writing programs in assembly language. People almost always prefer assembly language over machine language; they use a program called an **assembler** to translate mnemonic names in assembly language programs to corresponding numeric operators and operands. Although we do not show it here, assemblers allow the programmer to reserve and initialize memory for variables and constants. For example, location 59 would be reserved for *i*, and location 98 could be reserved for *eight* and initialized to 8.

STORING MACHINE INSTRUCTIONS IN WORDS

The values of variables of a program are stored in words of the computer's memory. In a similar manner, the instructions of the program are stored in words of memory. We can use two words to hold each VS instruction; one word for the operator and one word for the operand. Here we show three instructions stored in locations 18 through 23:

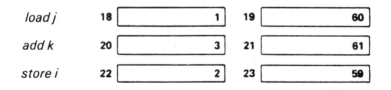

We could have saved space if the VS computer allowed us to pack the operator and operand into a single word. For example, the instruction

$$1 \qquad 59$$

could be packed into a single word as

$$1059$$

with the convention that the rightmost three digits are the operand and the other digits are the operator. Instructions for real computers are packed into words to save space, but to keep things simple, the VS computer uses two words for its instructions.

A *jump* instruction has as its operand the label of an instruction. When a *jump* instruction is written in machine language, the label must be a number. The number used is the location of the instruction being jumped to. Here is a translation of assembly language into machine language; the label *l* becomes 48:

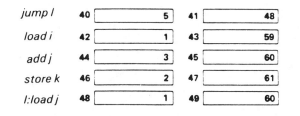

Just as the variables and instructions are stored in words in memory, strings such as *'powers of 2'* are stored in memory. In real computers this is done by packing several characters into each word. Since mixing characters and numbers is confusing, we will assume that the VS computer has a separate part of its memory used only for strings. Each string is saved in a different location in the special string memory. If the string *'powers of 2'* is in location number 1 in the special string memory, then we translate the statement

    print **,'powers of 2'*

to the machine instruction

       8   1   (putstr title)

We have now shown how to translate all VS instructions into numbers and thus into machine language. We will return to our program that outputs powers of 2 and will translate it to machine language.

STORAGE OF PROGRAM IN COMPUTER

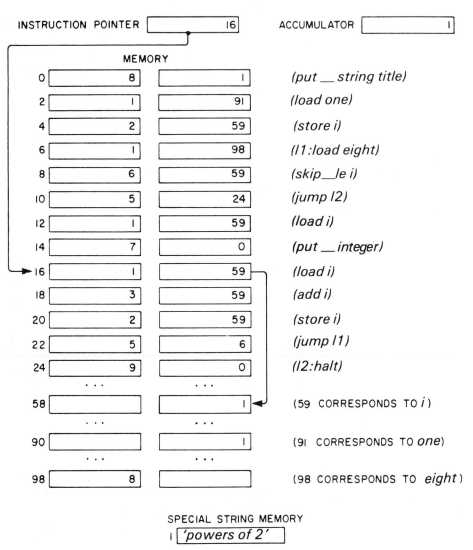

INSTRUCTION POINTER	16	ACCUMULATOR 1

MEMORY

0	8	1	*(put __ string title)*
2	1	91	*(load one)*
4	2	59	*(store i)*
6	1	98	*(l1:load eight)*
8	6	59	*(skip__le i)*
10	5	24	*(jump l2)*
12	1	59	*(load i)*
14	7	0	*(put __ integer)*
16	1	59	*(load i)*
18	3	59	*(add i)*
20	2	59	*(store i)*
22	5	6	*(jump l1)*
24	9	0	*(l2:halt)*
. . .		. . .	
58		1	(59 CORRESPONDS TO *i*)
. . .		. . .	
90		1	(91 CORRESPONDS TO *one*)
. . .		. . .	
98	8		(98 CORRESPONDS TO *eight*)

SPECIAL STRING MEMORY

1	*'powers of 2'*
2	
	. . .

A COMPLETE MACHINE LANGUAGE PROGRAM

We will assume that a VS computer always starts by executing the instruction in words 1 and 2. So we will place our machine language instructions in words 1, 2, 3, 4, ... We will continue assuming that variable *i* corresponds to memory location 59. The integer constants 1 and 8 will be represented by memory locations 91 and 98; these locations are initialized to hold the values 1 and 8 before the program is executed. We show the program as it would appear in memory after having executed instructions in locations 1 through 16. Up to this point the program has output

> *powers of 2*
>
> *1*

The VS computer has an **instruction pointer**, presently set to 17, that locates the next instruction to be executed. When an instruction has no operand, we give it a dummy operand of zero; for example, *halt* becomes 90.

SIMULATING A COMPUTER

A VS computer has never been built and undoubtedly never will be built. It might seem that we can never have a VS machine language program executed. But we can, by making an existing computer **simulate** a VS computer. This is done by writing a program, called a **simulator**, that acts as if it is a VS computer. We will discuss later in more detail the importance of simulators in computing, but first we will develop a Fortran subroutine that is a simulator for the VS computer.

The VS computer has an accumulator, which can be simulated by a variable declared by

> **integer** *accum*

It also has a memory containing 100 words. This can be simulated by an array:

> **integer** *memory(100)*

There is a special string memory. Assuming that the VS computer can hold, at most, 10 strings of length 20, we can simulate the string memory by another array:

> **character** **1 string(10,20)*

We need an instruction pointer to keep track of which instruction is to be executed next.

> **integer** *ip*

When the VS computer is executing, the instruction pointer has a particular value, say 10, indicating that word 10 contains the operator of the next instruction to be executed. Word 11 contains the operand. If *oprtor* and *oprand* are declared as integer variables in the simulator, then they should be given values by:

$$oprtor = memory(ip)$$
$$oprand = memory(ip + 1)$$

If the operator is 1, meaning *load*, the simulator carries out the *load* machine instruction by executing:

$$accum = memory(oprand)$$

If the operator is 2, meaning *store*, the simulator carries out the *store* instruction by executing:

$$memory(oprand) = accum$$

Similarly, the simulator can carry out the other VS instructions. After each instruction is carried out, the instruction pointer *ip* is incremented by 2 and operator and operand are set for the next instruction. When the instruction is a *jump* or *skip*, then the instruction pointer *ip* can be modified so an instruction other than the next sequential instruction will be selected. For example, if the operator is 6, for *skiple*, the simulator executes this:

    if *(memory(oprand)*.**le**.*accum)***then**
        ip = ip + 2
    end if

To make the simulator more readable, we will use mnemonic variables for each of the VS instructions:

    integer *load,store,..., halt*

We will initialize these variables to their corresponding machine language numeric values 1, 2, ...9. These declarations should be **common** to the simulator subroutine; the variables should be initialized before calling the simulator.

    Now we give the complete simulator as a Fortran subroutine. This subroutine assumes that the *memory* and *string* arrays have been declared and initialized.

```
        subroutine simltr
c       Simulates a very simple computer
        common/ core/ memory,string
        integer memory(100)
        character *1 string(10,20)
        common/ opcode/ load,store,add,sub,jump,skiple,putint,putstr,halt
        integer load,store,add,sub,jump,skiple,putint,putstr,halt
        integer accum,ip,oprtor,oprand,column
        character *1 outstr(20)
```

```
          ip = 1
          oprtor = memory(ip)
          oprand = memory(ip + 1)
5         if (oprtor.eq. halt) go to 30
              if (oprtor.eq. load) then
                  accum = memory(oprand)
              end if
              if (oprtor.eq. store) then
                  memory(oprand) = accum
              end if
              if (oprtor.eq. add) then
                  accum = accum + memory(oprand)
              end if
              if (oprtor.eq. sub) then
                  accum = accum - memory(oprand)
              end if
              if (oprtor.eq. jump) then
                  ip = oprand - 2
              end if
              if (oprtor.eq. skiple) then
                  if (memory(oprand).le. accum) then
                      ip = ip + 2
                  end if
              end if
              if (oprtor.eq. putint) then
                  print *,accum
              end if
              if (oprtor.eq. putstr) then
                  do 10 column = 1,20
                      outstr(column) = string(oprand,column)
10                  continue
                  print 20,outstr
20                format (' ',20a1)
              end if
              ip = ip + 2
              oprtor = memory(ip)
              oprand = memory(ip + 1)
              go to 5
30        continue
      return
      end
```

If you want to run a VS machine language program, you can write a main program to put the numbers representing the program and constants into the *memory* array, initialize the *string* array and then call the *simltr* subroutine.

USES OF SIMULATORS

We will now discuss some of the uses of simulators. Our simulator for the VS computer can be used to execute VS machine language programs. But it can serve another purpose, too. By reading the *simltr* subroutine, you can determine the actions carried out for each VS instruction; if you did not know how a VS computer worked, you could find out by studying its simulator. So not only can the simulator direct one computer to act like another, it can also show how a computer works.

Computer simulators are often used to allow programs written for one machine to execute on another machine. For example, a business may buy a new computer to replace an old computer. After the old computer is removed, programs written for the old computer can be executed by a simulator running on the new machine.

CHAPTER 17 SUMMARY

In this chapter we have presented features of machine language in terms of a very simple hypothetical computer called VS. The VS computer has an accumulator that is used for doing calculations. There are VS machine. instructions for loading, storing, adding to, subtracting from, and outputting the accumulator. There is a machine instruction for outputting strings. There are instructions for jumping to instructions, skipping ins,tructions and for halting. The nine VS machine instructions were sufficient for the translation of the example Fortran 77 program given in this chapter. Real computers typically have many more instructions. The following important terms were discussed:

Word — the computer's main memory is divided into words. Each word can contain a number. In real computers, a word can contain several characters, typically 4 characters.

Location (or address) — the number that locates a particular word in the computer's main memory.

Operators and operands — most VS machine instructions, such as

load i

consist of an operator and an operand; these are *load* and *i* in this example. Some instructions have an operator but no operand.

Mnemonic name — a name that helps programmers remember something. For example, *store* is the mnemonic name for VS machine instruction number 2.

Machine language — the purely numeric language that is directly executed by a particular type of computer. Some computer manufacturers sell families of computers, of various sizes and speeds, that all use the same machine language.

Assembly language — programs in assembly language use mnemonic names corresponding to the numeric operators of machine language. They also permit programmers to choose mnemonic names for the operands and labels.

Assembler — a program that translates programs written in assembly language to machine language.

Label — a name that gives the location of a machine instruction or a statement. The *jump* machine instruction, as written in assembly language, transfers control to a labeled instruction.

Simulator — a program that simulates some system such as a computer. A simulator treats a sequence of numbers as a machine language program and carries out the specified operations.

CHAPTER 17 EXERCISES

1. The VS computer described in this chapter does not have an instruction for reading data. Invent an instruction named *getint* that reads the next integer in the data into the accumulator. Show how to translate a read statement such as

    read **,k*

    into VS machine language, as augmented by *getint.* Show how the *simltr* subroutine given in this chapter can be modified to execute *getint* instructions.

2. Translate the following program into VS assembly language and then into VS machine language.

    integer *i,j*
    i=1
    j=5
    if *(i.*le.*j)***then**

```
        print *,'i is smaller'
   else
        print *,'j is smaller'
   end if
   stop
   end
```

3.   What will the following VS assembly language program output? Translate the program to both machine language and Fortran.

```
        load        zero
        store       previous
        load        one
        store       current
  k1:   load        fifty
        skiple      current
        jump        k2
        load        current
        add         previous
        store       next
        load        current
        store       previous
        load        next
        store       current
        putint
        jump        k1
  k2:   halt
```

4.   In this chapter an example program was given that outputs powers of 2. Have this program executed by the VS simulator given in this chapter. This can be done by writing a main program that initializes the *memory* and *string* arrays to hold the machine language version of the example program, and then calls the *simltr* subroutine.

Chapter 18

DATA STRUCTURES

In previous chapters we have shown that arrays provide a method of organizing data and that records can be used to structure data within a file.

All of the classifications: variables, arrays of variables, records, and files, are examples of what we generally call **data structures**. Just as we systematize our programs by attempting to write well-structured programs, we systematize the way in which data is stored. We structure data.

In this chapter we will describe other structural forms for data and give examples of how these structures are useful to us. We will describe data structures called **linked lists** and **tree structures**. There are many kinds of lists, for example **stacks, queues, doubly-linked lists**, and so on. Tree structures can be limited to **binary trees**, or may be more general.

These new data structures are not a part of the Fortran language as arrays are, so that when we want to store data in a linked list or a tree we use an array to implement them. We must program the structure.

LINKED LISTS

Suppose that we had a file of records stored in an array called *data*. The records are arranged in sequence on some key. For simplicity, we will consider that each record consists only of a single field which is the key to the ordering. We know that if the order is ascending and no two keys are identical, then

$$data(i+1).\text{gt}.data(i)$$

The difficulty with this kind of data structure for a file comes when a new item is to be added to the file; it must be inserted between two items. This means we would have to move all the items with a key higher than the one to be inserted, one location on in the array. For example, you can see what happens when we insert the word *dog* in this list:

	before	after inserting *dog*
data(1)	cat	cat
data(2)	duck	dog
data(3)	fox	duck
data(4)	goose	fox
data(5)	pig	goose
data(6)	-	pig

Any list that is changing with time will have additions and deletions made to it. A deletion will create a hole unless entries are moved to fill the hole.

When the list changes with time we can use the data structure called the **linked list**. In the linked list each item has two components, the data component and the linking component or **link**. We associate with each entry in the *data* array an entry in a second array called *link*. The number stored in *link(i)* is the index of the next entry in the sequence of the *data* array following *data(i)*. This means that the actual or **physical sequence** in the *data* array is different from the **logical sequence** in the list. Here is an example showing our previous list as a linked list. The start of the list is stored in the integer variable *first*.

	first	3	
data(1)	pig	*link(1)*	0
data(2)	fox	*link(2)*	4
data(3)	cat	*link(3)*	5
data(4)	goose	*link(4)*	1
data(5)	duck	*link(5)*	2
data(6)	-	*link(6)*	-

Here is a diagram of this:

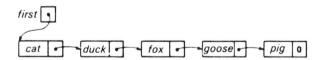

You can follow the list by beginning with the value of *first*, which is 3. The first entry will be in *data(3)*; it is *cat*. By looking then at *link(3)* you find a 5 which is the index of the next list item, *data(5)*, which is *duck*. You follow the list down until you reach a *link* whose value is 0; this is the signal that you have reached the end of the list. Other signals can be used, such as having a negative number.

INSERTING INTO A LINKED LIST

To see the merit of a linked list we must see how to insert new entries. We will add *dog* in its proper list position. We will do this first by hand; afterwards we will have to program it for the computer. We will place the entry *dog* in *data(6)* since it is an available or free location. We must now change the values of certain of the links so that the new entry will be inserted. We must put a value into *link(6)* and change the value of the *link* of the entry before *dog*, which is *cat*, to point to *data(6)*. This means that *link(3)* must be changed to 6 and *link(6)* must be set to 5 so that the entry after *dog* is *duck*, which is *data(5)*.

The linked list then becomes

		first	*3*
data(1)	*pig*	*link(1)*	*0*
data(2)	*fox*	*link(2)*	*4*
data(3)	*cat*	*link(3)*	*6*
data(4)	*goose*	*link(4)*	*1*
data(5)	*duck*	*link(5)*	*2*
data(6)	*dog*	*link(6)*	*5*

Here is a diagram:

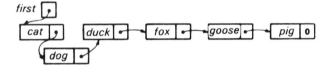

To add *dog*, one link must be changed and one set. No movement of the existing items in *data* is necessary. This is surely an improvement over moving half the list, on the average, to insert a new entry. The cost of this improved efficiency of operation comes in having to reserve memory space for the *link* array. This array gives the structure of the list and is stored explicitly for a linked list. In an array, the sequence or structure is implicit; each entry follows its neighbor. We will see several other kinds of structures that require us to store the structure information explicitly.

MEMORY MANAGEMENT WITH LISTS

With linked lists, some of the memory is used for structure information and some for data. For any list, as the list grows, we use more memory; as it shrinks, we use less. This means we must reserve enough memory to hold the longest list that we ever expect to have. But we should not waste memory. As we stop using certain elements of the array by deleting entries, we must keep track of where they are, so when additions occur we can reuse these same elements. To keep track of the available array elements we keep them together in a second linked list. The list of available array elements does not have any useful information in the *data* part, but it is structured as a list using values in the *link* part. We must keep track of the beginning of this list so we keep the index of its beginning in an integer variable *avail.*

Here is an array of 10 elements that stores our previous data items in a different set of locations and has the available space linked up:

	first	*10*		*avail*	*7*
data(1)	goose		*link(1)*	*9*	
data(2)	fox		*link(2)*	*1*	
data(3)	-		*link(3)*	*6*	
data(4)	duck		*link(4)*	*2*	
data(5)	-		*link(5)*	*0*	
data(6)	-		*link(6)*	*5*	
data(7)	-		*link(7)*	*3*	
data(8)	dog		*link(8)*	*4*	
data(9)	pig		*link(9)*	*0*	
data(10)	cat		*link(10)*	*8*	

In these arrays there are two linked lists, one containing the actual data, the other containing elements available for use. Each list has a pointer to its start; each has a last element with a link of 0. Every element of the array is in one list or the other.

The next problem is to write a subroutine for adding a new item to the list. We will develop the algorithm for this by step-by-step refinement.

SUBROUTINE FOR INSERTING INTO A LINKED LIST

The first step is to construct a solution tree. We will presume the value to be added is in the variable *value:*

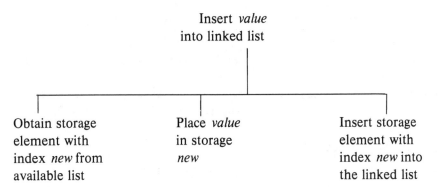

The expansion of the left branch of the solution tree requires us to find the index *new* of the first element of the list of available elements and remove the element from the list. Here is the program segment that does this:

$$new = avail$$
$$avail = link(avail)$$

The middle branch is also simple. It is

$$data(new) = value$$

We must expand the right branch still further:

Insert storage
element with
index *new* into
the linked list

if list is empty **then**
    Place element at beginning of list
else if *value* goes first in list **then**
    Place element at beginning of list
else
    Find place to insert *value*
        and adjust links to make insertion
end if

Here *value* will go first in the list if either the list is empty or *value* is less than the first element of the list. So we can write, "**if** list is empty," in this way:

if *(first*.**eq.** *null)***then**

We have assumed that the variable *null* will be initialized to zero. We can write, "Place element at beginning of list," in this way:

$$link(new) = first$$
$$first = new$$

For the part of the program after the **else** we need to examine the entries in the list and compare them with *value*. The index of the element being compared we will call *next*. The index of the element just compared previously we will call *prev*. We need to keep track of this previous element, because if

$$value.lt.data(next)$$

we must insert our element with index *new* between *prev* and *next*. Here is the program segment for this:

```
c         Find place to insert new value
          prev = first
          next = link(first)
5         if (next.eq.null) go to 10
              if (value.lt.data(next)) then
c                 Set next to force exit from loop
                  next = null
              else
                  prev = next
                  next = link(next)
              end if
              go to 5
10            continue
c         Adjust links to make insertion
          link(new) = link(prev)
          link(prev) = new
```

the whole subroutine can now be written out. Notice that *data, link, first, avail,* and *null* are **common** to this subroutine:

```
          subroutine insert(value)
c         Insert new value into linked list
          character *10 value
          common/ list/ data,link,first,avail,null
          character *10 data(30)
          integer link(30),first,avail,null
          integer new,prev,next
c         Obtain storage element for new value
          new = avail
          avail = link(avail)
c         Place new value in storage element
          data(new) = value
```

```
c       See if new value goes first in list
        if (first.eq. null) then
            link (new) = first
            first = new
        else if (value.lt. data (first)) then
            link (new) = first
            first = new
        else
c           Find place to insert new value
            (copy above program segment here)
        end if
        return
        end
```

DELETING FROM A LINKED LIST

Deletion is very similar. We will just record the final subroutine.

```
        subroutine delete (value)
c       Delete specified value from linked list
        character *10 value
        common/ list/ data, link, first, avail, null
        character *10 data (30)
        integer link (30), first, avail, null
        integer prev, old
c       Find the item to be deleted
        old = first
5       if (data (old).eq. value) go to 10
            prev = old
            old = link (old)
            go to 5
10      continue
c       Remove item from list
        if (first.eq. old) then
            first = link (old)
        else
            link (prev) = link (old)
        end if
c       Add storage element to free list
        link (old) = avail
        avail = old
        return
        end
```

Before using these two subroutines we must set *null* to 0, set *first* to *null,* set *avail* to 1, and *link(i)* to *i + 1,* with the exception of the last element which should have a *null* link.

MAINTAINING A LINKED LIST

Here is a main program that allows you to insert or delete names from a linked list or output it depending on which of three choices you make:

```
           program linked
    c      Permits insertion,deletion, and output
           common/ list/ data,link,first,avail,null
           character * 10 data(30),entry
           integer link(30),first,avail,null,i,reply
    c      Initialize all space to available
           null = 0
           avail = 1
           first = null
           link(30) = null
           do 10 i = 1,29
               link(i) = i + 1
    10         continue
    c      Find out what action is wanted
           print *,'Enter(1)insert,(2)delete,(3)output,(4)end'
           read *,reply
    20     if (reply.eq.4) go to 30
               if (reply.eq.1) then
                   print *,'Type entry to be inserted, in quotes'
                   read *,entry
                   call insert(entry)
               else if (reply.eq.2) then
                   print *,'Type entry to be deleted, in quotes'
                   read *,entry
                   call delete(entry)
               else if (reply.eq.3) then
                   print *,'Here is list'
                   call out
               end if
               print *,'Enter(1)insert,(2)delete,(3)output,(4)end'
               read *,reply
               go to 20
    30         continue
           stop
           end
```

```
        subroutine out
        common/ list/ data,link,first,avail,null
        character *10 data(30)
        integer  link(30),first,avail,null
        integer  i
c       Output list in alphabetic order
        i = first
10      if (i.eq. null) go to 20
            print *, data(i)
            i = link(i)
            go to 10
20          continue
        return
        end
        (copy insert and delete subroutines here)
```

STACKS

We showed how to insert and delete items for a linked list. The insertions and deletions could be anywhere in the list. In each case, as the list of data items was changed, a second linked list of available storage elements was maintained. A deletion from the list of data items resulted in an addition to the list of available elements; an addition in the data list produced a deletion in the available list. The actions involving the available storage list were much simpler. This is because the additions and deletions for it always were to the beginning of that list. A list that is restricted to having entries to or removals from the beginning only is called a **stack**. The situation is similar to a stack of trays in a cafeteria. When you want a tray you take it off the top of the stack; when you are through with a tray you put it back on the top. Stacks operate in a "last in first out" order, so they are sometimes called *LIFO* systems.

When a list is used as a stack, we often call the pointer to the beginning of the list *top*. When an entry is removed from the top we say we have **popped** an entry off. The value of *top* must then be adjusted to point at the next entry. When we add an entry we say we have **pushed** it onto the stack.

Because a stack change only occurs at one end, it is convenient to implement a stack without using a linked list; an ordinary array will do. In our examples, a linked list is necessary for our stack of available storage elements because they are scattered all over. Stacks have other uses so we will show how a stack can be implemented using an array. We will call the array *stack*. The bottom of the stack will be in *stack(1)*, the next entry in *stack(2)*, and so on. Sorry if our stack seems to be upside down! Here is a stack of symbols:

top	*4*
stack(1)	+
stack(2)	-
stack(3)	+
stack(4)	/

This sort of stack is often used in Fortran compilers for translating arithmetic expressions into machine language.

Before using the stack we initialize it to be empty by setting *top* to zero:

$$top = 0$$

To add an item to the stack we can call the subroutine *push*:

```
subroutine push(symbol)
character*1 symbol
common/ lifo/ stack,top
character *1 stack(20)
integer top
top = top + 1
stack(top) =symbol
return
end
```

To remove the top item from the stack we can call the subroutine *pop*:

```
subroutine pop(symbol)
character *1 symbol
common/ lifo/ stack,top
character *1 stack(20)
integer top
symbol = stack(top)
top = top − 1
return
end
```

The variable *top* and the array *stack* must be **common** to the *push* and *pop* subroutines and to the program that initializes the stack. Stacks may be implemented in other ways than shown here.

A PROGRAM USING A STACK

If we want to read a list of symbols and output them in reverse order we can program it this way to use a stack:

> Initialize the stack to empty
> **read** a *symbol*
> **if** *(symbol*.**eq.**' ') **go to** end of loop
> > push *symbol* onto the stack
> > **read** a *symbol*
> > **go to** beginning of loop
> > end of loop
> Output the *symbols* in reverse order
> **if** (stack is empty) **go to** end of loop
> > pop a *symbol* from stack
> > output *symbol*
> > **go to** beginning of loop
> > end of loop

Here is the program:

```
          program back
    c     Reads list of symbols and outputs them in reverse order
          common/ lifo/ stack,top
          character *1 stack(20),symbol
          integer top
    c     Initialize the stack to empty
          top = 0
          print *,'Enter symbols, one to line; end with blank'
          read 10,symbol
    10    format (1x,a1)
    20    if (symbol.eq.' ') go to 30
              call push(symbol)
              read 10, symbol
              go to 20
    30        continue
    c     Output the symbols in reverse order
          print *,'Here is reversed list'
    40    if (top.eq.null) go to 50
              call pop(symbol)
              print 45,symbol
    45        format (1x,a1)
```

```
                    go to 40
50                  continue
              stop
              end
```

(copy *push* and *pop* subroutines here)

QUEUES

Another specialized type of list is a **queue**. For it, entries are made at the end of the list, deletions are made from the beginning. Rather than search for the end of the list each time an entry is made, it is usual to have a pointer indicating the last entry. Queues involve using things in a manner referred to as, "First in first out" (*FIFO*) or, "First come first served" (*FCFS*). This is the usual way for a queue waiting for tickets at a box office to operate.

It is not as easy to implement a queue using an array. It is always growing at one end and shrinking at the other. If an array is used, when the growth reaches the maximum limit of the array, we start it at the beginning again. Here is a queue of users of a computer waiting for service. We have a maximum of 8 elements. Five people are in the queue. The next person to be served is named *Shum.*

first 6	*last 2*
queue(1)	*Lawrence*
queue(2)	*Johnston*
queue(3)	-
queue(4)	-
queue(5)	-
queue(6)	*Shum*
queue(7)	*Linnemann*
queue(8)	*Miao*

Here are subroutines used to *enter* or *leave* this queue. Before using these subroutines the queue can be initialized to be empty by setting *first* to 1 and *last* to 8.

```
          subroutine enter(name)
          character *10 name
          common/ fifo/ queue,first,last
          character *10 queue(8)
          integer first,last
          last = last + 1
          if (last.gt. 8)then
```

```
        last = 1
end if
queue(last) = name
return
end


subroutine leave(name)
character *10 name
common/ fifo/ queue,first,last
character *10 queue(8)
integer first,last
name = queue(first)
first = first + 1
if (first.gt. 8) then
        first = 1
end if
return
end
```

Queues can be implemented by linked lists as well as by simple arrays. Queues are used in the programs called **operating systems** that operate shared computer systems. Different jobs requiring service are placed in different queues, depending on the demands they are making on the system's resources and the priority that they possess to be given service. Also, in programs that simulate other systems such as factories, queues are maintained to determine the length of time jobs are required to wait to be served when other jobs are competing for the same production facilities.

TREES

A linked list is an efficient way of storing a list that is changing with time, but it introduces an inefficiency in retrieval of information from the list. In the chapter on sorting and searching we saw that a binary search for an item in a list is much more efficient for long lists than a linear search. Unfortunately, there is no possibility of doing a binary search in a linked list; we must start at the beginning and trace our way through. There is no direct access to the middle of a linked list. It is for this reason that a more complicated data structure called a **tree** is used. We can get the efficiency of a binary search by having the elements linked into a **binary tree structure**.

To show how a binary tree is formed, we will look at the example of our list of names of animals:

> *3* → *cat*
> *2* → *dog*
> *duck*
> *1* → *fox*
> *goose*
> *pig*
> *snake*

To do a binary search we should begin in the middle. We have added *snake* to the list so the list has a middle entry. If we are looking for the name *cat* we find that *cat*.**lt**.*fox*, so we then discard the middle entry and the last half of the list. The next comparison is with the middle entry of the remaining list, namely with *dog*. Since *cat*.**lt**.*dog* we eliminate the last half of the smaller list. By this time, we are down to one entry, which is the one we are looking for. It took three comparisons to get there. A linear search for *cat* would, as it happens, have taken only 1 comparison. On the **average**, the binary search takes fewer comparisons than a linear search. A short list is not a good example for showing off the efficiency of binary searching, but it is much easier to write out all the possibilities.

We will now look at the binary tree that would be used to give the same searching technique. Here it is:

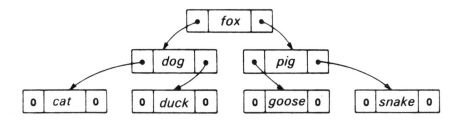

Each data element in the tree structure consists of three parts, the *data* itself and two links that we designate as *left* and *right*. The word *fox* is in a special position in the tree, called the **root**. From *fox* we have branches going to the left to *dog* and to the right to *pig*. In a sense, *dog* is in the root position of a smaller tree, what we call the **left subtree** of the main tree. The word *pig* is at the root of the **right subtree**. The words *cat, duck, goose,* and *snake* are at the end of branches and are called **leaves**

of the tree. All the data elements are in nodes of the tree; *fox* is the root node and *cat* is a leaf node. To search for an entry in a binary tree, we compare the element in the root node with the one we are seeking. If the root is the same, we have found it. If the root is larger we follow the *left* link to the next entry; if smaller, we follow the *right* link. We are then at the root of a smaller tree, a tree with half as many entries as the original. The process is then repeated until the looked-for data is found.

Here is our tree structure as it might be stored in three arrays called *data, left,* and *right.* The variable *root* holds the link to the root element. We have jumbled up the sequence to show that the actual order in the *data* array makes no difference. A zero link is used to indicate the end of a branch.

		root	4	
	data	*left*		*right*
(1)	*goose*	0		0
(2)	*snake*	0		0
(3)	*dog*	6		7
(4)	*fox*	3		5
(5)	*pig*	1		2
(6)	*cat*	0		0
(7)	*duck*	0		0

Starting at *root*, we find the root is in *data(4).* The pointer *left(4)* leads to *data(3)* which is *dog.* The pointer *right(3)* leads us to *data(7)* which is *duck.* You can see how it works.

A tree structure is a **hierarchical structure** for data; each comparison takes us one **level** down in the tree.

ADDING TO A TREE

To add a data item to a tree structure we simply look for the element in the tree in the usual manner, starting at the root. If the element is not already in the tree, we will come in the search to a link that is zero. This is where the element belongs. In our example, if we want to add *cow*, we would start at *fox*, then go to *dog*, then to *cat.* At this point we would want to follow the right link of *cat*, but we find a zero. If we stored the new entry in *data(8)*, we would change *right(6)* to 8 and set

data(8)	*left(8)*	*right(8)*
cow	0	0

As we add items to a tree, the tree becomes lopsided; it is not well balanced. Searching efficiency depends on trees being well balanced, so that in an information retrieval data bank using a tree structure, an effort should be made to keep the tree balanced. We started with a balanced tree and it became unbalanced by adding a new item. If a tree is grown from scratch using the method we have described for adding a new entry, it is unlikely to be well balanced.

DELETING FROM A TREE

Removing an entry from a tree is a more difficult operation than adding an entry. The same method is used to find the element to be deleted, but then the problem comes. It is not difficult if both links of the element to be deleted are zero, that is, if it is a leaf. We just chop it off and make the link pointing to it zero. If only one link is zero it is similar to an ordinary linked list and deletion is similar to that. We just bypass it:

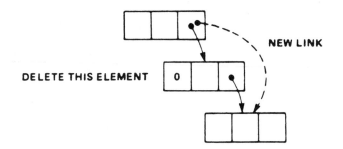

If neither link is zero in the element to be deleted, we must move another element into its position in the tree. In our original tree, if *fox* is to be deleted, it must be replaced by an element that is larger then all other elements in the left subtree or smaller than all the elements in the right subtree. This means that either *duck* or *goose* is the only possible choice. The one to be moved must be deleted in its present position before being placed in its new position.

Remember, in a linked structure, we never move a data item from its physical location in the data array; we only change the links to alter its logical position.

OUTPUTTING A TREE IN ORDER

Trees are used where searching and updating are the main activities. Sometimes we must output the contents of a tree. We must be systematic about it and be sure to output every node. We will show how to output it alphabetically.

An algorithm for outputting a tree alphabetically can be written in this way:

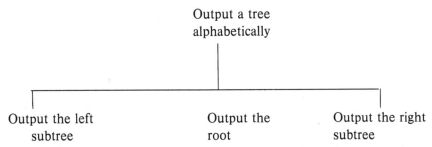

Output a tree
alphabetically

Output the left   Output the   Output the right
    subtree   root   subtree

We see that we have described our algorithm in terms of three parts. The middle part, "Output the root," is easy, but the other two require us to, "Output a tree." This is exactly what our problem is, to "Output a tree." We have defined the solution to a problem in terms of the original problem. This kind of definition is called a **recursive** definition of a solution. It seems rather pointless, as if we were just going in a circle, but it really is not. The reason it is not pointless is that the tree we are attempting to output when we say, "Output the left subtree," is a smaller tree than the original tree when we said "Output a tree." When we try to output the left subtree we get this solution:

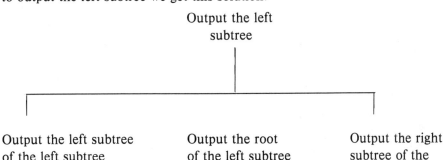

Output the left
    subtree

Output the left subtree   Output the root   Output the right
of the left subtree   of the left subtree   subtree of the
                                                          left subtree

This time the left subtree of the left subtree has to be output. It is smaller still. The algorithm is again repeated. Each application of the algorithm is on a smaller tree, until you reach a point where there is a zero link and there is no left subtree at all. Then the action of outputting it is to do nothing; no tree, no output. That is how recursive algorithms work.

In programming terms, the algorithm calls itself over and over, each time to do a reduced task, until the task is easy to do.

In many programming languages, such as PL/1, Pascal, or Turing a subroutine can call itself. This is not allowed in Fortran, but for the rest of this paragraph we will assume that Fortran allows such recursive subroutines. Here is a recursive subroutine for outputting a tree in alphabetic order, given that its root is *root* and its data and links are in *data, left*, and *right.*

```
            subroutine output(root)
   c        Recursive method of tree output (not allowed in Fortran)
            integer root
            common/ tree/ data,left,right,null
            character *10 data(30)
            integer left(30),right(30),null
            if (left(root).ne. null) then
                call output(left(root))
            end if
            print *,data(root)
            if (right(root).ne. null) then
                call output(right(root))
            end if
            return
            end
```

Each time the subroutine is entered for a new subtree, a different node is referred to by *root*. For this job, a recursive subroutine is very easy to program. In a recursive algorithm, each time a program calls itself, a record must be kept of the point in the program where the subroutine was called, so that control can return properly. As the subroutine recursively calls itself, a list is built of these points of return. Each point of return is added on top of the stack of other points of return. Finding the way back involves taking return points, one after the other, off this stack. For languages such as PL/1, Pascal, or Turing, this is all set up automatically by the compiler. In Fortran, we can still write a subroutine to output a tree, but since it cannot call itself, it is more difficult to program.

SORTING USING A STACK

A number of sorting methods that are very efficient require essentially recursive procedures. Since recursion is not available in Fortran these must be implemented in another way using a stack. One such algorithm is the Quicksort algorithm. Suppose that you have a list of integers that you want sorted. Quicksort divides the array into two partitions, the left partition and the right partition, by choosing an arbitrary element as the pivot. The pivot is usually the middle element. The next step is to arrange, by swapping that all the elements on the right of the pivot are greater than the pivot or all those on the left are less than the pivot. The pivot is considered part of the left or right partition depending on which of these holds. At this stage, the problem of sorting has been simplified in that we have partitioned our original list into two lists each of which can now be sorted separately. To sort each of the partitions, the same technique is applied recursively.

As the sorting proceeds each partition is partitioned into two, each of which must ultimately be sorted. The subdivision continues until only one element remains in a partition. We keep a stack to remember what partitions still need to be sorted. When the partition we are currently working on is sorted, we remove the top partition from the stack and start to sort it. When we create two partitions we stack the right partition and sort the left one. When no more partitions remain on the stack we are finished. For each partition we must keep the index for its left end and the index for its right end on the stack. These will be in array variable *lefts* and *rights*. The position of the stack top will be in *top*.

Here is a subroutine using Quicksort to sort an array *A* of *n* integers:

```
       subroutine quick(A,n)
       integer A(n),n
       integer temp,begin,end,top,lefts(50),rights(50),i,j,pivot
c      Initialize stack to contain complete array
       top = 1
       lefts(top) = 1
       rights(top) = n
c      Continue to sort as long as items are on stack
10     if (top.eq. 0) go to 100
c          Pop partition to be sorted off stack
           begin = lefts(top)
           end = rights(top)
           top = top - 1
c          Continue until only one element remains
20         if (begin.ge. end) go to 90
               i = begin
               j = end
               pivot = int((begin + end)/ 2.)
c              Continue while i.le.j
30             if (i.gt.j) go to 80
c                  Compare left items with pivot until bigger one found
```

```
40              if (A(i).ge.A(pivot)) go to 50
                    i = i + 1
                    go to 40
50              continue
c               Compare right items with pivot until smaller one found
60              if (A(pivot).ge.A(j)) go to 70
                    j = j - 1
                    go to 60
70              continue
c               If i is less than j swap elements i and j
                if (i.le.j) then
                    temp = a(i)
                    a(i) = a(j)
                    a(j) = temp
c                   Advance to next elements nearer pivot
                    i = i + 1
                    j = j - 1
                end if
                go to 30
80              continue
c               If there is a left part to sort, push right part onto stack
                if (i.lt.end) then
                    top = top + 1
                    lefts(top) = i
                    rights(top) = end
                end if
c               Set to sort left partition
                end = j
                go to 20
90              continue
            go to 10
100         continue
      return
      end
```

Here is a main program to test *quick*.

```
      program testqu
      integer list(20),i
      print *,'Enter 20 integers, one to a line'
      do 10 i = 1,20
            read *,list(i)
10          continue
```

```
        call quick(list,20)
        print *,'Here is the sorted list'
        do 20 i = 1,20
            print *,list(i)
20          continue
        stop
        end
```

(copy *quick* subroutine here)

Pretend that Fortran does support recursive calls to subroutines and write one for Quicksort. See how much easier it is!

CHAPTER 18 SUMMARY

In this chapter we showed how to build up data structures using arrays. Some of these data structures use links to give the ordering of data items. The link (or links) for a given item gives the array index of the next item. The following important terms were discussed:

Linked list — a linked sequence of data items. The next item in the list is found by following a link from the present item. The physical order of a collection of items, as given by their positions in an array, is different from their logical order, as given by the links.

Inserting into a linked list — a new data item can be inserted by changing links, without actually moving data items.

Deleting from a linked list — a data item can be deleted by changing links, without moving data items.

Available list — the collection of data elements currently not in use.

Stack — a data structure that allows data items to be added, or pushed, on to one end and removed, or popped, from the same end. A stack does not require the use of links. A stack handles data items in a last-in-first-out (*LIFO*) manner.

Queue — a data structure that allows data items to be added at one end and removed from the other. A queue handles data items in a first-in-first-out (*FIFO*) manner.

Binary tree — a data structure in which each item or node has two links, a left link and a right link. The left link of a node locates another node and with it a subtree. Similarly, the right link locates a subtree. There is a unique beginning node called the root. If both links of a particular node are null, meaning they do not currently locate other nodes, then the node is called a leaf.

CHAPTER 18 EXERCISES

1.   The *Fly-by-Nite* Airline company is computerizing its reservations system. There are four *Fly-by-Nite* flights with the following capacities:

flight # 1	*5 seats*
flight # 2	*5 seats*
flight # 3	*8 seats*
flight # 4	*4 seats*

The information for passenger reservations is to be stored in a linked list. At some point during the booking period, the following diagram might represent the current passenger bookings.

The above diagram shows the first element in each list holding the number of seats remaining. Each succeeding element holds the name of a passenger and either points to the next element or holds a 0 to indicate the end of the linked list.

In order to set up such a linked list system you will need four arrays. The first will contain the number of seats remaining. The second array holds the location of the first passenger of each flight.

The third array called *name* holds all the passengers. If all seats on all flights are taken, there will be 22 passengers. Hence *name* will need a maximum of 22 locations. The fourth array called *link* contains the location of the next passenger, if any. Before any events happen, the free locations must be linked together. Initially each *link(j)* contains a value $j + 1$, except *link(22)* which contains a 0 as end of the list.

A variable *avail* contains the location of the head of this chain of available locations. For the example given above, *avail* contains 10 and the *name* and *link* arrays could have these values:

name(1)Hamacher	name(5)Lehman	name(9)Vranesic
link 6	link 0	link 0
name Boulton	name Farkas	name
link 5	link 7	link 11
name Ham	name McNaughton	.
link 8	link 0	.
name Hehner	name Wilson	name
link 3	link 9	link 0

The reservation system is to accept four types of transactions:

Type 1 is a request for a reservation. The data entry contains the code word *res*, name of the passenger, and the flight number.

Type 2 is a request to cancel a reservation. The data entry contains the code word *can*, name of passenger, and the flight number.

Type 3 is a request to output the number of seats remaining on a specified flight. The data entry contains the code word *seats* and a flight number.

Type 4 is a request to output a passenger list for the flight indicated. The data entry contains the code word *list* and a flight number.

Each type of transaction is to be handled by a subroutine. Here are descriptions of the subroutines:

add(who,number). Adds passenger *who* to flight *number*. If that flight is filled, a message is output to that effect. The subroutine *add* uses a location in *name* and must update *avail.*

cancel(who,number). Cancels the reservation made in the name of *who* on flight *number*. The location in *name* is returned to the free storage pool. The variable *avail* must be updated.

info(number). Outputs number of seats remaining on flight *number.*

list(number). Outputs a passenger list for flight *number*.

The data entries should simulate a real reservation system in that entries of type 1, 2, 3, 4 should be intermixed. It would seem reasonable to assume that most cancellations would be made by persons holding reservations. However, people being what they are, you should not assume too much. In order to get your system off the ground, several reservation entries should be first.

Write and test each program as a main program before putting the subroutines together. Write *list* first and call it from *add* or *cancel* to help in debugging. Try several runs which show the capabilities of your system. Be sure to test unusual situations as well as the obvious ones.

2.   In this chapter there is a recursive subroutine for outputting a tree in alphabetical order. This is not a proper subroutine for Fortran. Write a non-recursive Fortran subroutine using the following algorithm. The algorithm uses a stack.

    a.   Initialize the stack to be empty and set index *n* (for node) to point to the root of the tree.

    b.   As long as the stack is not empty or *n* is not null (that is, 0), repeat steps c. to f., otherwise stop.

    c.   Keep pushing *n* onto the stack and setting *n* to be the left link *(left(n))* of its previous value until *n* is null.

    d.   Pop the stack and save the value removed from the stack as *n*.

    e.   Output the data stored in node *n*.

    f.   Set *n* to be the right link *(right(n))* of its previous value.

Test your subroutine. Can you see how the algorithm works?

Appendix 1:

SPECIFICATIONS FOR THE FORTRAN 77 LANGUAGE

In the interest of making Fortran 77 more suitable for pedagogic purposes, this book restricts or eliminates a number Fortran 77 features. For example, every variable must be declared. Features implied by the following terms are not included: pause, complex, implicit, equivalence, and namelist. Implicit conversions are not allowed among numeric, logical, and character types, thereby eliminating anomalies due to value representations.

Fortran 77 compilers do not enforce the restrictions that we impose on Fortran 77. As a result, errors such as failure to declare a variable (because in full Fortran 77 variables are declared implicitly) will not be diagnosed. The restrictions we have assumed are to make programs more understandable.

Language features introduced in various chapters are summarized in the following table.

Chapter	Features Introduced
3	Characters: letters, digits, and special characters Constants: integer, real, and character string Expressions: +, -, *, /, **, integer to real conversion Simple output: format-free output Mathematical built-in functions: mod, abs, sin, cos, atan, alog, exp, sqrt
4	Identifiers and variables Declarations: integer and real Assignment statements (with real to integer conversion) Simple input: format-free reading Parameter (constant) definition

5	Comparisons
	Logical expressions
	Selection: if-then-else
	Repetition: conditional loop and counted do loop
	Paragraphing
	Logical constants
	Logical variables
7	Character string variables (fixed length only)
	Character string comparison
	Catenation and substrings
8	Arrays (including multiple dimensions)
	Data initialization
10	Detailed control of input and output: formats
11	Subprograms: subroutines and functions
	Calling and returning
	Arguments and parameters
16	Files and records
	Initializing and closing off files
	Reading and writing records
	Random access to files

The following sections give detailed specifications for each chapter. In describing the specifications, we will use this notation:

[item] means the item is optional

{item} means the item can appear zero or more times

When presenting the syntax of language constructs, items written in **bold face** letters, for example,

return

denote keywords; these items appear in Fortran programs exactly as presented. Items written in lower case, non-italic letters, for example,

statement

denote one of a class of constructs; each such item is then defined as it is introduced. Words shown in *italics* are particular examples of such constructs.

CHAPTER 3: LITERALS, EXPRESSIONS, AND OUTPUT

A **character** is a letter or a digit or a special character.

A **letter** is one of the following:

> A B C D E F G H I J K L M N O P Q R S T U V W X Y Z
> a b c d e f g h i j k l m n o p q r s t u v w x y z

A **digit** is one of the following:

> 0 1 2 3 4 5 6 7 8 9

A **special character** is one of the following:

> + − * / ( ) = . , $
> b (blank)
> ' (apostrophe or single quote)

An **integer constant** is one or more digits optionally preceded by a minus sign (without embedded blanks), for example:

> 4 −19 243 92153

Note that an integer constant must not contain a decimal point.

A **real constant** can be one or more digits with a decimal point. Alternately, a real constant can be a significant digits part followed by an exponent part. The **significant digits part** must be one or more digits with an optional decimal point. The **exponent part** must be the letter *e*, followed by an optional plus or minus sign, followed by one or two digits. A minus sign may optionally precede the real constant. There must not be embedded blanks. The following are examples of real constants.

> 3.14159 −2. .0025 5.16*e*+00 50*e*0 .9418*e*24 1.*e*−2

There is a maximum size for an integer constant. This means that there is a maximum allowed number of digits in the significant digits part of a real constant and a maximum allowed magnitude of the exponent. (These maximum values will vary from compiler to compiler.)

A **literal** (or **character string constant**) is a single quote (an apostrophe), followed by zero or more occurrences of non-single-quote characters or twice repeated single quotes, followed by a single quote. The following are examples of literals:

> '*Fred*' '*x=24*' '*Mr. O''Reilly* '

There is a maximum length of character strings.

An **expression** consists of integer and/or real constants combined using:

+	addition
−	subtraction and negation
*	multiplication
/	division
**	exponentiation
( )	parentheses

Built-in functions can also be used in expressions. Two operators (among +, −, *, /, and **) cannot be adjacent to each other.

Real and integer values may be combined in expressions. When an integer value is combined with a real value, the result is a real value.

Evaluation of expressions proceeds from left to right, with the following exceptions. Multiplications and divisions have higher precedence than (that is, are evaluated before) additions, subtractions, and negations. Parenthesized sub-expressions are evaluated before being used in arithmetic operations. Division (/) should be used only when one or both of the operands have real values. Division of an integer value by an integer value is not advisable. Exponentiation has higher precedence than multiplication and division; exponentiations are evaluated from right to left. The following are examples of legal expressions.

$$-4 + 20 \quad 2 * 8.5e+00 \quad (4.0e+01 - 12.0e+01)/(-2)$$

The values of these three expressions are, respectively, 16, 17.0e+00, and 4.0e+01.

Character strings cannot be used in arithmetic operations. There are no implicit conversions from numeric values to character string values or vice versa.

A built-in function call is one of the following:

> *mod*(expression , expression)
> *abs*(expression)
> *sin*(expression)
> *cos*(expression)
> *atan*(expression)
> *alog*(expression)
> *exp*(expression)
> *sqrt*(expression)

The *mod* function accepts two integer expressions as arguments and produces an integer result. The *abs, sin, cos, atan, alog, exp,* and *sqrt* mathematical functions accept a single real expression as an argument and produce a real result. The function *iabs* will accept an integer expression as argument and give an integer result. Appendix 3 gives a more detailed description of Fortran built-in functions. In Chapter 3 only a small subset of the Fortran 77 specifications is introduced. Here are the definitions of statement and program as presented there:

A **statement** is:

> **print** *, output item {,output item}

A **program** is:

> **program** identifier
> {statement}
> **stop**
> **end**

Remember that the notation {statement} means zero or more statements.

A **program identifier** must be a letter followed by as many as five letters or digits.

An **output item** is a literal or an expression. The following is an example of a program:

> **program** *adds*
> **print** *,2,'plus',3,'makes',2 + 3*
> **stop**
> **end**

The output from this example is: **2 plus 3 makes 5**

Output produced by the **print** statement is placed in successive fields across the output line. The widths of these fields depends upon the compiler. Some compilers output integer values in fields just big enough to hold the integer others in 12-column fields, real values right-justified in 15-column fields, and character strings in fields as long as the particular string. Fields are separated by a blank column. Output lines always begin with a blank.

When a literal is output by a **print** statement, its enclosing single quotes are removed. In addition twice repeated single quotes in a literal are output as one single quote.

Fortran programs must appear in columns 7 to 72 of the input line. Continuation from line to line is accomplished by placing a plus sign (or a non-zero digit) in column 6 of each continuation line.

CHAPTER 4: VARIABLES, INPUT, AND ASSIGNMENT

A **variable identifier** (or **variable**) is a letter followed by more letters and digits. An identifier cannot contain embedded blanks. Most compilers allow identifiers to be at least 6 characters long. Some permit more characters but ignore those after the 6th.

A **program** is:

> **program** identifier
> {declaration}
> {statement}
> **stop**
> **end**

A **declaration** is:

> type variable {,variable}

A **type** is one of the following:

> **integer**
> **real**

A **definition** is:

> **parameter** (variable=value {,variable=value})

By Chapter 4 the possible kinds of statements is enlarged.

A **statement** is one of the following:

> **print** *,output item {,output item}
> **read** *,variable{,variable}
> variable = expression

In the Fortran 77 of this book all variables must be declared. An expression may be or may include a variable.

Real values may be assigned to integer variables. Any non-integer part of such a real value is truncated before the assignment without a warning message. Integer values may be assigned to real variables with automatic conversion.

The items in the data (the input stream from the keyboard) read by **read** statements must be separated by one or more blanks. When a **read** statement is executed, one data item is read for each variable in the statement. Each **read** statement begins reading at the beginning of the next line.

Each item in the input stream must be an integer constant or a real constant.

An integer constant can be read (and will be automatically

converted) into a real variable. However, a real constant can not be read into an integer variable. There are no automatic conversions from character string values to numeric values or vice versa.

A **keyword** is any of the special identifiers, for example, **real, print** and **end**, that are part of the Fortran syntax. A variable should not be given the same name as a keyword. In this book we use **bold face** for keywords.

Any number of blanks can appear between symbols, for example, between constants, keywords, identifiers, operators $+$, $-$, $*$, $/$, $**$, and the parentheses (and). When constants, keywords, or identifiers are adjacent, for example, **integer** and i, they must be separated by at least one blank.

A comment consists of the character c in column 1 and any characters (the actual comment) in columns 2 to 72 inclusive. Comments are continued by putting the character c in column 1 of succeeding lines (not by putting a plus sign in column 6). Comments cannot appear in the data. A blank line is accepted as a comment line.

CHAPTER 5: LOGICAL EXPRESSIONS, SELECTION, AND REPETITION

A **condition** is one of the following:

> .true.
> .false.
> .not. condition
> condition .and. condition
> condition .or. condition
> comparison
> (condition)

A condition is sometimes called a **logical expression**.

A **comparison** is one of the following:

> expression .lt. expression
> expression .gt. expression
> expression .eq. expression
> expression .le. expression
> expression .ge. expression
> expression .ne. expression

A **type** is one of the following:

> **integer**
> **real**
> **logical**

A **logical operator** is one of the following:

> .and.
> .or.
> .not.

Logical expressions can be operands in the logical operations of **.and.**, **.or.** and **.not.**. Real and integer values cannot be operands in logical operations. The **.and.** operator has higher precedence than the **.or.** operator.

There is no implicit conversion between numeric values (integer and real) and logical values. Logical values cannot participate in arithmetic operations.

A **statement** is one of the following:

> **print** *,output item {,output item}
> **read** *,variable {,variable}
> variable = expression

```
          if (condition) then
              {statement}
          {else if (condition) then
              {statement}}
          [else
              {statement} ]
          end if

          do label identifier = start,limit [,step]
              {statement}
label         continue

label1        if(condition)go to label2
              {statement}
              go to label1
label2        continue
```

In the counted **do** loop the label must be an unsigned integer that appears after **do** and is repeated in the label field (columns 1 through 5) of the **continue**. This label must be different from other labels in the program. The counter variable (identifier) usually is declared to be an integer variable. Even after arrays are introduced, the counter variable must still be simple, that is, not an array element. The step is optional; if omitted it is taken to be 1.

The start, limit, and step (if present) usually are given by integer constants, or integer variables, or integer expressions. The counter variable should not be changed inside the loop.

Initially the expressions for start, limit, and step are evaluated; the counter variable is set to the start value and, for positive step values provided this does not exceed the limit, the loop body is executed. At the end of the loop body, if the sum of the current value of the counter variable and the step does not go beyond the limit, then the sum is assigned to the counter variable and the loop body is executed again. Otherwise the loop is terminated, and the value of the counter variable is unspecified.

In the **if** (condition) **go to** conditional loop there are two different labels, label1 and label2. No two labels in columns 1-5 in a program can be the same. To make a program easier to read we give labels that have ascending values such as 10, 20, 30, and so on, but this is not necessary.

Paragraphing rules are standard conventions for indenting program lines. Some compilers may provide automatic paragraphing of programs. If this feature is available, it should be used.

A set of paragraphing rules can be inferred from the method used to present Fortran constructs. For example, the **if** (condition) **go to** loop was presented in the following form:

```
label1          if(condition)go to label2
                  {statement}
                  go to label1
label2          continue
```

This form means that the statements enclosed in an **if...go to** group should be indented beyond the level of the opening **if...go to** line. The **continue** which closes the group should be indented to the same level as the enclosed statements.

An alternative conditional loop (not used in this book) is:

```
label1          if (condition) then
                  {statement}
                  go to label1
                end if
```

The condition in this loop is the continuation condition for the loop and is the negative of the condition in the other form which is the termination condition.

The text of comments should be indented to the same level as their corresponding program lines. The continuation(s) of a long program line should be indented beyond the line's original indentation. If the level of indentation becomes too deep, it may be necessary to abandon indentation rules temporarily, maintaining a vertical positioning of lines.

CHAPTER 7: CHARACTER STRING VARIABLES

A **type** is one of the following:

> **integer**
> **real**
> **logical**
> **character***length

Variables declared to have the attribute **character***length are called character string variables. In the declaration of character string variables, length must be a strictly positive integer constant.

Each character string variable has a fixed length determined by its declaration. If the variable is assigned a string shorter than its declared length then the string is padded with blanks on the right to the required length. If the string is longer than the declared length, it may be truncated on the right to the required length; some compilers may consider such truncation to be illegal.

When character string values of different lengths are compared, the shorter is temporarily padded on the right with blanks to the length of the longer. Character string constants can be read from the data. Character string variables can be output.

There are string facilities for finding lengths, concatenating, or finding substrings but these are not particularly useful. The built-in function *len* has an integer value, the length of its argument. A character string variable has its declared length no matter what value has been assigned to it. Catenation is accomplished using the operator / /. Substrings of a character variable are defined by the form:

> character variable identifier (starting position: end position)

Single character substrings have the same starting and end positions.

There is no implicit conversion between character string values and numeric or logical values.

CHAPTER 8: ARRAYS

The form of declaration remains as it was:

A **declaration** is:

> type variable {,variable}

However, the form of variable is now allowed to specify array bounds. In a declaration, a variable is now:

> identifier [(range {,range})]

The range can begin at any integer m, positive or negative, and run to n (where $m <$ or $= n$). The range is then written as $m: n$. The maximum number of ranges is seven.

In an expression, or in a **read** statement, a variable has the form:

> identifier [(expression {,expression})]

where each expression is an array index. Each array index expression must have an integer value that is within the specified range.

Array elements may be compared, assigned, read, and output on an element by element basis, in the same way as single variables with similar attributes. Arrays can be read and output using implied **do** loops and a one-dimensional array, whose index goes from 1 to n, can be read and output without specific reference to the index.

A **data** definition for one-dimensional array variables with the same index is:

data (variable(index) {,variable(index)}, index=start,limit[,step])/value{,value}/

This is used to initialize the elements of an array.

CHAPTER 10: FORMATTED INPUT AND OUTPUT

Format-free **print** and **read** statements were introduced earlier. Here we introduce formatted **print** and **read** statements of the form:

print label {,expression}

label   **format**(control {,format item})

read label,variable {,variable}

label   **format**(format item {,format item})

In these statements, the label is a strictly positive integer constant that appears after **print** or **read** and is repeated in the label field (columns 1 through 5) of the corresponding **format** specification. Within the main program or in a particular subprogram, all labels in columns 1 through 5 must be different. We make a practice of placing the corresponding **format** specification immediately after the **read** or **print** statement that refers to it although this is not necessary.

It is possible to use both format-free and formatted **read** and **print** statements in the same program. Notice that the unformatted **read** and **print** use an asterisk instead of a format identifier label.

The control in a formatted **print** statement must be one of the following carriage control characters:

' '	(blank)	start a new line (single space)
'1'	(one)	start a new page
'0'	(zero)	skip a line then start a new line (double space)
'+'	(plus)	go back to beginning of current line (overprint)

The formatted **read** statement reads the next data line, skipping any remaining columns of the last read line. Carriage control characters cannot be specified in a formatted **read** statement. We have made it a practice to include a format item *(1x)* in each formatted **read** statement indicating that the first column of the input line is not to be used. This allows us to line up input data entries with prompt headings more easily.

A format item is one of the following:

nx   Skips next n columns.

iw   Outputs or reads an integer right justified in a field of *w* columns.

fw.d   Outputs or reads a real quantity without an exponent, right justified in a field of *w* columns. The number of digits to the right of the decimal point is given by *d*.

ew.d   Outputs or reads a real quantity with an exponent, right justified in a field of *w* columns. The number of digits to the right of the decimal point is given by *d.*

aw   Outputs or reads *w* characters. If a literal or character variable of fewer than *w* characters is output, it is right-justified in the field of *w* characters and padded on the left with blanks.

naw   Outputs (reads) *n* sets of *w* characters from (into) a one-dimensional array of *n* **character** **w* elements. This is the only format item that transmits an entire array.

The following restrictions and details should be noted. Each of *n, w* and *d* must be unsigned non-zero integer constants, as in *80a1.* All real quantities are rounded off before output.

Numbers read or output by the *i, f,* and *e* format items are right justified in their fields. The variable or literal that corresponds to *aw* must be *w* characters long.

Each variable in a formatted **read** or **print** must correspond to an *i, f, e,* or *a* format item. The *x* format item can precede or be intermixed with *i, f, e,* and *a* items, but must not be last in a list of format items.

When reading character values, if fewer characters are entered than required by the length of the variable that is to receive the string before the return is pressed, the remaining characters on the right of the variable will be assigned blanks.

When reading integers, any blank columns are considered to be zeros, so that if the data is not right justified in its field, it is scaled. If data read using *fw.d* does not contain a decimal point, then one is assumed to be *d* digits from the right of the field. If the data read using *fw.d* contains a decimal point, then it over-rides the *d* in the format item. Numbers read using *fw.d* must not have exponents.

Numbers read using *ew.d* can have exponents, but do not need to. If the decimal point is entered then the *d* is ignored. If it is not entered, it is assumed *d* digits from the right of the significant digits part.

CHAPTER 11: SUBPROGRAMS

Here the form of a program is extended to allow the specification of subprograms.

A **program** is:

> **program** identifier
> {definition}
> {statement}
> **stop**
> **end**
> {subprogram}

A **subprogram** is one of the following:

> **subroutine** name[(identifier {,identifier})]
> {definition}
> {statement}
> **return**
> **end**

> type **function** name(identifier {,identifier})
> {definition}
> {statement}
> **return**
> **end**

A **definition** is one of the following:

> type variable {,variable}
> **parameter** (variable=value {,variable=value})
> **common** /identifier/ variable {,variable}
> **data** (variable {,variable})/value {,value}/

The list of variables in a **data** definition may be replaced by an implied **do** for array variables. The form for one-dimensional array is:

> array variable(index),index=start,limit [,step]

Notice that a "definition" can be a declaration.

The **call** statement is introduced:

> **call** subroutine name [(expression {,expression})]

As well, **return** now becomes a statement:

> **return**

When a **stop** is executed in the main program, it terminates the entire program's execution. When a **return** is executed in a subprogram, it causes return to the calling main program or subprogram.

All parameters for a subprogram must be declared and must have the same types, ranges, and lengths as their corresponding arguments. There is no automatic real/integer conversion for parameters/arguments. A parameter array range may be given as another parameter if that parameter is a simple (non-array) integer. Lengths of character string parameters may be given as *.

Assignment of a value to a parameter will cause the value to be assigned to the corresponding argument. If the argument is a constant or an expression containing operators, then an assignment must not be made to the parameter. Similarly if the argument is a **do** loop start, limit, step, or counter variable, then an assignment must not be made to the parameter. Functions must have at least one parameter but subroutines can have none.

Each definition of a particular **common** block must specify the same names of variables in the same order. These variables must be declared to have the same types, ranges, and lengths as in other specifications of the particular **common** block. Every **common** block must be defined in the main program.

A subroutine subprogram is invoked by the **call** statement. A function subprogram is invoked by using its name with argument(s) as required in an expression. Each subprogram (or the main program) that invokes a function must contain a declaration giving the type of the function. For example, if *area* is a function then the declaration

integer *area*

must be included in the main program and subprograms that invoke *area*. Inside a function, the name of the function acts as a simple variable without further declaration. This variable must be assigned a value before returning from the function and this provides the function's value.

Subprograms cannot be recursive, meaning they may not invoke themselves directly or indirectly.

Within a particular subprogram, or in the main program, all names of accessible variables, subprograms, and common blocks must be unique and labels must be unique. Names and labels need not be unique from subprogram to subprogram to main program.

CHAPTER 16: FILES

This introduces the use of external files other than keyboard input and screen output. A file is sometimes called a data set. A file consists of records and may be sequential or direct access each record consists of fields. Each field has a value of one of the Fortran types: integer, real, logical, or character string of a particular length. The template of a record is the sequence of types of its fields. Each record in a particular file must have the same template.

Before a seqiential file can be written on or read from, it must be initialized by the statement:

open (file number, **file**='file name')

Each file number must be an unsigned, non-zero integer constant. On Vax computers sequential files are opened at the end of the file rather than at the first record. For these you must include after the **open** statement the statement:

rewind file number

Records are added as the next record of a sequential file by the statement:

write(file number,format identification)variable{,variable}

Each transmitted variable must be a simple (non-array) variable or an element of an array. The list of variables constitutes one record that is added to the end of the file. The record must be formatted. After the final record of a file has been written, the file must be ended by the statement:

close (file number)

The next record is read from a sequential file by the statement

read(file number,format identification)variable{,variable}

Each variable in the list must be a simple (non-array) variable or an array element. The next record is read into the list of variables. The record template defined by the types of the variables in the list must be the same as the template of the records on the file. Reading must not go beyond the final record written on the file.

Once a sequential file has been initialized (by **open**) it can be either written or read but not both. A sequential file that is being written can be ended (by **close**), initialized (by **open**) and then read or re-written in the same program. A file that is being read can be initialized (by **open**) and then written or re-read. Every time the writing of a file starts (after **open**), any previous contents of the file are lost, and once the writing is completed, the file must again be ended (by **close**).

(Some compilers require that any transmitted record be at least 16 bytes long. Real, integer and logical values each take up 4 bytes and character strings take up one byte per character. For example, a record consisting of two integers, a real value, and a **character***5 value would be acceptable because it is 17 bytes long.)

For random access files the initialization for reading and writing is:

open (file number,**file**='file name',[**status**='**new**',]**access**='**direct**', [**form**='**unformatted**',]**recl**=number of characters)

To read a record from a random access file the form is:

read (file number,format identification, **rec**=record number) variable {,variable}

To write a record in a random access file the form is:

write (file number,format identification,**rec**=record number) variable {,variable}

To close a random access file use:

close (file number)

Appendix 2:

SYNTAX OF FORTRAN 77

A **program** is

>**program** identifier
>{definition}
>{statement}
>**stop**
>**end**

A **definition** is one of the following:

- a. type variable {,variable}
- b. **common** /identifier/ variable {,variable}
- c. **parameter** (variable=value {,variable=value})
- d. **data** (variable {,variable})/value {,value}/

A **type** is one of the following:

- a. **integer**
- b. **real**
- c. **character***length
- d. **logical**

A **subprogram** is one of the following:

- a. **subroutine** name[(identifier{,identifier})]
  {definition}
  {statement}
  return
  end

- b. type **function** name(identifier{,identifier})
  {definition}
  {statement}
  return
  end

A **statement** is one of the following:

a.		**print** *,expression {,expression}
b.		**read** *, variable {,variable}
c.		**print** label {,expression}
	label	**format**(control {,format item})
d.		**read** label, variable {,variable}
	label	**format**(format item {,format item})
e.		variable = expression

f.
```
        if(condition) then
            {statement}
        {else if (condition) then
            {statement} }
        [else
            {statement}]
        end if
```

g. label1
```
        if(condition) go to label2
            {statement}
        go to label1
```
    label2 **continue**

h.
```
        do label identifier = start,limit [,step]
            {statement}
```
    label1 **continue**

i.		**call** subroutine name [(expression{,expression})]
j.		**return**
k.		**stop**
l.		**open**(file number,**file**='file name',[**status**=**new**] [**access**=**direct**, [**form**=**unformatted**] [**recl**=number of char])
m.		**close** (file number)
o.		**read** (file number, [format identification,] [**rec**=record number]) variable {,variable}
p.		**write** (file number),[format identification,] [**rec**=record number] variable {,variable}
q.		**rewind** file number

Notation: [item] means the item is optional.
             {item} means the item is repeated zero or more times.

Appendix 3:

BUILT-IN FUNCTIONS IN FORTRAN 77

Here is a list of the most used built-in functions.

a. Integer built-in functions.

> mod(i,j)-remainder of i divided by j; i and j must be integer values. The result is integer.
> $iabs$(x) - absolute value of x
> $adim$(x1,x2) - absolute value of $(x1-x2)$
> $max0$(x1,x2,...xn) - maximum of xs
> $min0$(x1,x2,...xn) - minimum of xs

b. Real built-in functions.

For these functions, the arguments must be real. The result is real.

abs(x)	- absolute value of x
sin(x)	- sine of x radians
cos(x)	- cosine of x radians
$atan$(x)	- arctangent of x in radians
$asin$(x)	- arcsine of x in radians
$acos$(x)	- arccosine of x in radians
$sinh$(x)	- hyperbolic sine of x
$cosh$(x)	- hyperbolic cosine of x
$tanh$(x)	- hyperbolic tangent of x
$alog$(x)	- natural logarithm of x
$alog10$(x)	- logarithm to base 10 of x
exp(x)	- e to the x power
$sqrt$(x)	- square root of x
dim(x1,x2)	- absolute value of $(x1-x2)$
$amax1$(x1,x2,...xn) - maximum of xs	
$amin1$(x1,x2,...xn) - minimum of xs	

c. Double-precision functions

Largely the same as those for real arguments. The names of the double precision version of the functions a *d* in front of the real name with the exception of *amax1, amin1, alog,* and *alog10* where the leading *a* is replaced by a *d.* For example, *dmax1* or *dlog,* the arc functions are exceptions, for example, the name *datan* is used for the double-precision arctangent.

dprod(x1,x2) - double-precision product of *x1* and *x2*

d. Character built-in functions

index(string,substring) - gives the starting position of the first occurrence of substring in string. If there is no occurrence the value is zero.

len(string) - length of string literal, variable, or expression.

e. Type conversions functions.

ichar(character) - position of the character in the collating sequence
char(x) - character in position *x* of the collating sequence
dble(x) - converts *x* to double precision; *x* can be real or integer.
int(x) - converts *x* to integer by truncation
nint(x) - converts *x* to integer with rounding
real(x) - converts *x* to real
sngl(x) - converts double precision *x* to single precision
dnint(x) - converts double precision to nearest whole number

Appendix 4:

THE OPERATING SYSTEM

BEGINNING A SESSION ON THE COMPUTER

After your program has been composed on a piece of paper you are ready to enter it into the computer to see how it works. You will be typing each line on the input keyboard just as you would on an ordinary typewriter. As you type, the letters, digits, and special characters appear on the screen. A flashing symbol on the screen, called the **cursor**, shows you where the next character you type will go.

Before you can begin entering your program you must get the input-output terminal going (if it is not already turned on) and make contact with the operating system. This procedure varies from one operating system to another. If you are sharing a computer among many terminals, you will be required to **log in** to the system and identify yourself.

For many systems all that is required to initiate the log in procedure is to depress certain keys on the keyboard. When you do, there appears on the screen a request for you to identify yourself. This consists of a word, such as **Name**: appearing at the top of the screen. To this prompt from the system you must respond by typing the name (or number) under which you, personally, have been authorized to use the computer. When you have finished, press the return key so the computer will know you are done.

In order to protect you from having other users giving your name (or number) and gaining access to the files you have stored in the system, or perhaps taking computer time at your expense, most systems use a **password**. The password should be known only to yourself. The operating system will prompt you to enter your passwrod by displaying something on the screen such as **password**:. You type your password then press the return key. (Whenever you have finished a response of more than one character you will be pressing return.) usually the password is not displayed on the screen as you type it. This is to prevent anyone reading it over your shoulder.

After the logging in process is complete the computer will prompt you in some way to indicate that it is ready for a system command.

SYSTEM COMMAND LANGUAGE

You may think that it is quite enough to learn to program in the Fortran language without learning a second language. But it is essential to learn the **system command language** if you want to enter your Fortran programs, save them in a file, execute them, edit then when they have errors, and run them again.

Each operating system has its own command language. But there are features common to many systems. A command is often given to the computer by pressing the key that corresponds to the first letter in the command word. For instance, typing the letter *e* (for *edit*) might be the command to begin editing. Sometimes two letters are required for the command, such as *ed* (for *edit*). These abbreviations cut down on the amount of typing that you have to do.

Many command languages have **levels**. At each level there are a certain number of different commands available; some of these commands take you to a lower level, some return you to a higher level from which you came. We say then that the command language has a **hierarchical structure**. For example, when you have just logged in you will be at the top level of the command structure. At this level there will be several possible commands that you might give. Some systems state the level and list the available commands in a **prompt line** at the top of the screen. In other systems you may ask for help by typing a **help command**. In still others you just have to remember what level you are at and what commands are available at that level.

Each person using a shared computer system will be permitted to store a number of files in secondary storage. Each of these files has to be given a **file name** so that it can be retrieved from storage when you want it. Before you begin to enter your program you must indicate what name you intend to use for the file that will contain your program. You may use the same name that follows the keyword **program**, but any name will do. File names are often limited in the number of characters they may contain. Every file you have must have a different name. The names of our Fortran programs are limited to six characters.

As you type your program it will not go directly to the secondary store but instead will remain in the high-speed memory in a **workfile** or **buffer** until you give the command to store it away. If you do not **write** the workfile into the permanent file in secondary memory before you **log off** it may be lost. Usually the program must be written into the secondary file before it can be compiled and executed. To cause the program to be executed you would give the **execute command** naming the file to be executed.

After establishing the name of the file that you are about to enter, you are ready to type the program. From the top level you must give the command to enter the **edit mode** (or **level**). There are two quite different kinds of editors: **line editors** and **full-screen editors**. We will describe these two separately and you will have to find out which kind of editor is used on your system. Some systems permit either kind of editing. Full-screen editing is perhaps easier to understand, but line editors can be more efficient.

To begin entering your program with either kind of editor you will have to give a command that takes you to a third level in the hierarchy which we will call the **enter text mode**. Some editors call it **insert mode**, others call it **append mode**. In any case, any characters you type in this mode will be taken to be part of your own program, rather than system commands. There are some special characters on the keyboard, such as **backspace**, (or **left-arrow** or **delete**) **return**, or **escape**, which cause respectively: movement of the cursor back one space, with erasure of the character just typed; a movement of the cursor to the start of the next line; and, for some systems, escape causes a return to the edit level.

The kind of editor you have does not change the way you enter your programs initially. But the method used to make changes in a program — to correct errors or to modify it — is quite different in the two systems.

FULL-SCREEN EDITORS

To make corrections to programs using a full-screen editor, in the edit mode you move the cursor to the place where an **insertion, deletion**, or **substitution** is to occur. This is done using special keys on the keyboard for movement of the cursor: right, left, up, or down. These may be keys that are in a separate section of the keyboard in a **keypad** which does not correspond to anything on a normal typewriter keyboard. Cursor movement may instead require you to depress a special key called the control (*ctrl*) key and another key such as the letter *c* at the same time. This would be stated as *ctrl-c*. You must learn what produces cursor movement in your own system. Often the keys are labelled with arrows pointing in the direction of the movement you can achieve.

To delete something you would position the cursor at the place where the deletion is to start, enter the **delete mode** by giving a system command then move the cursor over each character to be deleted. (If you backspace the character reappears.) After the deletion you must return to the edit mode. This return is achieved by pressing one key if you want the deletion to be incorporated and another if you have changed your mind and want it left as it was. Insertion is similar. After entering the **insert mode** you type in the material to be inserted just to the left of the cursor's position on entry. The rest of the line will be automatically spaced over.

To substitute one string of characters in the text, called a **target string** by a **substitute string**, we would first enter the **substitute mode**, then type these two strings with a **delimiter**, such as a slash character (/) before and after each string. The first occurrence of the target string in the text, following the position of the cusor on entry to the substitute mode, is replaced by the substitute string.

LINE EDITORS

In line editors, changes to the text are made be referring to particular lines of the text by number. Lines of the text that you have entered are numbered sequentially 1 to the total number of lines. A line is whatever you type up to the time you press the return key which starts a new line. At any time the editor is positioned at a particular line of the text, called the **current line**. This is always the last line upon which an action was taken. Lines may be displayed by giving a line number, or range of numbers, followed by a command to display the line.

Insertions can be made just after (or just before) the current line by entering the insert mode and typing additional lines. As you return you must be sure the insertion is accepted. To delete a line you need only position the editor at the line to be deleted and give the delete command. There may be a second command you can give to restore the line if you deleted it by mistake. This must follow immediately after the deletion.

Changes in lines are similar to insertions except that the line you type in replaces the current line.

Substitution of a part of the current line is accomplished by giving a substitute command followed by the target and substitute strings, surrounded by delimiters. The substitution applies only to the first occurrence of the target string in the text starting at the current line. Substitution of every occurrence of the target string in the text can be accomplished by giving a command for a **global substitution**.

Blocks of text may be moved by stating the range of lines to be moved and giving a **move command**. This move often requires the use of a temporary file to store the block to be moved before it is inserted in another location. It is sometimes called a **cut and paste** operation.

FILING OF PROGRAMS

Programs should be saved in disk files. There will be a **file directory** listing all the programs that you have saved. This group of files may be added to, or deleted from by systems commands given either from the **edit mode** or from a **file mode** depending on what system you are operating under. Any files that you have may be read into the high-speed memory for editing or insertion into other files. This is done by a **read command**. Files may be written from the workfile into the permanent file by a **write command**. Files may also be deleted when you no longer want them.

The nature of the editors and filers varied from one operating system to another. In this chapter we can only mention a few things that are common to many systems. The details of your own system will have to be obtained elsewhere.

In Appendix 5, we present details of the Unix*tm* operating system. In particular we will describe its line editor. Unix is a trade mark of Bell Laboratories.

In Appendix 6 we present details of another commonly used operating system the VAX/VMS system, devised by the Digital Equipment Corporation.

When you have finished a session at the terminal, you must **log off**.

APPENDIX 4: SUMMARY

In this chapter, we explained in general terms how to enter a computer program into the computer, file it, run it, save it, and edit it. Details of two commonly used operating systems are given in the appendices. The following important terms were presented.

Operating system — the program that is controlling the computer and which permits you to enter, edit, file, compile, and execute your Fortran programs.

Cursor — a small flashing signal such as a rectangle or underline which is displayed on the screen of a computer input-output terminal. It is used to indicate to the user where the next character to be typed on the keyboard will be located. As each character is typed the cursor moves one position to the right along the line. If the return key is pressed the cursor moves to the first position of the next line.

Full-screen editor — a system of editing text on the screen of a computer terminal where the cursor may be moved anywhere on the screen by pressing keys that move it left, right, up, or down. Insertions, deletions, and changes take place at points in the text indicated by the position of the cursor.

Line editor — a system of editing text on a screen where insetions, deletions, and changes take place on certain lines of the text at which the system is positioned. Lines can be referred to by number and the line at which the system is positioned, the current line, is the one upon which action last took place.

Log in — the procedure that you must go through to begin a session at an input-output terminal of a shared computer system. After pressing some key (or keys) on the keyboard, a prompt from the system appears on the screen to begin the log in.

Authorized user — a person who has been given permission to use a computer system. Each authorized user has a name (or number) that identifies the user to the system. Files may be stored and programs executed by authorized users.

Password — most systems protect the privacy and security of users by having a password (known only to the user) required to be entered before access to the system is permitted. Passwords are requested by the system at log in time. Usually they are not displayed on the screen as they are entered so as to maintain their secrecy.

Command language — a repertoire of instructions that can be given to the operating system to achieve certain results involved in entering, editing, running, and filing of programs. Many command languages have a hierarchical structure involving levels. To give a command you type certain characters, often single letters.

Level or mode — a stage in the hierarchy of a command language. After completing the log in procedure you are in the top level of the command language. By typing the edit command, you will be put in the edit mode which is a second level. From there typing the insert command might take you to a third level. At each level there is a range of commands that can be given and at least one way to return to the higher level.

Edit mode — a second level in the command hierarchy used when you want to enter or change a program.

Insert mode — used when material is to be inserted in a program. With full-screen editors, the cursor is placed on the character position just following where the inserted material is to go, before the insert mode is entered. With line editors, the system is positioned at the line following (or before) which the insertion is to occur, before the insert mode is entered. After entering the insert mode, the new material is typed. The command is then given to return to the edit mode with the insertion accepted.

Delete mode — used when material is to be deleted from a program. With full-screen editors the cursor is placed on the first character to be deleted. After the delete mode is entered, spacing the cursor right deletes material; backspacing restores deleted characters. With a line editor the system is positioned at the line to be deleted. Giving the delete command deletes the line.

Substitute mode — used whan a string of characters called the target string is to be replaced by another string called the substitute string. With full-screen editors the substitution applies to the first occurrence of the target string in the text following the cursor's position. With line editors the substitution applies to the first occurrence of the target string starting at the current line. If all occurrences are to be substituted we say it is a global substitution.

File directory — a listing, by file name, of all the programs that you have stored in secondary memory. Commands can be given to read a certain file into the high-speed memory in a location called the workfile or to write the workfile into the secondary memory. The file directory itself can be displayed by giving a command.

Appendix 5:

THE UNIX COMMAND LANGUAGE

In order to enter programs via an input-output terminal the computer must have an operating system. One operating system that is widely used is the Unix*tm* system which was developed by Bell Laboratories. We will describe the command language that enables the user to enter, edit, file, compile, and execute programs using the Unix line editor. The basic terms used have been introduced in Appendix 4.

Unix commands are given using lower case letters and are, in general the first letter of the command word. Commands are usually typed starting in the first column or the first column after any prompt symbol.

To log in: turn on terminal; press *ctrl-d*, word **login**: appears; you type your name (or number) followed by return; the word **password**: appears; you type your password then return. The computer will signal that you may proceed by displaying a single character (say $) as a prompt. A display of the character ? means the computer does not understand. Try again. When you have logged on you are at the **top level** (or **shell level**).

To enter your program: starting after the $ prompt symbol type *ed* (for edit) followed (after a space) by the name of your program then return; the computer will respond that it is a new file. This means that you have no program on file with that name and are starting fresh. (If you have a file by that name, it will be read into the workfile (buffer) where it may be edited and the number of characters in the file will be displayed.) At the **edit level** the prompt symbol is an asterisk. Next you type *a* (for append) and return. You are now in the append mode which is the level below the edit mode and you may proceed to type in your program. There is no prompt symbol now. If you type an incorrect character backspacing (or perhaps delete or rubout) will erase it. After you have finished typing in your program you must return to the edit mode. This is done by typing a period in the first column followed by return. The asterisk prompt will reappear.

To save your program: whatever is in the workfile is saved by typing *w* (for write) followed by return. If no file name is given after *w* the file is written under the name you established when you first entered the editor. You can write it into another location by giving a new name after the *w*. Files that have been modified should always be saved before you leave the edit mode to go to the top level. To leave the edit mode and return to the top level, type *q* (for quit) then return. The $ prompt symbol will reappear.

To execute your program: from the top level type the command that causes compiling followed by the name of your file; to execute the program just compiled type the execute command; the output of the program, either at compilation time or execution time appears on the screen. The exact commands for compilation and execution vary from one system to another. In one version, program file names must end in *.f.* To compile a program give the command

　　　f77 name.*f*

This stores an object program as name.*o* and an executable program in *a.out*. To cause execution give the command *a.out*. The *a.out* file should be moved to another file such as name.*x* if you want to save it for the future. This saves compilation time.

To modify a program: bring it into the workfile; make appropriate modifications by insertion, deletion, substitution, or movement of blocks of lines. To make modifications you must position the system at the line to be modified. To begin you need to see where you are. You can display the program that is in the workfile by using the *p* (for print) command from the edit mode. Preceding the *p* you type the line number or range of line numbers that you want to see displayed. For example, *5p* displays line 5; *3,5p* displays lines 3 to 5. At any time after a display, pressing return will result in the line following the current line being displayed. Pressing − (minus) before return will cause the previous line to be displayed. If you use *n* (for numbered) instead of *p* the line number will be displayed beside the line. The metacharacter period stands for the current line, the $ for the last line. Typing .,$*p* causes the lines from the current line to the last line in the file to be displayed. To find out the number of the current line you type . =*p*. You can display a line that is 10 lines on from the current line by typing . +*10p*. By using the display command you can position the system at any line you wish to modify. The current line is always the last line displayed.

To delete the current line: type *d* (for delete). Repeated use of the delete command will delete successive lines.

To insert a line (or more) ahead of the current line: type *i* (for insert); this puts you in the insert mode; now type the line (or lines) to be inserted; type period in the first column to return to the edit mode with the insertion completed. If you use *a* (for append) instead of *i* (for insert) the material is added *after* the current line rather than *before*. This can be used to add text to the end of the file.

To substitute: position the system at the line where substitution is to take place; type *s*/target string/substitute string/ ; if you want to see the result type a *p* after the last slash before you return. The first occurrence of the target string in the line is substituted. If you type a *g* (for global) after the last slash all occurrences in the current line are substituted.

To change one line for another: position at line to be changed; type *c* (for change); in the change mode enter new line or lines; then type period followed by return to go back to the edit mode.

To move lines to a new position: type number (or range of numbers) of line (or lines) to be moved then *m* (for move) followed by the number of the line that will just precede the moved block in its new position. If you wish to copy a set of lines from one location into another use *t* (for transfer) instead of *m*.

To incorporate another file: if you want the other file at the end of the workfile type *r* (for read) followed by the file's name; if you want it inserted after the current line type .*r* followed by the name of the file.

To undo a substitution: if you change your mind or have made an error you can undo any substitution by typing *u* (for undo). This reverses the immediately preceding substitution.

To search for a string: the command /string/ will output the first occurrence of the string starting at the current line. The next occurrence of the same string can be found by giving the command // followed by return. All occurrences are displayed by the command g/string/. The search may be used to position the system at a line containing a target string for a substitution. The command that searches and substitutes is /target string/*s*//substitute string/*p*. If *g* precedes this and also a *g* precedes the *p* all occurrences in the file are substituted.

Applying operations to a range of lines: the operations of deletion, change, printing, or substitution can be applied to a range of lines; the range is stated before the command by: first line, last line. The symbol $ stands for the last line of the text so that a range *1*$ means to all lines of the text.

Special symbols: the symbol $ means the end of a line or the last line of the text; the symbol ˆ means the beginning of a line; square brackets around a range of characters, such as [*a-z*] means any character from a to z.

An ampersand, &, used in the substitute string means anything mentioned in the target string. A null target string means that the string should be the same target string as mentioned in the previous command.

Examples:

(a)   *1,$s/^[0-9]///gp*

would find all occurrences of lines starting with a digit and delete the digit. The last occurrence only would be displayed.

(b)   *.,$-10 d*

would delete lines starting at the current line and going up to 10 lines from the last line.

(c)   *s/$/;/p*

would place a semicolon at the end of the current line and display (print) it.

(d)   *s/do/& 10/*

would add 10 after the word *do* in the current line.

(e)   *g/income/s//pay/gp*

would search for all occurrences of the target string *income* and substitute the string *pay*, each occurrence would be displayed. Note: the target string in the substitute command can be written as *//*, since it is the same as the string in the global search command.

The following can be accomplished by commands at the top (shell) level.

To list the directory of your files: type *ls.*

To print a file on the line printer: type *lpr* followed by the name of the file.

To log off: From the top level type *logout* or *bye* (or *ctrl-d*).

To redirect output to a file instead of the screen: follow the execution command by the > symbol and the name of the file where data output is to be stored. For example, the command

> *a.out > output*

will send the output to the *output* file rather than to the screen.

To read data from a file instead of from the keyboard: follow the execution command by the < symbol and the name of the input data file. For example,

> *a.out < input*

will read data from the *input* file rather than from the keyboard.

To rename a file: at the top level give a command of the form:

> *mv* old name   new name

This is called a move command.

To delete a file: at the top level give a command of the form:

> *rm*   name of file

This is a remove command. To remove a file its full name must be given but if an asterisk is used for part of the name all files with the other part will be removed. For example,

> *rm addup.**

will remove files named *addup.f* and *addup.0*. Care must be used as you may lose valuable files this way.

To display a file: at the top level give a command of the form:

> *cat* file name

This stands for catenate. Several file names may follow the cat command. The command

> *cat* file1, file2 > file3

catenates file1 and file2 and stores it as file3.

To copy a file: at the top level give a command of the form:

> *cp* original name   copy's name

Appendix 6:

THE VAX/VMS
COMMAND LANGUAGE

Before you can begin entering your program you must get the terminal going and make contact with the VAX/VMS operating system. This part of the procedure varies from one type of terminal to another. A common procedure would be to: Turn on the power to the terminal, make connection by a telephone call to the VAX computer system if the terminal is not permanently connected, then press the return key or the control key and at the same time the letter *y* (*ctrl-y*). You will have to find out exactly what the procedure is for the particular terminal you are using.

When you have made contact with VAX/VMS you will see on the screen the word **Username**:. The cursor is now positioned right after the prompting word **Username**:. You respond by typing your name, in the form under which you are authorized as a user, followed by pressing the return key. The system then displays the word **Password**:. After you finish typing the password, again press the return key. The computer signals to you that you may proceed by displaying a message saying, for example

WELCOME TO VAX/VMS VERSION 3.0

followed on the next line by a single character (a $) prompt symbol. If the prompt character appears, this means that the system is ready for a system command.

VAX/VMS commands can be given using upper or lower case letters and are often abbreviated to the first few letters of the command word. We will use lower case letters and show the entire command word. You can experiment to see how few letters are really needed. Commands are usually typed starting right after the prompt symbol.

The VAX/VMS command language has a hierarchical structure. When you have logged in you are at the top level of the VAX/VMS system. You can tell you are at this level because there is a $ prompt symbol. In this top level there are various commands that you can give. These include the edit command, the compile command, the link command, and the execute command. As well, there are commands for finding out: the time and date, and the description in the VAX/VMS manual of any system command. These will be described in detail later.

We will be describing the particular editing system called EDT. In EDT there are two modes of operating: one is line editing, the other is full-screen or keypad editing.

Each person using a shared computer system will be permitted to store a number of files in disk storage. Each of these files must be given a **file name** so that it can be retrieved from storage when it is wanted. Before you begin to enter your program you must indicate what name you intend to use for the file that will contain your program. All programs in Fortran must have names of one to six characters followed by *.for.* You may use the same name as you have already given to your Fortran program and simply add the *.for*, but any name will do. Files that are not Fortran programs should not have names followed by *.for.* The *.for* is called the **file type**. Each file is specified by a file name followed by a file type.

ENTERING A PROGRAM

To input the program, type the command *edit* followed, after a space, by the file name you have chosen for your program, the *.for*, and then return. This takes you to the EDT editor. The message

> **Input file does not exist**
> **[EOB]**

appears. If you already have a file by that name the file you have named will be brought from disk memory to the file buffer when the *edit* command is given. If you do not name a file after the command *edit* but instead press the return key, a prompting message saying

> **$_File**:

will appear and you can then enter the file name and type.

When you enter the edit mode the first line of the file with that name is displayed followed by **[EOB]**. In our case, since it is a new file, there is no first line. Now you are in the edit level or mode which is part of EDT and is a second level of the hierarchy below the top command level. In this level there is an * (asterisk) prompt symbol. We will first describe the line editing mode of EDT as it is perhaps simpler. You are automatically in the line editing mode when you have given the *edit* command at the top level.

Before you begin to type your program you must go to the next level, to the text entry mode, which is done by typing *insert.* The characters you type in this mode will be taken to be part of your own program, rather than system commands. What you type in the insert mode will be stored in the high speed memory of the computer in the file buffer. The text you enter must be saved in the file in secondary storage before you next return to the top command level or it will be lost. We will say how to do this later.

So now you can type your program. If you make a mistake in typing a character, you can press the delete key on the main part of the keyboard and this will back up the cursor one space and you can type the correct character. You could wipe out a whole line by deleting repeatedly until the cursor is at the start of the line but instead you can delete a whole line by pressing *ctrl-u* then return, rather than pressing the delete many times.

Type in your program, trying to make as few mistakes as possible and correct them as soon as you detect them. When you are finished, you are ready to return to the edit mode. This is done by typing *ctrl-z* followed by return. This causes you to escape from the insert mode and go back to the edit mode.

RUNNING THE PROGRAM

You have now entered your program and are back in the edit mode. The file that you have created in the insert mode must be saved before you return to the top command level for program compilation and execution. To do this, type *exit* followed by return. Whatever is in the buffer is saved under the file name that you established when you entered the edit mode. Files that have been just entered or modified should always be saved before you leave the edit mode to go to the top command level. To leave the edit mode and return to the top command without saving the buffer type *quit* then return. If you want to save the buffer in another file rather than the one whose name you gave on entering the edit mode, use the edit command

> *write* file name

followed by *quit.*

Now you are ready to compile your program. We will give the commands for the VAX-11 Fortran. To do this type the command *fortran* which is the command which will change your Fortran program into an object program that will be stored in a file of the same file name as your Fortran program but whose type is *.obj* rather than *.for.* The command *fortran* is followed by the file name, which may, but need not, be followed by the type of your program file, then return. The transformation now takes place. If you have made any syntax errors these will be reported on the screen . The lines that have errors are displayed and pointers to the errors are given. If you have many errors you might just make a note of them to remind yourself when you are correcting the program.

Suppose for the present that you get no error messages. Your next move is to give the command *link* followed by the file name (with or without *.obj*). This prepares the compiled program for execution and stores the final version of the compiled program under the same file name with type *.exe*. You can then give the command for execution which is *run* file name (with or without .exe).

For our first program, which we called *addup*, the file name with type might be *addup.for*. After it had been entered we could give the command *fortran addup.for* (or just *fortran addup*) which would compile the program and store the object program in *addup.obj*. We could then give the command

> *link addup.obj* (or just *link addup*)

which would put the translated program, ready for execution, in *addup.exe*. Execution can then be obtained by giving the command

> *run addup.exe* (or just *run addup*)

You may run this program at anytime in the future without recompiling.

To see a program file on the screen you can give the top level command *type* followed by the file name with its type. If the length of the file is more than the screen will hold, the display will keep moving upwards with lines disappearing off the top and new lines appearing at the bottom. This is called scrolling. You can stop this scrolling at any time by typing *ctrl-s*; to start again, type *ctrl-q*. If you are not interested in looking at any more output, type *ctrl-y* to escape back to the top command level. Do not try to look at files that are in code, that is, any translated programs.

You can see a list of the names of all your files in a directory by typing the top level command *directory*. The file names are all shown in capital letters even though you may be using small letters. When you are editing files each new version of a file is kept. The **version number** of a file is part of its complete **file specification** which has the form

> file name. type; version number

If no version number is specified, say in the *edit* command, the latest version is the one you get. When you list the directory all versions are shown. To get rid of files you do not want any more you can give the command

> *delete* file specification including version

Frequently you want to delete all but the highest numbered version of a file. This can be done by the command *purge* specification of file with type but without version

All versions of a file can be removed by using the *delete* command followed by the file specification with an asterisk in the place of the version number. We call the asterisk here a **wild card**; it stands for any number whatever. To rename a file give the command *rename* followed by the old file specification and the new file specification, in that order. To create a copy of a file, rather than move it, give the command *copy* followed by the file specification of the file to be copied then the file specification the copy is to have. The command

delete addup.*;*

would delete all versions and types of all files whose name was *addup*.

OBTAINING PRINTED OUTPUT

If for some reason you want a hardcopy record of what you have in your file you can do this by giving the top level command

print file name .type; version

So there is no problem about getting a printed listing of your Fortran program. But how do you get a printed listing of error messages, or the output from a program's execution? These things are normally displayed on the screen but not stored in a file. It is possible to redirect the output from the screen to a file instead. This is done by assigning a different file name to the normal file names, used by default, which send the error messages and the output to the screen. The **logical name** of the file where the error messages are sent is *sys$error*, so to change it from its normal assignment which is your terminal to a disk file, called *addup1.err* for example, you precede the compilation command by the command

assign addup.err sys$error

To return error messages to the screen give the command

deassign sys$error

An alternative way to obtain a hardcopy of error messages is to give the compiling command in the form

fortran/list program name

This stores the error messages in a file whose specification is

program name .*lis*

This can then be printed if you want. To have the program's output sent to a file instead of to the terminal, precede the *run* command by the command

> *assign addup.out sys$output*

Again you must give the command

> *deassign sys$output*

to return the output to the screen. To print these two disk files you give
the command

> *print addup.err, addup.out*

To see them on the terminal give the command

> *type addup.err, addup.out*

To see the whole file that is in the buffer at any time displayed on the
screen you can give the edit command

> *type whole*

You will notice when you display a file using the edit *type* command that
the program is indented on the left, that each line is numbered, and that
[EOB] is on the line following the last line. The edit mode prompt symbol
* is on the bottom line of the display. To correct errors we must edit the
text of a program.

THE EDT LINE EDITOR

As the program is being translated from a Fortran program to a
machine language program, as happens with the *fortran* command, the
translator detects and reports errors in the form, or syntax, of the statements in your program. The lines with syntax errors are displayed along
with error messages. An error message includes a pointer to the part of the
statement containing the error. You must fix all errors. To do this you
must edit your original program. Changes are made by insertion, deletion,
substitution, and movement of blocks of lines.

To modify a program: enter the edit mode with the *edit* command followed by the name of your Fortran program with type. You will see only
the first line of your program displayed, but the whole program is in the
buffer. The VMS text editor that we will describe first is the **EDT line editor**. To make changes you must position the system at the line to be
modified. Often you refer to the line by number. You can display any line
of the program in the buffer by using the *type* command followed by the
line number or range of line numbers that you want to see displayed. A
range is expressed as

> first line number: last line number

This *type* command, which is at the edit level, is different from the *type* command of the top level which requires a file specification as a **parameter**. For this *type* command the parameter is a word like *whole*, or a line number, or range of line numbers. For example, *type 5* displays line 5; *type 3:5* displays lines 3 to 5. The current line is the last line displayed. At any time after a display, pressing return will result in the line following the current line being displayed. The lines displayed are numbered and indented on the screen.

The metacharacter period stands for the line number of the current line. The command *type .* causes the current line to be displayed. The command *type before* causes all lines in the buffer up to the current line to be displayed. The command *type rest* causes the display of the rest of the program including the current line. The first line of the buffer can be referred to as *begin*, the empty line after the last as *end*. The command

> *type .: end*

is equivalent to

> *type rest*

By using the *type* command you can position the system at any line you wish to modify. The current line, remember, is the last line displayed. If the whole file buffer is displayed (including [**EOB**]) the current line becomes the first line of the buffer.

To delete the current line: type *delete*. Repeated use of the *delete* command will delete successive lines. The *delete* command can be used with a line number, or the range of lines, to be deleted specified.

To insert a line (or more) just before the current line: type *insert*, this puts you in the insert mode; now type the line (or lines) to be inserted; type *ctrl-z* at the end of the last line to be inserted to return to the edit mode with the insertion completed. When an insertion takes place, line numbers are given appropriately. If the insertion of three lines takes place preceding line number 4, the new lines are given the numbers 3.1, 3.2, and 3.3. To insert before any line other than the current line just put its line number after the *insert*. For example, *insert end* will cause the insertion at the end of the buffer.

To substitute: position the system at the line where substitution is to take place; type

> *substitute*/target string/substitute string/

The first occurrence in the current line of the target string is substituted. If you type *whole* after the last slash all occurrences in the text starting at the current line and going to the end are substituted. The total number of substitutions is displayed along with each line in which a substitution occurred.

To change one line for another: position at line to be changed; type *delete* then, after return, type *insert*, in the insert mode enter new line; then type *ctrl-z* followed by return to go back to the edit mode.

To move lines to a new position: type *move* followed by the number (or range of numbers) of the line (or lines) to be moved, followed by the word *to* then the number of the line that will just follow the moved block in its new position. If you wish to copy a set of lines from one location into another use *copy* instead of *move*.

To incorporate another file: if you want the other file at the end of the buffer, type *include* followed by the file's specification followed by *end*; if you want it inserted before the current line omit the *end*. Appropriate line numbers are given to the new lines.

To search for a string: the command "string" will output the first occurrence of the string starting at the current line. All occurrences are displayed by the command *type all* "string". The search may be used to position the system at a line containing a target string for a substitution. For example, to search for the word *program* give the command "*program*".

THE EDT FULL-SCREEN EDITOR

So far we have been describing one way to enter and edit the text of programs. It is based on making changes to individual lines of the program which are often referred to by line number. The **EDT full-screen editor** uses a **keypad** which is part of the keyboard of the terminal. The illustrations on the next page show the keypads of two commonly used terminals.

The keypads are different for the different kinds of terminals. By pressing keys near the keypad the cursor can be moved anywhere on the screen: up or down, left or right. For the VT100 terminal the cursor moving keys are in a row to the left of the keypad. for the VT52 terminal the cursor moving keys are in a column on the right side of the main keyboard. Each key of the keypad can perform two different functions. One is the **normal function** and is listed first on the key; the other is the **alternate function** which is listed below the normal one on the key. To obtain the alternate function press the key on the upper left corner of the pad (known as the **gold key**) before you press the **function key**.

Keypad 1:

	10	11	12
GOLD	HELP	DEL L UND L	UP REPLACE
7 PAGE COMMAND	**8** FNDNXT FIND	**9** DEL W UND W	**13** DOWN SECT
4 ADVANCE BOTTOM	**5** BACKUP TOP	**6** DEL C UND C	**14** RIGHT SPECINS
1 WORD CHNGCASE	**2** EOL DEL EOL	**3** CUT PASTE	**15** LEFT APPEND
0 LINE OPEN LINE		**16** SELECT RESET	**21** ENTER SUBS

Keypad 2:

	10	11	17
GOLD	HELP	FNDNXT FIND	DEL L UND L
7 PAGE COMMAND	**8** SECT FILL	**9** APPEND REPLACE	**18** DEL W UND W
4 ADVANCE BOTTOM	**5** BACKUP TOP	**6** CUT PASTE	**19** DEL C UND C
1 WORD CHNGCASE	**2** EOL DEL EOL	**3** CHAR SPECINS	**21** ENTER SUBS
0 LINE OPEN LINE		**16** SELECT RESET	

KEYPAD OF VT100 TERMINAL

The locations of any of the keys we refer to can be seen in the diagrams of the two keypads.

The **EDT keypad editor** is an alternate to the line editor which is the normal editor. To change from the normal EDT line editor to the EDT full-screen or keypad editor give the edit command *change*. (This means that the full-screen editor of EDT is at the third level, one below the edit level.) When you do this, the first 22 lines of the file in the buffer are displayed on the screen. There are no line numbers now as we do not use them in full-screen editing; nor is the text indented. To make alterations in the text you must move the cursor to the place where the alteration of substitution, insertion, or deletion is to occur.

How to move the cursor: The four basic cursor moving keys are used but they are not the only ones that move the cursor. The **end of line** (EOL) **key** moves the cursor to the end of the line it is on; the backspace key of the main keyboard moves it to the beginning of the line; the **word key** (WORD) moves the cursor to the beginning of the next word; the **section key** (SECT) moves it on 16 lines of text to the next section. The **top key** (TOP) moves it to the start of the file in the buffer; the **bottom key** (BOTTOM) to the end.

You can move the cursor backwards (instead of forwards in the text) by pressing the **backup key** (BACKUP). All cursor moves are reversed until the **advance key** (ADVANCE) is pressed to reset the direction.

How to delete text: Move the cursor to the first character to be deleted then press one of the three delete keys: **delete character key** (DEL C), **delete word key** (DEL W), or **delete line key** (DEL L). Each of these three can be undone if you immediately press the appropriate **undelete key** (UND C, UND W, or UND L). The DEL L key deletes from the cursor's position to the end of the line and moves the next line up to the cursor. The DEL EOL key deletes the rest of the line but does not move the next line up.

How to insert text: Simply place the cursor where the insertion is to occur and type the insertion. The text to the right will move to make room. Text of a new file can be entered in this way.

How to move text (a process called cutting and pasting): Select the range of text you want to move by placing the cursor at the beginning and pressing the **select key** (SELECT). Now move the cursor one character past the end and press the **cut key** (CUT). The text selected vanishes from the screen but is stored in the **paste buffer**. To put it into its new position move the cursor to that new position and press the **paste key** (PASTE). Several copies of what is in the paste buffer can be placed in the text if desired; the contents of the paste buffer are not changed until the next cut is made.

If you make the wrong selection of the beginning of a cut you can undo it by pressing the **reset key** (RESET).

To substitute text: Use deletion and insertion. The contents of the paste buffer can be substituted if you select text as for a cut then press the **substitute key** (SUBS).

To find a particular string in the text: Press the **find key** (FIND). The prompt **Search for:_** will appear at the bottom of the screen. Enter the string to be sought followed by pressing the **advance key** (or the **enter key**). The cursor is automatically positioned at the start of the first occurrence of the string. To find the next occurrence press the **find next key** (FNDNXT).

To store the changes you have made in the buffer file: Return to the line editor by pressing *ctrl-z* and proceed as before. An alternative way is to enter the command mode by pressing the **command key** (COMMAND) then type the command *exit* followed by return.

To get help: Press the **help key** (HELP).

OTHER VAX/VMS COMMANDS

There are other commands that are available at the top level.

To have the date and time displayed: type *show time*.

To have the VAX/VMS instruction manual displayed: type *help* followed by the top level command that you want explained. For example, typing *help fortran* will produce a display that tells you all about the *fortran* command.

To change your password: type *set password*. The system responds by asking you to enter your old password. If you do this correctly the system then asks you to enter the new password. Passwords should be at least six characters long if they are all lower case letters. The maximum length is 31 characters. If you forget your password, only the person in charge of the system can help you. After you have entered your new password, which as usual is not displayed, the system asks you to type it again just to be sure. (The prompt says *Verification*.) If they match the change is made.

To terminate a session at the terminal: type *logout*.

Appendix 7:

LIST OF APPLICATIONS

INDEX